IMPARTING CITY

TANJA SIEMS

IMPARTING CITY

METHODS AND TOOLS FOR COLLABORATIVE PLANNING

Birkhäuser
Basel

TABLE OF CONTENTS

FOREWORD

FROM BARBARA CAMPBELL-LANGE

The growing international awareness of environmental and societal inequities presents us all with a collective challenge and responsibility to act: we need to reduce waste, increase wellbeing, and better cherish our limited resources of people, time and materials. Following Bruno Latour, urban designer and educator Tanja Siems supports an ethos that encourages greater sharing, where we can rally around such 'matters of concern' and consider possible ways forward for the design of our environments. Her exemplary work urges us to detect bias, unfurl assumptions and use this information to change our usual methods and processes.

The projects in this book explore modes of engagement that have not only been designed but also tested. They reveal the complexity of our urban context, its formation as a manifold and extraordinary palimpsest of social and physical conditions and constraints, where everything and every decision lies in contingent relation to something or someone else. Siems presses for 'mediation', for different kinds of conversations among diverse groups of actants, for dialogues that harness the advantages of virtual as well as physical communication. She suggests different kinds of measures in different kinds of spaces – mechanisms that activate greater inclusion and, above all, increase trust. Combining an unfailing spirit of generosity with practical acumen, her practice endeavours to enfold the overlooked and the less heard. For Siems, recognising varied cultures of experience and expression and acknowledging disparate concerns and agendas is an essential step towards improving our environment.

As part of this transformation and shift towards new forms of collaboration, Siems takes education outside the framework of the university and its institutional spaces. Her methodology of participatory urbanism causes students to improvise spatial settings in the city as stages of inquiry, often working for long stretches of time directly on site. The immediacy of researching real places in real time as participant observers enables students to survey different kinds opportunities and challenges alongside local citizens, socio-political organisations and authorities. Remarkably the Siems' team has situated these participatory practices inside exceptional historical buildings such as an abandoned Train Station in Wuppertal, the vacant Birker Bath in Solingen and an old empty radio shop in Remscheid.

International interdisciplinary research projects such as 'Solar Energy in an Urban Development Context' have extended this out-of-studio approach. Here Siems' masters students were able to discuss ideas and experiment onsite during a month-long summer school at Berlin-Adlershof, evolving a sustainable urban plan for the area. Importantly this collaborative work was embedded with the knowledge of local people as well as insights from a network of experts based in socio-economic as well as creative disciplines.

This direct fieldwork approach allows students to explore urban questions in distinct ways. Siems eshews standardised planning tools, predefined answers and variations of tired typologies. Instead she enables projects that can independently identify issues leading to the co-creation of innovative, locally relevant proposals. Her students are empowered to design their own site-specific design processes, to follow their intuition and to be open to alternative and unusual possibilities. By relying on genuine interest and care for a place, looking closely at what actually exists, engaging directly with people, the resulting projects display a wide spectrum of novel approaches and intelligent propositions.

Siems advocates for a closer connection between pure and applied knowledges, where the valuable speculative adventures of imaginative design can more coherently and effectively respond to the challenges of real clients and budgets. She is committed to interdisciplinary projects in both higher education and the built environment industry. To do this, she aims to create non-hierarchical interfaces and networks where different worlds and different viewpoints can co-exist and intersect, opening up seams of enquiry that enrich and inform decision-making.

Siems encourages us to think otherly, to sidestep 'business as usual' and to be mindful, in any project, of its many histories and possible futures while actively operating in the 'now'. She dares us to 'design the design', to reconsider and adapt planning processes in the built environment to make them more fluid, inclusive and adjustable. Conveyed through images, diagrams and texts, the projects in this book demonstrate that her work is continually growing and innovating, offering new approaches and fresh means of cooperation. Yet, beyond this, what gives Siems' projects a unique ethos of care is her profound understanding of the inevitably incomplete and imperfect nature of participatory and mediating processes. Through her work she gifts us possibilities, sustainable and resilient strategies, unusual methods and inventive tools that inspire all of us to try harder, to collectively find ways, large or small, direct or indirect, to engage, protect and enhance our cultural commons.

Professorin Barbara Campbell-Lange
The Bartlett School of Architecture, UCL

INTRODUCTION

APPROACHES TO PARTICIPATORY PROJECTS

Communicating design ideas and processes is one of the most important tasks of creative work. Only through communication can complex tasks be deeply understood and supported sustainably. In no other field than urban design is this task multi-faceted and extremely fascinating. The city itself reflects manifold interactions within our society in its full complexity. Occurrences of everyday life intersect with culture and leisure. Therefore urban space defines our identity and the way we live together, in all its dimensions. Understanding planning, however, is significantly different from this immediate view of the city. Urban design ideas are often developed on the basis of a plan, from an abstract top-down vantage point. On the one hand, this approach contradicts our immediate view in terms of scale and dimensions. On the other hand, urbanity today is defined by the capacity for adaptation and transformation. Hence, the task of a forward-looking urban design is to permit related processes and, at the same time, create reliable framework conditions and circumstances for expressing these developments.

A functional urban fabric always encompasses a balanced mix of interactions – ranging from cultural and social dynamics to a conscious and balanced way of dealing with the immediate environment and its resources. Each of these individual factors requires viewing them as initiators of their respective counterparts. In the context of comprehensive urban planning and design, they cannot function forever in isolation. At the same time, urban transformation processes need to take place faster than in previous decades, since it is also necessary to advance integrative and participatory processes within the planning of cities and their urban life. A diverse set of approaches and strategies exists to implement this in practice. At the Urban Design Institute in Wuppertal we have developed approaches and strategies over recent years and demonstrated their implementation in various applied projects. This handbook is intended to assemble them in the context of an experimental mode of urban research, while offering recommendations for action and impulses for creative collaboration.

Understanding spatial design as a comprehensive texture composed of multi-faceted actors and urban elements requires an approach that avoids standardisation or doctrinal subordination and, instead, responds to each of the existing circumstances in a targeted way. Deliberating on our own approach, we have indeed learned much from Bruno Latour's ideas – ever since he held his first architectural lecture in 1999 at the Architectural Association School of Architecture in London, where he spoke of Paris and the manifold ways of reading the city. An analytical and networked mode of action as a basic precondition of our work is clearly apparent in many of its aspects. A systematising analytical approach that Latour, for instance, proposes for the examination of environmental changes in Africa's steppe, as described in *Pandora's Hope*, constitutes a decisive example of establishing a basis for any and all large-scale observations. Even if all data and facts are at hand, the systemic deliberation on these data is decisive in order to visualise findings for comparison and application. It is therefore a central task of urban design to display as many interrelations as possible within a seemingly objective totality, in order to identify what Latour describes as "matter of concerns", or the transformative elements of each specific case. The relevance of Latour's description of the principle of a "circular reference", according to which things are to be observed simultaneously from multi-faceted points of view, becomes particularly clear in the dimension of urban design-related situations. Latour asks how we can recognise the totality, while also recognising the respective components and smallest elements. When applying this to the city, we can ask the question of how these components and elements can be understood in their totality from a bird's eye perspective and, at the same time, from the viewpoint of the respective urban actors. We need to repeatedly switch between these positions, in order to achieve a comprehensive understanding of the structures of things and social networks (Latour 2005).

In his current endeavours, Latour invites us to expand this view even further and act responsibly within "Gaia's" all-encompassing orbit. Activities must no longer be isolated compromises. Every form of action is partial to the tenuous situation of a divided environment and, thus, lacks influence on our common and future existence. From the analysis of specificities to a consciousness of divided, comprehensive responsibilities, Latour further inspires us to change our principal point of view and engage in approaches that do not build upon meeting predetermined goals. Instead, the aim is to not lose sight of the big picture. By doing so, it becomes possible to adjust the respective and specific tasks at any time and actively achieve far-reaching improvements.

This publication is intended to present multi-faceted approaches that contribute to a better understanding of the urban situation and do justice to the communication and implementation of new planning schemes and developments. In order to convey this understanding to a new generation of planners and embrace processes of perpetual change, a conversation on teaching, research and practical implementation is essential. The related dynamics are reflected in the principle of teaching as research and simultaneous research as teaching. Based on this principle, planning is not considered something that has been determined in advance, something that is rigidly imparted within teaching. Instead, it becomes a research process of perpetual advancement that simultaneously influences teaching. Research and teaching, from this point of view, are no longer limited to educators and students of architecture and urban design. Even more so, they are intended to include other creative and planning disciplines. In order to yield sustainable effects, the process of teaching and research needs to be perpetuated within professional practice and urban society itself in an enduring way. Only continuous exchange on all levels and between the individuals that actually influence urban space can, as a result, produce a dynamic understanding of the city.

Hence this publication is aimed at all urban stakeholders and participants wishing to develop and realise diverse urban planning strategies. The used and generated methods and tools of participatory processes are visual and graphically presented in this handbook. These methodologies range from an analytical approach to concrete concept strategies and are shown as a realisation of participatory projects in various case studies. An open and creative experiment within a scientific urban testing ground supports the urban mediation process and therefore fully moderates its outcomes.

As a catalogue of methods and applied tools, the book as a guide demonstrates real and directly implementable principles of actions for an exploratory urban research within the design and planning institutions.

Cooperative approaches in teaching and research

Creative work processes as described above are subject to continuous further development. The publication in your hands presents related examples of my applied teaching, research and practice activities, viewed from different perspectives. For years, we have been successfully connecting practice, teaching, and research at the Institute in Wuppertal and at the Architectural Association (AA), as well as our interdisciplinary planning office T2 Spatialwork in London. We deliberate deeply on integrated urban design concepts and the positive impact inter- and transdisciplinary teamwork liaisons can have within planning and design processes. The ways architectural and urban design projects are implemented are an integral part of our teaching courses. As fields of research in a scientific context, they serve to develop comprehensive strategies with a diverse set of involved actors. In a similar sense, scientific methods derived from recent research projects at the institute are put to the test in the context of planning practice.

Creative negotiation and communication between urban elements constitute significant tasks of contemporary urban planning. From this perspective, mediation describes more than the simple communication of information on urban conditions and needs, or establishing an amicable compromise. More so, the term refers to the creative process within phases of planning and implementation and, thus, itself becomes a central element of the concepts mentioned above. Within the Bachelor and Master programmes modules, the method of communicating and conveying information through mediation and interaction is subject to comprehensive and focused research and testing design or urban strategies within these courses. One significant aim of communication and mediation is to visualise the complex urban design process continuously and intelligibly for all parties involved to see. Most of all, this requires and depends on the open-ended character of the process. For this purpose, again and again, our team asks the following questions within the related teaching modules: how we sustainably integrate mediation as a method in the urban design discipline and urban research in the future? Can we create an interactive urban interface as a medium and surface for communication? Which design-based content can be interweaved with cultural, social, political, ecological, and economic aspects? How can we use these to design future scenarios that are sufficiently flexible and open to sustainably deliberate on all factors relevant to the design process?

Research questions and urban design tasks

In order to meet the complexity and multi-faceted character of urban design assignments, it is necessary to develop different points of origin and approaches for each respective contextual situation. Two major approaches to site-specific assignments and related research and design questions specifically attuned to the object of inquiry are the cornerstones of our work. We will introduce them in the following.

A site-specific approach begins with clearly delineating and defining the object of inquiry or an area under observation. In many cases, scientific institutions or cities and municipalities interested in entering into an academic collaboration specifically indicate which areas are envisioned for research. In most cases, this type of assignment specifies a site intended for planning or particular typologies of built structures. However, the topic of the inquiry itself and the development of a functional programme remain open. As a result, in the context of urban design pedagogy, we find it an interesting and important task to develop such topics on the basis of a specific situation in a comprehensive manner and in cooperation with the students. Within an established open framework, application-oriented method of urban analysis can serve to generate new strategies and propose recommendations for action to the areas which are under consideration.

In the case of a research-oriented approach, this procedure is turned “upside down”. From the very beginning, assignments encompass a clearly defined research and design question, a specific goal or a stipulated guiding idea. A predetermined place or design object does not exist when the assignment begins. Instead, the application of methods established on the basis of the research question and the following specification of a site becomes the focus of the assignment. Following this notion, the different methodical approaches are examined, evaluated, and implemented under close consideration of the essential practical requirements.

Neither approach is ever mutually exclusive. Instead, they generate alternating cycles and "feedback loops" that enable proposing sustainable answers to the hypothetical core of the ongoing assignment. To us, it therefore becomes imaginable and desirable that a specific place with its particular socio-economic circumstances provokes the formulation of research questions in the course of the assignment that, in a further step, allow examination in terms of their general applicability. In reverse, a specification of locations within predefined research assignments can also inspire new research questions, or expand and revise the original question.

Integrated urban design instruments and tools

We do not dictate general principles to students in a top-down manner. Instead, we show them planning processes that experience a creative development with real-life projects on their own terms. In particular, this approach is applied to a diverse set of tasks directly aimed at the urban design context – a context in which planners are confronted with actors on many levels and a diverse range of circumstances. Examinations of traditional knowledge on spatial, political, social, ecological, and economic framework conditions, as well as the deliberation on future-oriented, inter- and transdisciplinary theories, are just as necessary as the development of competence in initiating and tolerating comprehensive urban development processes.

The concept of applied types of urban strategies with integrated design and planning approaches is essential to all areas of our academic teaching and scientific research activities. Basic teaching courses introduce historical urban planning theories, guiding images, and principles – not only in terms of theory, but always in parallel with exercises and designs and with attention to comparability. Particularly within the Master's research study in our institute, design as such is only a partial aspect of student assignments. The urban design-related planning process and its impact on the different urban stakeholders are fundamental to practice-oriented assignments. Such processes always produce results, even when the design itself is still under negotiation. How can we advance such complex interrelations, step by step? Here, the exchange between students and experts, and the introduction of practical knowledge into conceptual work and in the context of existing national and international networks is of particular importance.

Students do not develop their projects in a hypothetical condition of isolation. Instead, they have to actually apply and justify them, again and again, to experts and in public. An important element of urban design assignments is to communicate each individual design in spatial terms and according to different dimensions and interrelations. From the viewpoint of the urban design discipline, communication that actually conveys these issues needs to be interdisciplinary and enable direct exchange with the public and political actors. This interaction is based on a reciprocal exchange that enables the transformation of the original design concept in a perpetually sustainable way, instead of letting false compromise constrain its relevance.

Former tried and trusted approaches to urban design processes and their implementation are becoming less and less effective, given contemporary challenges. The related problems increasingly require open-ended planning approaches based on creative solutions. Different methods of illustration and communication developed in our institute support the aim of presenting creative solutions envisioned on the basis of related experimental and scientific approaches in a manner that is comprehensible to all.

The process of systematising and structuring a diverse set of information and data is an important element of teaching. For this purpose, we employ didactical and analytical tools that are subject to continuous further development within the design process. Comprehending and evaluating complex urban patterns and structures is a prerequisite for scientific analytical work. It forms a basis for deriving differentiated and integrated design strategies. Multi-dimensional graphic illustration types are particularly suitable for an analytical approach to multi-faceted urban design systems.

Urban and architectural spaces are designed by the use of drawings that serve to define and specify connections and transitions, patterns and principles by use of a diverse set of graphic illustration types. Different dimensions of planning are compiled within the process of drawing and draughting that also result in a form of illustration that no-experts can also understand. An important element in this regard is the development of an urban design matrix. The difference between an urban design analysis and a problem of natural sciences is the ambiguous and often contradictory character of urban systems. A matrix is a tool that serves to filter data and information that appear difficult to compare at a first glance and, by their juxtaposition, can generate new knowledge. As a form of graphic illustration, it is capable of describing confusing terrain through systematising, connecting, and superimposing information that originates in different topical fields. As a result, unexpected opportunities arise and are revealed.

Spatial implementation through self-initiated urban labs

The space in which participatory projects are intended to take place needs to be designed creatively. It also needs to allow interaction, with the support of urban design approaches that are capable of adaptation. In recent years we successfully implemented and demonstrated this in our urban research laboratories. For this purpose, a diverse set of architectural and urban spaces were reconfigured in order to inspire a creative exchange between students, educators, experts, and local actors directly on site.

Examples include our variable labs, which we design and implement in the context of an experimental research and teaching approach. A former swimming pool in the inner city of Solingen offered us the opportunity to generate a creative exchange with all stakeholders on site. This was possible through the adaptive reuse of the existing spatial configuration of the building complex. Based on this spatial change, we were able to advance political and societal discussions on urban transformation. The redesign of a storefront in the centre of Remscheid resulted in the creation of a neutral, yet simultaneously creative space. It allowed the bringing together of local actors and decision makers, newly inspiring them, with a focus on the topics at hand. Within our research endeavours, an inflatable research lab represented water-sensitive city concepts in public space. It supported us in conveying results to different municipalities. The bright and airy structure allowed the creation of spaces that served to discuss these complex topics with experts and laypeople in a different manner than is usually the case.

Interdisciplinary frameworks as basis for encounter

Living labs and participatory events are mostly and directly aimed at a singular topical field and a particular urban design-related, societal situation. Their intention is to find and communicate answers and solutions aimed at the tasks at hand by a targeted use of developed spatial tools and instruments. When such a framework is defined early on, successful communication is often limited or tedious, if opinions have already solidified beforehand. This raises the question how, at the very beginning of the process, all involved parties can enter into a form of agreement that can serve as a true point of origin. This can offer all participants a fresh look at the tasks at hand, from different perspectives and, at the same time, in a comprehensive manner. Such a point of origin needs to become an experience that is broadly understood and can be shared by all partners. This "common ground" needs to be applied and implemented as a starting point and framework in order to generate sustainable effects. In this context, both thematically and topically, cultural events and projects have proved just how exceptionally successful they can be. Not only can they offer a neutral basis and a shared experience for many different involved actors. They can also take place at the same time as the actual process and complement it, incrementally or cyclically. The publication in your hands illustrates this approach. It does so, to a major degree, by presenting examples of the work of the Interprofessional Studio and its "Master of Fine Arts in Spatial Performance and Design" course, which I co-founded a decade ago at the Architectural Association in London. Projects that have been initiated throughout the years, in collaboration with a cultural centre in Madrid, as well as various cultural institutions in Cologne and London, clearly show how engaging a creative dialogue within gridlocked existing planning structures can promote sustainable effects.

Application in building practice

The projects of the respective teaching modules and research projects demonstrated within this publication always refer to real-life scenarios. They shape the related tasks in terms of urban design and society. In a further step, this publication shows how these principles are applied beyond the realm of teaching and research, according to projects of building practice. One major example is the following urban and infrastructural design project in Brussels. Our interdisciplinary planning office, T2 Spatialwork, realised it in close collaboration with the Brussels-based architectural office B612 Architects. Within this multi-faceted urban project, the principles of "planning as communication" by use of mediation tools were employed, as well as the principles of an open design process that allows continuous development through negotiation, facilitated by applied partial projects. Based on the complex political, demographic and organisational situation, this case study clearly indicates the opportunities and, most of all, the potentials of "urban planning through communication". The realisation project also demonstrates to its observers current limitations in planning practice, which need to be creatively overcome. Against its background, the need for further change in contemporary practice – often perceived as too bureaucratic – and thus, the need for closer ties with teaching and research within practice become obvious.

1 LEARNING FROM PRACTICE

In cooperation with Theo Lorenz

Madrid project profile

Project initiators and cooperation partners

AAIS Interprofessional Studio London, Director: Theo Lorenz
BUW Wuppertal, Urban Design Institute: Tanja Siems and Rocio Paz
in cooperation with Matadero Madrid: Pablo Villanueva and Ariadna Cantis

Important data and facts

Arganzuela, a district of Madrid, covers an area of 6.55 sq km with a population of about 150,000. The site occupied by the cultural centre Matadero encompasses roughly 120,000 sq m. More than 500 individuals from the arts and culture sector are active there. The century-old cattle market is now dedicated to the dissemination, exploration, and creation of cultural projects and offers a diverse range of activities.

Madrid project profile

Research question and project goal is the integration of the local population in the newly developed cultural centre Matadero in Arganzuela, based on participatory workshops, events and festivals.

Project timeline

Within a timeframe of three years, nine research project meetings were held, in combination with international festivals, local events, summer schools, and workshops.

Culture as shared basis for collective action
"Common Ground", Matadero Madrid

In a complex area of creative work, such as urban planning, it is particularly obvious how difficult it is to find a common denominator for everyone involved. This becomes particularly clear when the goal is not simply the lowest common denominator, but instead a result that creates lasting effects. Many ideas that are good in themselves fail not because of the planning or anticipatory elaboration, but because they cannot be communicated to the various groups involved.

For this reason, forms of active participation that include as many actors as possible in the planning process are an important basis for a sustainable urban design practice. Participatory instruments that accompany the entire process in the form of citizens' forums, exhibitions and publications to clarify and explain the various propositions are an integral part of urban planning projects. Such events and actions serve to communicate proposals to all parties involved, through lectures, talks, and comprehensible visualisations. They allow citizens to express their concerns and expectations regarding the proposals, which in the best case will be taken into significant consideration in the further development of the projects.

In addition to these rather passive forms of participation, there are usually more extensive instruments existing for active participation. In particular, surveys and workshops aimed at different planning topics find use here and can ideally serve to actively integrate the range of opinions of different involved groups in the process. The prerequisite for all of these forms of participation is to actually reach the different actors and bring them into a dialogue. So how do you initially manage to awaken their interest in the existing tasks at hand and how can we manage to generate a desire for exchange and consensus?

Creating a dialogue through transparency

Hardened fronts between actors all too often do not allow for dialogue right from the start. In many cases, an integrated form of educational work, for instance in the context of a forum or workshop alone, is not enough to clarify common interests or goals. Neither mutual interests, nor set goals become clear, since an existing and very basic form of scepticism prevents the establishment of a consensus. Finding this consensus becomes a fundamental component of urban design practice. It is crucial to build mutual understanding on an equal footing on newly created "neutral ground". The related work hardly calls for planning new and additional interventions. Instead, the task is to include the totality of existing ideas and initiatives, newly evaluate it, situate it within a specific context and restructure it in temporal terms.

To achieve this, a range of different aspects requires attention. This range extends from deliberations on a specific urban project to far-reaching cultural and social considerations. Aside from examining a specific project, it is important to analyse what earlier alternative developments and historical approaches were existing. This investigative research should include comparable case studies or case stories (action research). Such comparative surveys serve as basis for testing which initiatives, institutions and actors are decisively involved, how great their influence was – or still is – and what their interrelations are.

Based on how initiatives, for instance political groups or associations, are enmeshed with local actors and institutions – such as cultural facilities, restaurants, businesses – particularities within the area under planning become apparent. Furthermore, they can be directly integrated in the planning process. In many cases it is of particular importance to go further in this regard. This becomes clear when the task is to approach groups that are not directly embedded within the professional process. However, they may be decisively impacted by the developments taking place. The sustainable success of a project often specifically depends on including these groups.

In this context, it is necessary to broadly interpret the idea of a developmental task. In any social context, many activities take place that are often merely considered an add-on or even trivial. But it is precisely the basic element of the urban way of life as a result of long and ongoing processes that demonstrates their impact across generations and demographic groups. The fear of losing these aspects of culture and heritage repeatedly results in resistance against renewal. If we succeed in proactively identifying and integrating these aspects of culture based on their shared character from the very beginning of a process, then we have made the first step in formulating shared goals.

However, the related approaches are not suitable as generic, off-the-shelf solutions. Thus, each individual project requires newly discovering and decoding them. To choose

Opening event, Matadero Madrid cultural centre

Matadero Madrid photographic workshop with local actors

this path forward, an urban perspective of the task at hand and the related multi-faceted urban design tools and instruments is essential. For this purpose, the areas under research should be embedded in a precisely specified framework in combination with further connective elements. Then we can create a new basis for our work, together.

Creating a shared framework

In order to transfer this approach into the realm of application, we consider events or festivals as suitable formats. Such festivals thrive on the interaction and simultaneity of manifold ideas, rather than demonstrating a singular and self-contained approach. The connecting framework of individual initiatives that are embedded in the process itself can be extraordinarily diverse. Such frameworks can encompass comprehensive and, as a result, much more independent procedures with regard to formal and topical orientation than the actual subject matter, strongly connected to the process.

This independence yields a certain degree of neutrality. Culture, in all its manifestations, is particularly suitable as a vehicle for mediation. Events that embrace artistic, performative, yet also culinary elements as a shared basis appear to be particularly successful in this regard. Such productive approaches support the development of far-reaching research questions, methodologies and tools, based on multi-dimensional, yet specific case studies. By creating a neutral point of origin, further topical fields can be accessed that otherwise are overlooked or incorrectly evaluated in terms of their relevance within the urban design process.

This method of performative spatial work beyond the actual tasks of planning is a decisive basis for the work of the Interprofessional Studio (AAIS) at the Architectural Association in London. The "Master of Fine Arts in Spatial Performance and Design" was co-developed by Theo Lorenz and me with the aim of actually implementing applied projects that have a sustainable impact on the involved creative networks. This impactable effect is intended to encompass the involved projects as well, thus expanding the definitions of architecture, urban design, and art in a sustainable and evident manner. The projects developed within this studio are particularly suited to exemplify and illustrate the principle behind "common ground" as an element of a design process. In recent years we have established a sustainable symbiosis between the work conducted at the Interprofessional Studio at the Architectural Association and the Urban Design Institute at the University of Wuppertal. Identifying and testing new methodical approaches and topical fields of application within the interweaved, performative mode of work at the AAIS contributes to further independent steps undertaken by the Institute in Wuppertal. These result in rephrasing research questions aimed at generally applicable principles of urban design. Within applied projects, they are once more and collaboratively tested and evaluated.

Participatory workshops with local actors and the cultural centre

The multi-faceted and repeated cooperation with Matadero in Madrid, most of all, descriptively documents the expanded opportunities this mode of work offers. Matadero Madrid is one of the largest European cultural institutions. It was opened in 2011 on the site of a former industrial meat processing facility, far away from the cultural establishments of the inner city. From the very beginning, this adaptive reuse project, located within a historically developed demographic context where cultural life was seemingly absent, faced the risk of gentrification processes. At the same time, it also offered the potential for new and future developments.

The collaboration with the Matadero Madrid began even before the site was actually open to the public. First, in cooperation with the Interprofessional Studio in London, we

Dance workshop with local and international artists

co-developed an urban design workshop together with the Urban Design Institute research assistant Rocio Paz Chavez in Wuppertal and curator Ariadna Cantis from Madrid. The different institutions met for an initial exchange of ideas and approaches in this creative environment. Different expert lectures featured presentations of the greater urban planning strategy of the city of Madrid. This especially concerned the area along the river Manzanares, directly bordering the site of the Matadero. Alongside, new cultural and art initiatives were introduced by several promising artists and architects. The discussion first took place on a local level and then progressed into an international debate. The applied project methods of the Interprofessional Studio and the academic projects of the Urban Design Institute were confronted with the new context on site. The basic precondition of establishing shared knowledge of the site and its genius loci served to initiate the actual interdisciplinary cooperation.

Within a two-week workshop, the students from both institutions jointly researched the district. In this context, they participated in a dérive on site, together with six architects from Madrid: in situations aimed at "becoming acquainted" with something, the dérive as a method is a suitable means of intensively comprehending and experiencing an area of the city and all its peculiarities. This can include local participants and those from abroad, while supporting the generation of new and independent approaches to "becoming acquainted" with the city. In the workshop, the different groups discovered unique elements that transcended the scope of official planning concepts and analysis undertaken by local planners. In particular, the communal way in which people of different generations and age groups interacted in the area became apparent. The existence of multi-layered, site-specific traditions was expressed and illustrated in plans and maps, based on the visionary perambulation of the site, facilitated by the dérive. The evaluation of the resulting maps and the illustration of the distribution of functions in the district indicated that the area features many positive cultural achievements and multi-layered characteristics. Particularly in the culinary realm, this offered potential for the further development of the site.

Active participation through creative events

Based on a creative approach to urban spaces, it soon became clear that further applied steps needed to occur in order to actually achieve a more expansive result. For the following year, in the context of the opening of the cultural centre, we planned a series of workshops and events. The intention was to provide members of the public with a diverse set of opportunities to become acquainted with the new cultural institution in the district. But most of all the workshops and events were aimed at the local population. The students of the Interprofessional Studio initiated a series of workshops with members of different age groups. This included photo and scientific workshops as well as applied dance, sound, and music seminars with children and adolescents to test the results in various performances in which young people and adults could participate.

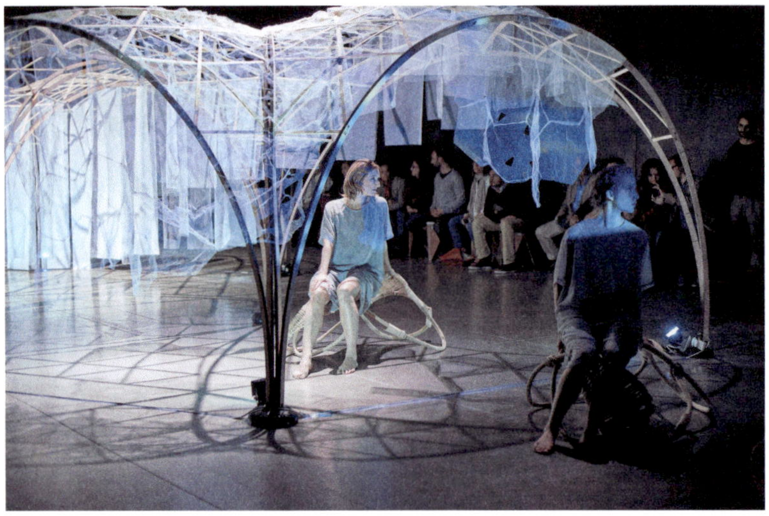

Dance performance, New Movement Collective

Food tasting with local gastronomes

Creative dinner as a discussion platform

Local market with local producers

The point of origin of all workshops was to support people in becoming acquainted with each other and the site. Some workshops were oriented on becoming acquainted with the area according to new criteria, in detail. For this purpose, documentary and forensic photography and sound recordings were created and related installations were set up. In parallel, the active dance workshops and those with artistic intent served to familiarise the residents with the new cultural opportunities and institutions. Therefore, step by step they became participants of the new cultural centre before it even was actually open to the public.

These individual workshop-type events were embedded in a dance performance, designed and realised by the students in collaboration with the New Movement Collective dance ensemble. The grand finale attracted more than one thousand visitors on the occasion of the opening of the centre. It was decisive for the events to not be predetermined, commercially oriented festivals. Instead, they were supposed to originate in creative and international collaborations, oriented on the moment of coming together as a team. The open network behind this ensured equal access to the site for all parties involved, which initiated new connections between the local actors. The approach allowed us to ensure that the community experienced immediate participation in these cultural activities. As a result, the site became the place of action and participants were able to perceive it in a different manner than usual in the context of the events.

Principal elements of participatory processes

The previous demonstrated forms of participation are basic modules for ongoing urban development processes. They enable an integrated way of becoming acquainted with otherwise abstract or impersonal planned and realised projects, in a manner that can be easily accessed and experienced. For enduring effects, further steps in the process are necessary. The example of the Matadero shows that the participation of guests alone is neither sufficient to establish an enduring connection to the immediate neighbourhood, nor between the local creative actors and the cultural centre. Sustainable participation should offer all parties involved further and enduring advantages and opportunities for development.

On this basis, together with the team of the cultural centre Matadero, we developed a festival for the following year. In addition to workshops and performances, we invited a diverse range of new actors to actively participate. We intended to embed local knowledge and capacities in the events and, as a result, activate them in an enduring way. For instance, a bunch of non-professional local dancers were integrated in the dance performance featuring internationally renowned professional dancers. Beyond that, local restaurant owners offered a variety of culinary events in cooperation with the artists.

The local market became a particular focal point of sustainability and success. The market vendors and merchants occupied structures the AAIS students created for the performances during the festival. Here, a diverse range of local products were made available and culinary food tastings offered a creative built upon knowledge and ideas of local business and urban actors. This way, the project did generate a sustainable effect for the site and long-lasting after-effect for the community. The market has by now become an established feature at the cultural centre and the restaurants that participated in the festival were also able to permanently operate on site or in the area. New forms of symbiosis were created on a basis that was established by all participants together.

Throughout the years, the stages undertaken for the series of projects that we developed and accompanied can be summed up as methodical principles of "common ground" procedures. By doing so, they can be identified within other projects or applied repeatedly. These methods of participative and collective teamwork can build upon each other. In a simplified manner, they can be summarised as "identifying characteristics", "shared discoveries and experiences" and "enduring creations".

Interactive strategy table, *Thames Gateway Assembly* exhibition

“Identifying characteristics” using urban design tools

Thames Gateway Assembly Project, London

Again, at the beginning it was important to identify the characteristics of the site and the specific cultural particularities and products, based on corresponding analysis with multiple feedback loops. This collective investigation is, on the one hand, oriented on individually gathering and objectively evaluating data. On the other hand, it is necessary to include existing planning schemes and ideas early on, based on the exchange with multi-faceted local initiatives, and to reciprocally engage in their renewed evaluation. This multi-layered approach allows us to take a new look at existing circumstances and, thus, discover specificities, differences and intersections.

In the case of the Matadero, the exchange with local planners, young creative actors, and residents of the area made two things apparent: one, the existing distance between the cultural centre and the local population, and second, the shared interests in relation to culinary activities. In other cases, the very same approach can result in very different and also very multi-faceted insight. An example for this is the multi-dimensional Thames Gateway Assembly project, which we present in the following.

For decades, the extensive Thames Gateway Quarter with its population of 1.45 million was home to new urban design ideas, initiatives, and project development. The London Thames Gateway Development Corporation constituted an institution exclusively responsible for the development of the area, covering 100,000 ha. The enormous amount of different planning ideas and opinions of participants made it extremely difficult to produce a comprehensive picture of the situation and its potentials. Due to this circumstance, it was even more difficult to assemble the range of different actors, in order to make their commonalities visible and design the process in a more transparent manner. For this purpose, the AA Diploma Unit 14, led by Theo Lorenz in collaboration with Peter Staub, Neil Davidson, and myself, generated an urban design charrette in the form of an exhibition including all existing project ideas.

Conveying urban processes through interactive exhibitions

The “Assembly” exhibition as an urban construct allowed us to bring together a most diverse set of stakeholders – the different agencies and departments of municipal administration and committees of local political actors, corporations and associations, various expert audiences, as well as the common urban public – in order to start a conversation. Within the Thames Gateway “Assembly”, a seven-metre-long strategy table served to encompass more than 30 historical and contemporary architectural and urban design concepts authored by experts and students. The proposals were made accessible through an interactive planning tool integrated in the strategy table surface. Users were able to contextualise them and as a result became subject to negotiation. This way, participants were able to encounter each other within a now “realised” framework, discover shared interests, and provide new impulses for a joint discussion on the proposals.

Building upon the multi-layered characteristics and identified potentials, a series of different initiatives formed. These initiatives included seminars and scientific publications, as well as student projects that were integrated into actual planning schemes for the area. Some initiatives influenced urban design strategies of the city of London, such as the ALGG policy framework “All London Green Grid” (reference to publication *Mediating Architecture*, Lorenz 2011).

Multi-disciplinary event at the Design Quarter Ehrenfeld

Dance performance with New Movement Collective

"Shared discovery" – exploring the city with analytical methods
Cologne-Ehrenfeld: A festival for the district

Another important step of participatory work can be described as a form of shared discovery. Based on the specific circumstances of a district, quarter, or neighbourhood, activities can be retraced, resulting in the creation of new interrelations through shared discoveries. These immediate activities can comprise guided photographic, audio and film recordings or dance workshops aimed at physically and sensorily experiencing the environment differently from usual, through new patterns of movement. As just one outcome, new situations can be discovered. This approach can include shared activities, such as gathering plants or collecting objects within a certain area. The basic premise is to create a form of shared perception that is easily accessible to all participants – even if they are guided by different attitudes and assumptions. A further collaborative project of the Interprofessional Studio and the Chair of Urban Design serves as an insightful example.

Two years after the Interprofessional Studio had begun its workshops and performances in collaboration with the Matadero in Madrid, this experience served as the basis for the conceptual development of a festival for the "Design Quarter" in the Ehrenfeld borough of Cologne. The area surrounding the Helios site in Ehrenfeld is characterised by long-term disputes between different stakeholders. This area, defined by its industrial history and factory buildings that eventually offered plenty of room for activities in the realms of nightlife, art, and culture, was recently under planning by an investment group with the aim of building a large shopping mall. Our intention was, as neutral and independent observers – "outsiders" even – to create a shared experience, aimed at stakeholders with greatly differing interests. A dance event integrated in the festival once more served as a neutral attraction. This allowed an offering of various workshops as extensions of the event. They became an opportunity for creative encounter and inspired cooperation between local actors. For methodical purposes, two workshops will be highlighted in the following.

Creative workshops for connecting stakeholders

The photography or film workshops, for instance, brought together participants from different stakeholder groups. They explored the area together, created a storyboard and established therefore an artistic demonstration of it, using photographic or filmic representations. The creation of static and moving images allows all participants to see the area from a different perspective. It also allows them to depict the area, free from intentions of overwhelming the other participants with their creation or convincing them of their own experience by insisting on a unique and singular characteristic. Participants were able to recognise, reveal, and document many specific characteristics of the area, as well as the extensive decay of the entire district.

The second approach to shared discovery, a dance workshop in the "Design Quarter Ehrenfeld" was offered to the community. Physical participation in this context serves as an instrument that connects and transforms. By learning choreographic procedures, the workshop generates an understanding of the event itself. The underlying premise is that all participants can become acquainted with, experience, and respect their own potentials and limitations, as well as those of the other participants, within a discipline they are not familiar with. At the same time, the intention is to achieve a harmonic shared result, despite the existing limitations.

In the course of one year, the different proposed workshops overcame the protracted, pre-existing conflicts between political representatives and district residents through moments of togetherness. As of today, neither is a shopping mall under development on the site any longer, nor a cinema or nightclub. Instead, the aim is to build a primary and comprehensive school. Its pedagogic concept seeks to create a symbiosis between school education and university training.

AAIS "Re-Dial" festival in Hackney, London

"Re-Dial" structure as a walkable model

“Shared experience” through interdisciplinary workshops
“Re-Dial”: An event in Hackney, London

Through their performances and integrated workshops, shared cultural events and festivals, such as planned by us cooperatively in the case of the “Design Quarter”, can be interpreted as a further principle of participation. The shared experience of stimulating activities such as performative events that impact a specific place or produce culinary happenings enables encounter on equal footing. At the same time, they comprise realised projects. The project-as-event becomes the non-judgemental host of the event. This principle can be applied to many projects of the Interprofessional Studio, including the studio’s urban and architectural concepts, collectively created by tutors and students. In relation to the city as phenomenon, this form of participation is particularly visible in the case of the “Re-Dial” project in London. The project, based on an urban installation in the London Borough of Hackney, served to test the different interdependent and interactive forces impacting humans, nature, and the city within a walkable model. All elements of the event were aimed at facilitating a shared experience. Aside from culinary events, including a supper club, most of all the public performances became an extraordinary experience. Impulse lectures and round-table discussions that took place during dinner or between performances offered the opportunity to newly debate and negotiate controversial topics within a neutral, yet creative context, despite how gridlocked urban processes may have become.

The different urban factors, such as environmental conditions due to noise emissions, intense sunlight, or wind stress can become something to be visualised and experienced within a sound-based or multi-media performance. We oriented them on a walkable model. The built timber construction comprises a walkable topographical artefact within a defined grid that is intended to represent the urban environment at an urban design scale. Different pendulum types integrated in the built structure became active based on the interrelations of the different represented urban forces and energies. The different formations and juxtapositions of visitors and their movement, as well as environmental and technological triggers such as street noise, wind, and sun, served to activate the different pendulum types. The actual performance combined all of these energies into a comprehensive choreography. Visitors and dancers jointly moved through the model in a targeted way. They were also guided by the sounds and movements of the musicians and their instruments. The result was a shared experience of urban design factors that typically remain abstract or subjective. City, nature, and humans became one within an all-embracing experimental fabric.

"Seed to Scene" festival, participatory workshop in Covent Garden

"Creative Industries" round-table discussion during the "Seed to Scene" festival

Generating sustainable effects and "enduring creations"

Covent Garden, London

As the Matadero case study in Madrid demonstrates, it is important to establish commonality between all participants from the beginning. This "common ground" is supposed to lead to the creation of "fertile ground". This also means that all commonalities eventually need to find fertile ground in order to thrive. In this regard, how can we generate enduring effects, instead of only triggering short-term, singular occurrences? Sustainable outcomes can reveal a very diverse and multi-faceted character. In an ideal case, an individual project can generate a multitude of sustainable initiatives among participating actors.

The concluding example in this chapter is the "Seed to Scene" festival, which we developed for the Covent Garden district of London. The project arose from a specific occasion in this urban area in central London. From the 1970s onwards, the site surrounding the former flower market developed into a centre for innovative art and cultural activities. Urban actors and artists had succeeded in preventing the demolition of the flower market halls and, thus, the complete redesign and gentrification of the entire site.

In recent decades the area increasingly became a popular tourist location and, to a major degree, a place oriented on purely commercial musical, theatre, and opera performances. These changes also led to a certain set of buildings that received permits exclusively for cultural uses yet were eventually no longer suitable for such purposes in commercial terms. As a result, following the turn of the millennium, the related buildings remained vacant for many years. The Interprofessional Studio succeeded in acquiring one of these buildings for the purpose of a two-week festival. Our aim was to recreate culturally oriented public events, to underline the character of the area as a creative and independent location. We generated and did build innovative, adaptable structures that are attractive to several cultural uses. Immediately following our events, the entire block was comprehensively renovated to build a space for creative individuals. Its mixed-use character has become a unique feature throughout the entire district. It currently houses an independent film school as well as young start-up firms active in the creative industry sector, these new residents are generating a permanent creative community.

Discovering and networking multi-faceted initiatives

The comprehensive effects and sustainable impacts of such specific creative uses are important. Our festival was a "seed" – an urban incubator that promoted the founding of different endeavours. Essential in this context are the multi-faceted initiatives that can generate particular key moments during a festival. The most successful initiative from the various multi-disciplinary collaborations during our "Seed to Scene" festival is the dance company called "New Movement Collective", which was actually founded during this collaboration. We created together with the dance company "spatial choreographies" that comprehensively combined architectural structures and the movements of performers within a unique build form. The festival further set creative impulses for the area and marked the beginning of a successful international collaboration between music producer Andrew Dean, renowned singer David McAlmont and ourselves – Theo Lorenz and Tanja Siems – establishing a creative, performative, interdisciplinary team which has lasted for years now. Beyond that, the festival laid the groundwork for David McAlmont's "performance presentation" format, taking place in different European cities as performative lectures oriented on politics and art history.

The after-effect as a catalyst: the multi-dimensional legibility of demonstrably enduring results, often transcending the envisioned scope of the actual project and its aims, becomes the measure for the success of participation efforts within projects. The creation of a diverse set of innovative initiatives during such performative festivals on site is, to us, enduring proof of the effectiveness of our methodical and applied approaches within the Interprofessional Studio.

Brussels project profile

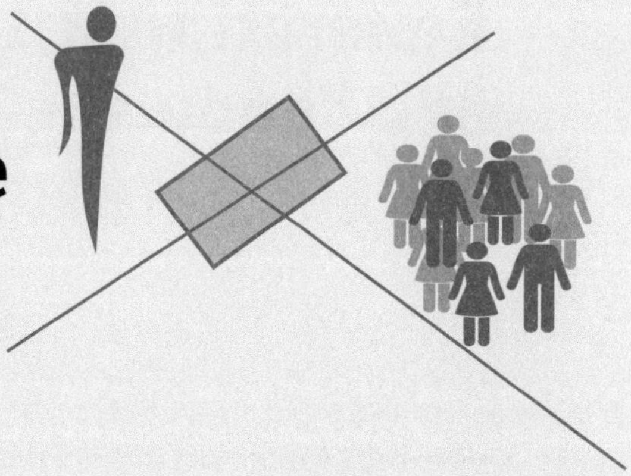

Project initiators and clients

The City of Brussels, represented by Pascal Smet,
Minister of Mobility and Public Works;
The community of Berchem-Sainte-Agathe,
represented by Mayor Joël Riguelle;
STIB Société des transports intercommunaux
de Bruxelles (Brussels Municipal Transport Services).

Participating partners and institutions

B612 Architectes, Brussels. Directors: Olivier Mathieu, Li Mei Tsien;
T2 Spatialwork Ltd., London. Directors: Theo Lorenz, Tanja Siems;
Workshops for the master plan in the second planning phase with
JES (Jongeren maken de Stad) and Yota!, Brussels.

Important data and facts

The area of Berchem-Sainte-Agathe municipality is 2.9 sq km; in 2019 the population was 25,500, of which 51.5 per cent were female and 48.5 per cent were male; the age distribution is as follows: 25.2 per cent in age group 0 to 17, 59.4 per cent in age group 18 to 64, and 15.4 per cent aged over 65.

Project objectives and goals

Developing a master plan for Dr.-Schweitzer-Square in the municipality of Berchem in Brussels based on sustained participatory integration of all those involved throughout the entire planning and implementation process. Redesigning the intersection that is heavily trafficked by personal motorised vehicles to create a comprehensive space for movement and leisure of all users.

Design project timeline

Analysis phase: investigation of the situation, listing of defects and qualities (0.5 years)
Participation phase in parallel with the analysis and development phase, with various workshop offerings (2 years)
Development phase: urban development strategy and revision of master plan (1.5 years)
Development phase of urban furniture, pavilion and tram stops (1 year)
Building phase: layout of square, traffic infrastructure and architectural elements (2.5 years)

A PARTICIPATORY IMPLEMENTATION PROJECT
BRUSSELS

Presentations of the master plan development to local actors, such as schools and restaurateurs

As planners, we set a framework that aims for high quality in both the urban development process and the design. This will always be maintained and intensified through our negotiation and mediation. The Dr.-Schweitzer-Square implementation project in Berchem municipality in Brussels, which was completed by our practice T2 Spatialwork in cooperation with the B612 architects practice in Brussels, can be used as a practical example. The project illustrates, very clearly, this mediating planning and design process, which we further developed with the acceptance and participation of the citizens and users.

From the very start, the basic principle involved a design process that does not view the design concept presented as a fixed and predetermined element from which there should be as little deviation as possible, but instead as a proposal that encourages all participants to take part in its further development. Each step of the design process is understood to be a shared design task that leads to the next step. This iterative process does not view the interim results or the overall result as the smallest common denominator of ideas to be achieved, but it tests and evaluates the implementation of the nuanced ideas of all participants (refer to the theory of the "design of the design process", Lorenz et al, 2011). The implementation project is therefore not just a built project that is finite in itself, but also serves as proof of the conceptual validity of the approach.

Our design process is based on the principle of directly involving all those with an interest in the planning – from the beginning of the design process through to its completion. Each and every community has committed actors who are brought together with the help of our mediating communication methods and who participate in the overall planning and building process. This means that, with this innovative participatory process, the urban development project is not just reduced to the smallest common denominator based on compromises agreed; rather, it can develop further in a sustainable fashion.

Mediatory communication methods with model and master plan; workshop with local seniors

Promoting cooperation between the different professional disciplines in the planning departments through mediation

Concepts for barrier-free access implemented at Dr.-Schweitzer-Square

GENIUS LOCI:
THE PLACE AND ISSUES TO BE ADDRESSED

The City of Brussels and the Mayor of the Berchem community organised an international public competition for the redesign of Dr.-Schweitzer-Square. The square, which is located to the west of Brussels' inner city, turns out – after intensive urban design and transport engineering investigation – to have a complex infrastructure with a very confusing intersection for all traffic participants.

There are no areas with sufficient quality to make people want to linger, nor any areas for active use by the different age groups; neither are there any clearly defined pedestrian and cycle through routes.

With the help of our urban development approaches and methods, the existing situation was recorded and analysed; for further evaluation, this was compared with historical images and sketches as well as with the current plan documents. The results were directly incorporated in the planning for the different areas of the square, as well as in the systematic redesign of the transport system and the urban strategy to be developed.

Today it is possible to view the entire redesign of Dr.-Schweitzer-Square from a bird's eye view and satellite perspective using Google Earth. The former disorganised, obscure, and unsafe situation for all traffic participants throughout the entire street area can now still be seen via Google Maps – just like in time travel – by viewing the no-longer-existing street at the crossroads of Avenue Josse Goffin and Chaussée de Gand directly opposite Rue Openveld.

From the very beginning, the planning task was beset by considerable obstacles and hindrances that had to be overcome during the entire participatory planning process. One of the most difficult obstacles was the lack of cooperation between the specific disciplines in some of the departments involved in the planning. Even though many of these employees work in the same building, sometimes even on the same floor, they do not use that as an opportunity for in-depth communication. At the very start it was clear to our design team that they had to create a strategic space in which cooperative planning could take place between all participants on neutral ground. We equipped this place with current planning documents, an ideas board, and a suggestion box for concerns and needs. We held on-site planning and discussion rounds and presented the results of these on a weekly basis, which led to a better exchange between the various disciplines.

A similar approach was taken to mediation between the different clients involved in this prestigious Belgian project. Each one of them felt that they were the only contract partner for this project. However, when important decisions had to be made, none of the parties felt able to take responsibility. This was exacerbated by the poor information flow between the different planning authorities – starting with the City of Brussels and the respective Federal Ministries responsible, via the planning departments with the various responsibilities that actually sit at the same level, and the STIB Brussels Municipal Transport Services and its engineers, through to the local Mayor of the Berchem community. This situation made it difficult for us to encourage open communicative exchange.

Mediatory communication methods

In each public forum in which we presented the ongoing design and planning in real time, opening it up for discussion, we managed not only to invite the clients but also to encourage them to attend and take a committed part in the discourse, primarily using the applied communication methods of the different forums. Achieving and even guaranteeing a transparent planning process was only possible through ongoing, interactive exchange of information between these institutions and departments, with their different agendas, covering the respective planning phase.

Another obstacle, and often a big hurdle preventing interested actors from participating in the process, is the very different languages which are spoken. There are already three languages that are referred to as official – Flemish, French, and German. These were spoken within the interest and stakeholder groups, as well as English, and in many cases, North-African Arabic. Consequently, one of the most important tasks for our team was to produce the planning documents in such a way that they could be read and understood not only by experts but also – and especially so – by laypeople. We could therefore guarantee that at least three languages were spoken in the participatory workshops. Our planning team is a multilingual entity, which was therefore able to bridge language barriers directly in the various workshop offerings, public conferences, and forums through appropriate translation and, at the same time, was also able to convey content of a planning nature. In addition, in exceptional cases, local translators were also engaged in order to build up and strengthen trust in the various aspects of the implementation project.

Our planning and building process was further hampered by the worldwide and local financial crisis in 2007 and by the political uncertainty resulting from the 2010 government crisis in Belgium, which meant that there was no acting government for a period of almost one hundred days. As in other projects, our planning included the possibility that there would be a change in the funding situation. Of special importance was to ensure that the individual elements were scaleable. For planning and developing an urban development strategy for the district and for developing the design concept at the Chaussée de Gand, this meant, for example, that the solutions offered were flexible and allowed for continuing synergies.

In the context of planning the development of the infrastructure and its technical details we first had to adopt rules for cycle traffic and the required installations. These were necessary to generate a comprehensive mobility strategy for the district, and thereby to create a stimulus with respect to the entire traffic infrastructure for the city of Brussels. These necessary planning rules and a tried-and-tested framework for technical installations ensuring barrier freedom did not yet exist at the time we were involved in planning the square. For the traffic strategy, we have applied a mixed principle of the existing and well working rules in Germany and Great Britain. The principle of separate cycle routes was developed using dedicated lanes on the street or on the pavement, using a combination of separate cycle and pedestrian pathways. This combination was tested beforehand using a simulation of the traffic flow of the different types of traffic in the different areas. In order to afford cycles a head start compared with motorised traffic, dedicated areas for cycles were planned at the traffic lights in front of crossroads, allowing cyclists to start immediately ahead of the motorised traffic when the lights turned green.

To create barrier freedom, we relied upon studies and actual traffic schemes in other European countries as tried-and-tested examples. By using special design patterns as well as specifically selected materials for the surface finishes we were able, in our design, to create a strategy for people with various disabilities. Using raised and dropped areas in the right places it was possible to ensure that the footpaths were safe and barrier free. The choice of materials and their arrangement allowed for good orientation for people who are blind or partially sighted. Later on, these concepts and implementation strategies that we developed for cycle traffic and barrier freedom were adopted as principles in the statutory guidelines for the city of Brussels.

Furthermore, no explicit guidelines for the participatory involvement of citizens and actors in the planning process existed. As a planning team, we initially proceeded intuitively and developed the workshops from our experience of the teaching and research methods in such a way that they could be made suitable for the participation of groups of different ages and experience. Our participatory approaches (as described below) with the different interest groups within the four planning phases represent the most important prerequisites for the development of a sustainable concept for Dr.-Schweitzer-Square.

URBAN DEVELOPMENT METHODS AND PARTICIPATORY PROCEDURES IN THE PLANNING PHASES

From the very beginning, our planning team had agreed to develop the urban strategy as well as the new concept for the square in a comprehensive manner, and to integrate the urban actors from the various walks of life from the very beginning in the design and planning process. After our outline design had passed through various competition stages and presentation rounds in front of clients and stakeholders, our international and interdisciplinary planning team received the commission for planning the square. In that decision, an important criterion was the fact that we emphasised the need for participatory integration of all parties involved as part of our planning assignment.

In order to better understand the place, we systematically carried out analytical steps with various evaluation rounds during the first planning phase for the urban strategy. The interdisciplinary nature of our planning network made it possible for us to ensure that we did justice to the situation of the place and the infrastructure requirements. Furthermore, the evaluation confirmed what we had already discovered during our first on-site visits: the plan area is extremely confusing and unsafe for both pedestrians and traffic.

Design alternatives within the planning process

As already mentioned, we faced the challenge of bringing together around a table the experts from the different planning departments, as well as interested actors, using interdisciplinary workshops. In this context we had a special interest in bringing about a comprehensive dialogue by providing a natural and comfortable setting. Owing to our open participatory process, we were always able to discuss the design alternatives with the wider public within the ongoing planning steps. This made it possible for us, throughout the planning process, to bring the master plan and the design concept up to the current planning status and to communicate this to all involved parties using various presentation methods and a number of different platforms. Using interest group analysis at an early stage, we identified those parties with an existing interest in the planning project, as well as other people whom – although interested – were not yet involved. The methods used in interest group analysis are described in the systematised dictionary, together with a description of various urban development methods. This analysis then made it possible to personally invite the local citizens and owners – such as shop owners, children, and young people, as well as employees and seniors with their various spheres of interest – to the planned participatory workshops, which were subdivided into subjects and working groups.

This diagrammatic overview shows the workshops, conferences, and forums, with the actors and respective subjects, which took place in parallel with the planning process in the four planning phases. In the category headed "Participation of actors", the duration, method of approach, and number of people are set out within the different workshop offerings. Each icon used in the illustration represents ten people in the real context of the workshops. The bars on the flags indicate the duration of the various events, which lasted between two and eight hours.

Participation of actors and stakeholders in the development of the master plan

We subdivided the planning for the infrastructure-dominated square into four phases. The first phase started with the development of the urban strategy and the master plan, and ended in the participatory design process with the design of the urban and architectural elements. For us it was important to allocate the actors and stakeholders, from the very beginning, to different working groups using different working formats such as workshops, conferences, and forums. The first focus group with up to thirty people consisted of citizens of various age groups and social backgrounds who, with the help of creative, moderated ideas, workshops, and working groups, assessed and evaluated the planning for the square and contributed additional ideas. Another focus group consisted of staff from the city department and planning experts. Using monthly conferences with up to fifty people it was possible to have in-depth discussions, check the content, and further develop the designs for the master plan and the urban elements in working groups set up for the purpose.

The citizens' parliament, the largest interest group with up to two hundred people, comprised urban players and actors such as local entrepreneurs and inhabitants. Using interest group analysis at an early stage, we had identified those parties with an existing interest in the planning project, such as the stakeholders, as well as other interested people who were not yet directly involved in the project. These

PLANNINGPHASE 1
Urban Strategy
-Masterplan-
during competition phase

Focusgroups

Workshop
+- 8H

- Poll / Survey / Interview
- Idea workshop (Schools)
- Idea workshop (Associations)

Children / Seniors

Departments/Experts

Conference
+- 4H

- Organisied walks
- Conferences with large groups

Strategic focus: Traffic

Interest Groups

Forum
+-2H

- Poll / Survey / Interview
- Panel: Future visions

Stakeholder

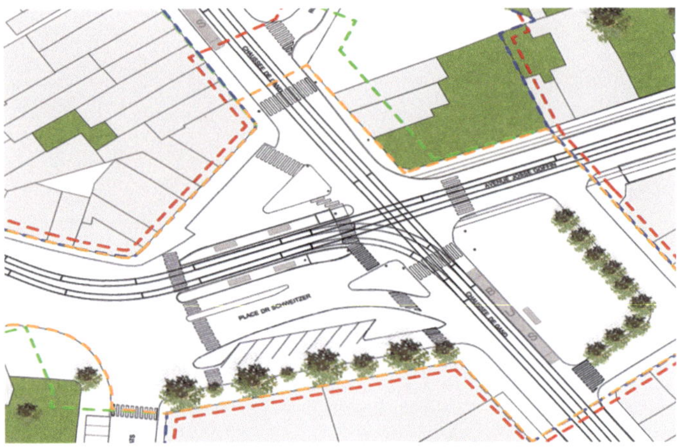

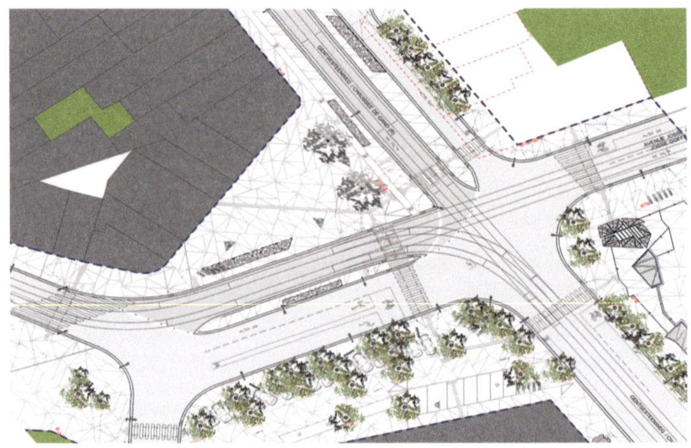

PLANNINGPHASE 2
Participatory Pavilion
-Masterplan-
through Participation

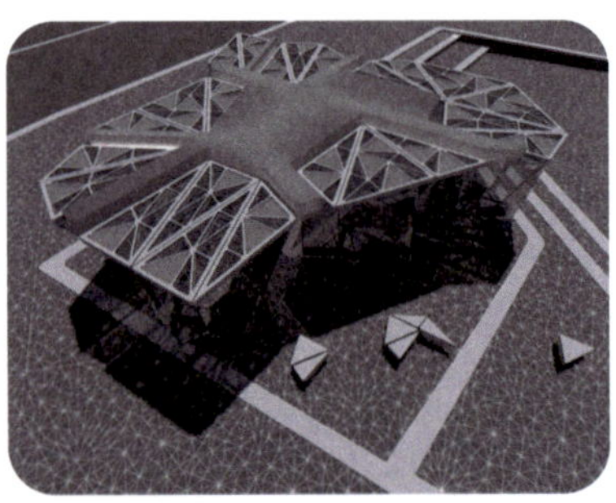

Focusgroups

Workshops
+- 8H

- Organised walks
- Working groups (selected)
- Idea workshop (open)

Young people / Seniors

Departments/Experts

Conference
+- 4H

- Idea conference
- Working groups (selected)

Strategic focus: Urban

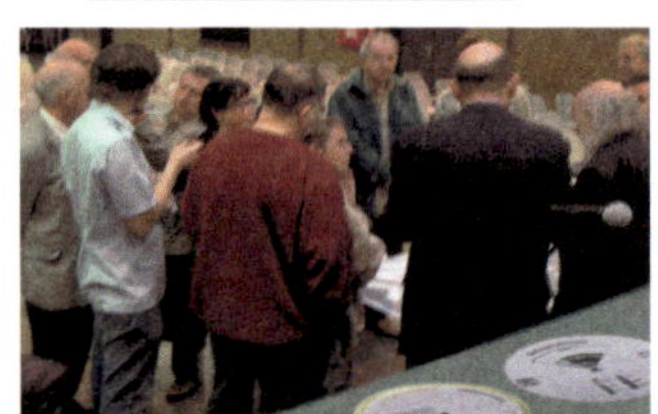

Interest Groups

Forum
+-2H

- Citizen parliament
- Prospect workshop

Stakeholder

Presentation of the "Phases and participatory involvement within the entire planning process"

PLANNINGPHASE 3
Urban Elements
-Street furniture-

Focusgroups

Workshop +- 8H

- World Cafe
- Working groups
- Idea workshop (open)

Children / Seniors

Departments/Experts

Conference +- 4H

- Idea conference
- Research group (selected)
- Working groups

Focus: Landscape

Interest Groups

Forum +-2H

- Urban quarter Workshop
- Citizens' Jury (Presentation)

Stakeholder

PLANNINGPHASE 4
Architecture
-Bus and Tram Stops-

Focusgroups

Workshop +- 8H

- Research group (selected)
- Idea workshop (selected)

Young people / Seniors

Departments/Experts

Conference +- 4H

- Idea conference
- Working groups (selected)
- Working groups (open)

Focus: Architecture

Interest Groups

Forum +-2H

- Urban quarter Workshop
- Citizens' Jury (Presentation)

Stakeholder

Kick-off event: Workshop format "future forum"

were brought together in a kind of planning cell and, in the further course of the planning stages, this cell was subdivided into working groups. Within the quarterly forums, this planning cell was able to query the urban development strategies and architectural objectives we had developed in the setting of "future conferences" as well as "perspective workshops" and then to develop detailed proposals, which – at the end of the event – were presented in the forum and discussed again.

For us as the planning team, the most important assignment within the design and planning process was to generate a balance between the different modes of transport with a view to developing a more generally applicable urban strategy. This would improve ecomobility and, at the same time, provide new high-quality open areas for people to move about or to rest and meet other people. The urban neighbourhood, which hitherto had largely been dominated by private motorised traffic, now featured four different areas with different uses and complementary atmospheres that were clearly defined in the strategic master plan and served the different modes of transport. In addition, it was possible to create safe traffic routes for pedestrians and cyclists by efficiently relocating the road layout with a systematic concentration of the specific routes for motorised private traffic and local public transport. In a first kick-off event we presented the urban development strategy alternatives we had developed to the public. Between the different presentations which, step by step, systematically illustrated the urban and infrastructure strategy with its planning elements for the neighbourhood and the square, a number of question rounds were inserted in order to establish tangible exchange by way of direct debate. These strategy plans were put on display in the auditorium directly after our presentation of the individual steps.

Participatory workshop processes

We carried out the kick-off event as a "future forum", with a subsequent perspective workshop using a charrette format, in order to discuss, in depth, the content of the alternatives presented by ourselves with the two hundred interested people. The public consisted of involved citizens as well as people from various public domains, such as representatives of the client, the City of Brussels, the Mayor of Berchem municipality, and the staff of the town planning and transport planning departments. The forum was used to publicly discuss the status quo, to exchange different viewpoints in a dialogue, and finally to work out practical proposals for the next planning steps. Within this kick-off forum and during forums over the following months, the group of participants was randomly subdivided into small heterogeneous groups of up to thirty people. One expert was assigned to each group to answer questions. These experts rotated between the individual working groups. At the end, the discussion was summarised in a type of short report; it was then presented to the entire interest group and the discussion was opened up again.

Because it was not possible for all participants to speak within such a format, we organised further workshops with different interest and target groups during the following months. In the first citizen forum it was possible to foster a valuable exchange with the citizens and stakeholders. This

"Interviews with stakeholder local actors"

led to many suggestions for the development of the urban strategy, which we were able to work into the urban development and infrastructure concept alternatives in the subsequent planning steps. Carrying out this interactive citizen forum at precisely this early point in the planning process was extremely valuable, since it was possible – through the open exchange – to overcome existing conflicts between the actors in the community and to accelerate and creatively support cooperation between them. At the end of the chapter we will again discuss in more detail the different methods used in the workshops as well as during the conferences and forums.

Interviews and tours with participants on site

In order for us planners to comprehend the situation of the square even better and to drive detailed information collection, we carried out random interviews and surveys as well as site inspections and guided tours, paperchases, or similar games with the residents and interested people. This procedure supported the collection of additional information which, beyond the analytical urban development method, provided detailed information about the district.

First of all, we conducted open interviews directly on site and, after that, guided interviews with active citizens of the district whom we had already identified. In this way we were able to capture experiences and impressions of the residents and actors who were active in the various associations and to obtain further critical information about the district. Based on the evaluation part of the urban development analysis we were able to distil concrete criteria and work them into a catalogue of survey questions. With the help of this catalogue the people surveyed were able to provide answers relating to the strengths and weaknesses of the district and to offer direct suggestions for improvements.

In addition to these survey sheets, we produced easy-to-read planning documents that were added to the survey catalogue in order to convey the concept ideas we were promoting. Subsequently, these materials were distributed in the form of a mailshot and, in addition, were uploaded to an easy-to-use online platform. After a few weeks the results of the online survey and the mailshot were collected and the deficits and qualities of the neighbourhood highlighted by the respondents were compiled in a table. The contributions were compiled in a cluster and hierarchically ordered by urgency. This systematic listing helped us to obtain detailed statements for the next planning steps.

In order to keep this analogue and digital dialogue process going, we started further surveys. In view of the fact that the response to the second survey was very poor compared with the previous one, we decided to use other methods to obtain additional information. We therefore began to organise open walkabouts and guided tours with the urban actors, and to carry these out over a longer period. As part of these creative tours, the method of trail-finding can be helpful for exploring the history of the place and local knowledge. At the end of the walkabouts and tours there were feedback sessions in order to retain and graphically capture the key impressions and also – in some instances – to compile the design

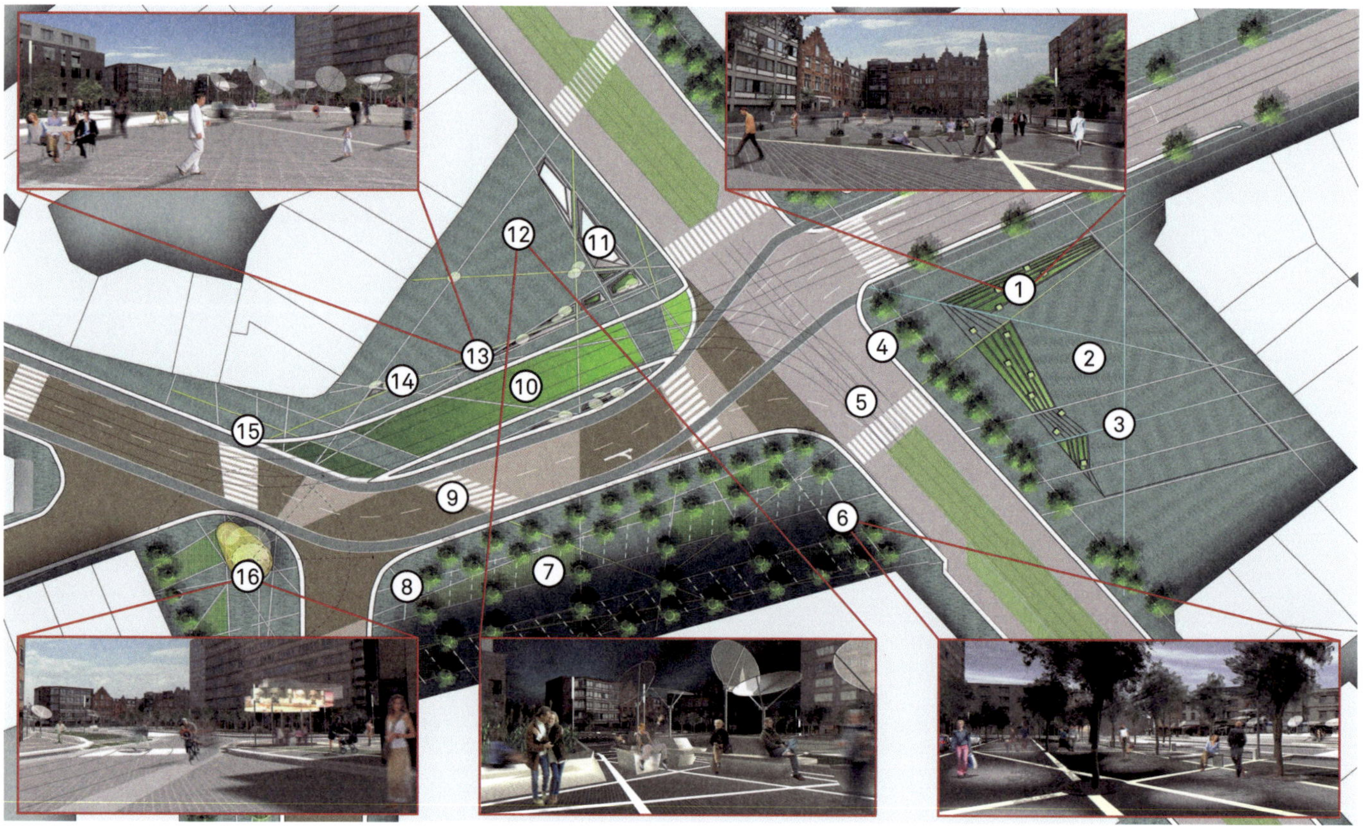

Montage of the street furniture and spatial elements for guided tours

proposals offered by the group. Our task as designers and planners was to evaluate the entire group's ideas and visions and to check them for their potential feasibility. This can be done using a kind of points system that makes it clear to all participants which contributions can be adopted in the ongoing planning and design process.

In contrast to the open walkabouts carried out by ourselves, the tours around the neighbourhood guided by the experts informed the participants about the planned urban development and infrastructure concepts. Similar to the open walkabouts, these tours were followed up with direct questions to the group regarding their impressions, comments, and suggestions. We then recorded these. The open walkabouts and the expert-guided tours were intended to provide information that was still lacking, and to further encourage dialogue between the participants.

This method of "on-site reconnaissance" with the help of interviews, surveys, walkabouts, and tours supports the collection of information, the aim of which is to obtain a better feeling for the place and its genius loci, and also to encourage all participants to identify with the place. We carried out these local inspections with the help of committed residents, for example those who were very active in various associations. In this way we were able to obtain information about the neighbourhood, which we would not have obtained to this degree using the purely classical survey method.

With the help of this informal information, and using other information from photo documentation, existing plans and maps, as well as studies, guiding images, statistics, and cadastres, our planning team was now able to produce clear and easy-to-read plans and drawings. In turn, these plans supported us in the next planning steps in the organisation of productive participatory workshops. We were able to use this material not only as a planning device, but also as a device to support mediation in the continuing events involving residents and stakeholders as members of the ongoing focus and interest groups.

Master plan and architectural concept put up for discussion

In the following workshops, working groups, and conferences, the further evolution of the urban development strategy and the master plan, as well as the architectural design of the various items of street furniture and spatial elements, were put up for discussion. The design of the four areas involved, i.e. Water Garden (Nos. 1 to 4), La Plazza (Nos. 11 to 14), Orchard (Nos. 6 to 8) and Forum (No. 16), was also continually checked against the urban strategy and the master plan developed therefrom. The terraced Water Garden with its fountains and water features creates a tranquil and restful area; La Plazza, with its cafés, restaurants, and the tram station, invites people to take an active part in what is happening. The Orchard is a flexibly usable parking place that provides areas for stationary vehicles as well as for

Rendering of the participation pavilion as mediation element

temporary market stalls during the weekly market. The Forum, with its interactive mediation pavilion, invites citizens to actively participate in the master plan and its implementation.

The elements designed for the master plan, such as seating areas, planters, streetlamps, and lights integrated in the paving, set the overall design framework for the whole of Dr.-Schweitzer-Square and the adjoining neighbourhood. These elements were designed in a way that revitalises the area, not only by day but also by night. They were put up for discussion in the focus groups during the workshops involving school classes, young people, and local employees as well as retirees. Within these creative workshops, imaginative and unusual ideas and solutions were generated by the focus groups using playful processes. In the individual workshops, each focus group broke into small groups and worked through the following three phases: (1) Discussion of the urban development and architectural designs, as well as the overall concept. (2) Creative solutions to be developed from the critique and evaluation, as well as a review of the results in terms of realistic implementation. (3) At the end of these subject-related workshops, the solutions produced were recorded and documented with the help of a supporting expert using sketches, cognitive maps, or physical models. Our planning team then upgraded these in terms of graphics to make the material suitable for technical and design-related evaluation, and to make it possible to arrive at a comprehensive summary for revision of the master plan.

Development of a participation pavilion

The media installation at the Forum that we developed in the context of the master plan was intended, as an interactive mediation space, to virtually demonstrate to interested citizens the future development of Dr.-Schweitzer-Square even before its implementation, and to illustrate the various steps of the development and the resulting construction phases using an easy-to-operate digital platform. In the ongoing work with the interactive media installation, it became clear in the workshops with the different age groups that this installation should not just be used as a participation element. For this reason we developed a pavilion that, in its design and form, visually reflects the entire square as a walk-in model. In this way it was possible to three-dimensionally simulate the planned development of the traffic intersection, as well as the individual areas on site, as part of the overall planning and implementation process. The pavilion as a participation element was a three-dimensional structure that showed the citizens the designed space to scale. The photo shows our first mock-up of the pavilion, which we erected at the square as a test installation during an earlier phase of the master plan preparation, and which remained there for several months.

Once the master plan had been substantially revised by our interdisciplinary planning team, with the help of the participants' suggestions, we invited the different interest groups as focus groups to more ideas and planning work-

Mock-up of the pavilion as a participation element at the square

shops, as well as round tables, to initiate further communication at this planning stage. We selected the following methods for the workshops: in the focus groups for children, youngsters, and seniors we used planning games such as digital and analogue models and board games on site, as well as paperchases, to get to know the terrain and obtain a better understanding of the district. This made it possible to comprehensively display – in a playful way – the conceptual and technical elements of the urban development planning and architectural aspects. With the shopkeeper focus group, we proceeded in a similar way. Using these creative methods to communicate the planning process, we conveyed extensive design and planning information about the next planning steps to a wide range of interest groups, stimulating their very active involvement and, above all, their participation.

Revision of the urban concepts with the help of participatory design strategies

The subjects in the first planning phase, i.e. urban strategy and master plan development, dealt with safety in the infrastructure system; here, the focus of the experts and participants was primarily on managing the traffic. With the help of the workshops, conferences, and forums, we were able to compile the results of the different working groups and adopt these in the next planning steps. This prepared the ground for starting the next planning phase to deal with the revised master plan after the participatory input. The result was that the different working groups confirmed our plan objectives, which were to make the street narrower and further reduce motorised traffic using it. Furthermore, the working groups also came out in favour of integrating separate cycle paths and public transport tracks in the plan proposal.

This made it possible to develop new design strategies for the previously identified sub-areas, i.e. the Water Garden, La Plazza, the Orchard, and the Forum, with more available space and areas for flexible use. Certain design principles were considered important by our design team. Therefore, the Water Garden was designed with active and passive areas for the respective user groups. The planting areas provided at the edge of the square were slightly raised in order to create a terraced effect, and thereby to generate areas for rest, for pathways cutting through, and for play areas. We selected the layout of the plants in the raised area of the Water Garden in such a way that, with an irrigation system, they were play-

Planning simulation in the form of an analogue board game

fully and sufficiently supplied with water and nutrients using the water elements we included in the design – such as a water seesaw, the irrigation pump, and the water feature. In this way it was possible to make economies with respect to the cost of plant maintenance.

The area called the Orchard is an actual orchard with fruit trees and design elements that we chose, as well as seating and a sufficient number of planters. This area is noteworthy for the flexibility of its use, which includes areas for stationary vehicles and also for market stalls. During the daytime, the areas for stationary vehicles were made available to local market stalls because the parking spaces are primarily used by commuting local residents. In order to achieve an attractive landscape design, we selected trees that were either flowering or that produced foliage throughout the year, thus producing a range of colours across the seasons. We selected trees that do not shed their fruit in order to avoid damage to parked vehicles.

La Plazza is an area that was created by the infrastructural change and the new layout of paths and tracks that we devised. This area has been designed with seating, inviting passers-by to rest. With the street furniture that we developed, a new quality was created that made new innovative spaces possible, attracting the foot traffic necessary to resolve the problem of vacant shops. Shops had their former owners returning, while others opened with new retail concepts.

During the design phase, the Forum – the place for debate and participation – was still dominated by an interactive piece of artwork. This had been planned as a kind of urban "stethoscope" with which observers could perceive the entire planning of the square in panoramic fashion. However, during the process of implementation it became immediately clear to us planners that this had to be developed even further in order to achieve the objective, which was to initiate an interactive participation process directly on site. For this reason, this interactive sculpture was developed into a participation pavilion, which opened up new possibilities for participation.

In the next step, the design elements we developed further for the four sub-areas described above were incorporated in the master plan. During another set of participatory workshops in the second planning phase, the current plan status was discussed and again presented to the participating citizens and actors for discussion. Further participation workshops were organised and expert urban designers and town planners were invited to run them. Key design subjects

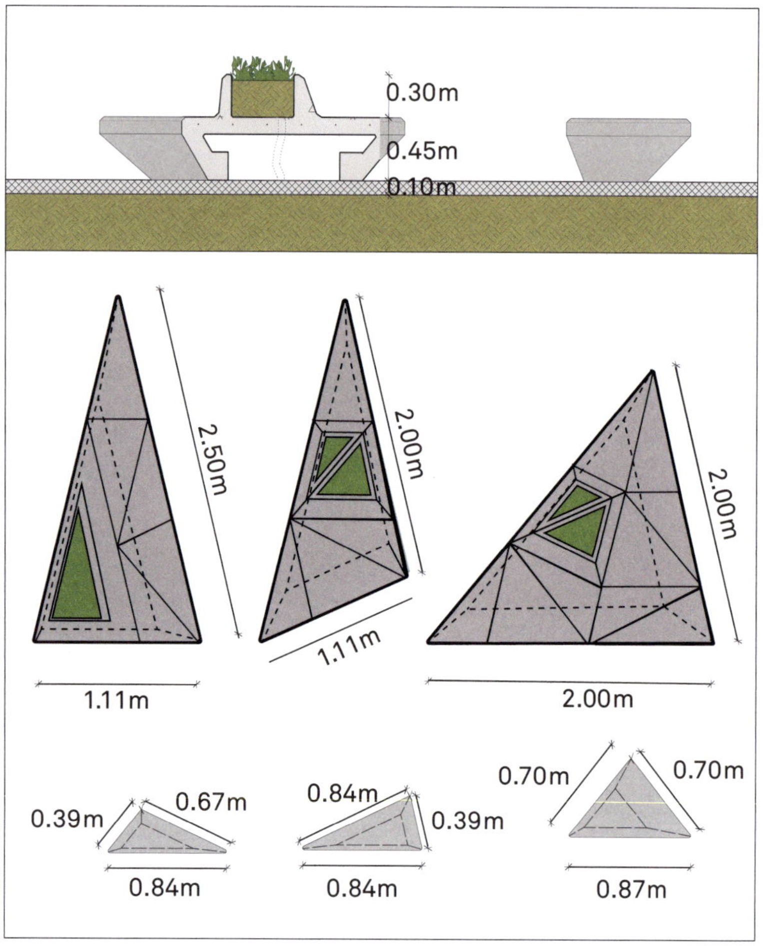

The Orchard provides an area for local market stalls

for the further development of the master plan within the workshops revolved around materials and scale. For these workshops we developed planning documents that contained the details of the design elements.

Easy-to-grasp design levels for a participatory process

The first plan level shows the horizontal level of the square in its entirety, including the materials we selected. At the next plan level, the small, round, mostly stand-alone seats are shown, which are made of light-coloured concrete at the right height for seating. The next plan level details the street furniture with its integrated planters, which were aimed at enhancing the overall design quality of the square. The shape and height were chosen to ensure that the seating areas and the backrests are in ideal proportion to each other. The trough planters are behind the backrests and function as dividers between the seating. The fourth plan level contains a scale representation of the proposed bus and tram stops, and the participation pavilion. For the next workshops in the following planning phase, the structure of the participation pavilion was completed to ensure that it could be erected at Dr.-Schweitzer-Square as a three-dimensional manifestation and be used to drive the discussion relating to design questions.

The focus group workshops in particular supplied extensive suggestions for developing the street furniture and installations within the context of the master plan. The compiled views and statements were discussed, summarised, and evaluated, and we compared the results with the more advanced ideas produced by the different working groups during their workshops; they could then be directly incorporated in the third planning phase – the development of the street furniture. Most of the participants agreed that this made it possible to actually perceive the different scales of the square's design elements. By using a uniform pattern for the setting of the different areas, it was possible to create a new framework in the overall design. This sample pattern was then to be replicated in the design and the selected materials, thereby providing stimulating input for the working groups.

The third planning phase focused primarily on the revision of the design of the street furniture and the tram stops. By determining the new pattern for the square as a new framework it was possible to clarify many design questions that had previously remained unanswered – for example, how to handle the design of barrier freedom and street furniture. The design of the square pattern was based on the calculation of triangular angles by the mathematician, Ludwig

Workshop with schoolchildren – here with the analogue model

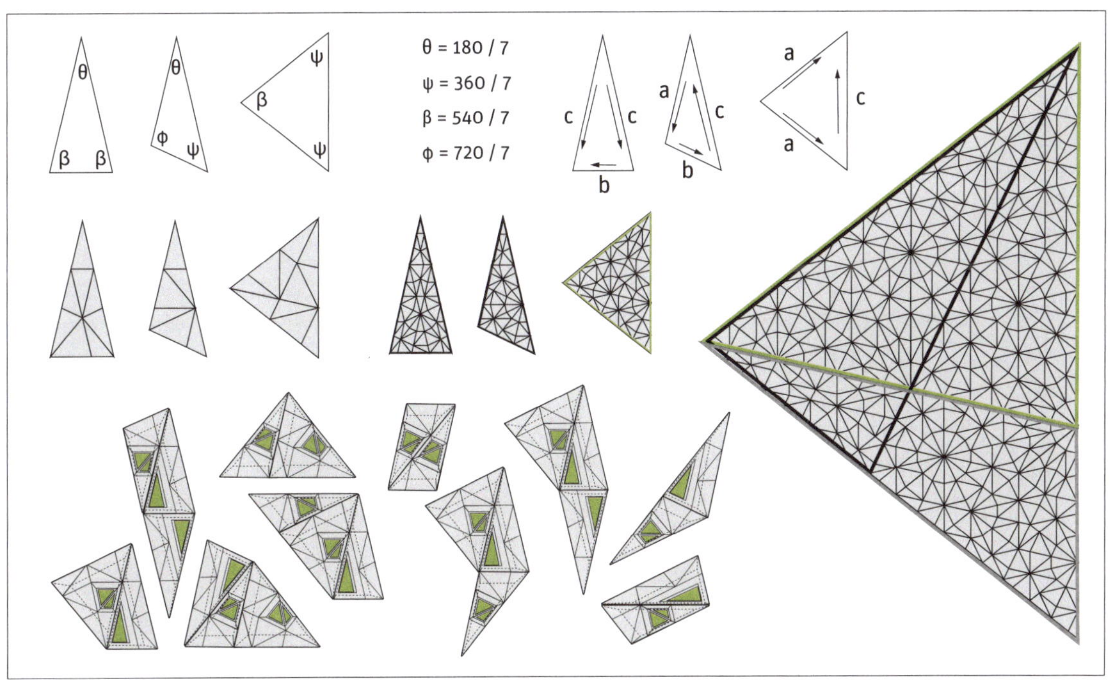

Danzer's principle in the design pattern of the square

Danzer. With the help of this mathematical concept it was possible to devise a wide range of design patterns for the paving of the entire square, and to calculate the size and proportionality of the seating and pavilion. Each element fits into the next larger component, which means that the small seating elements can be inserted directly into the paving pattern, and the triangles of the seating elements can be found again in the pavilion.

Architectural design of elements enhances the character of the square

The architectural design of the square, the different types of seating (with and without planters), the bus and tram stops, and the participation pavilion were extensively discussed and evaluated in different working groups within the interest groups. In these various workshops, people of differ-

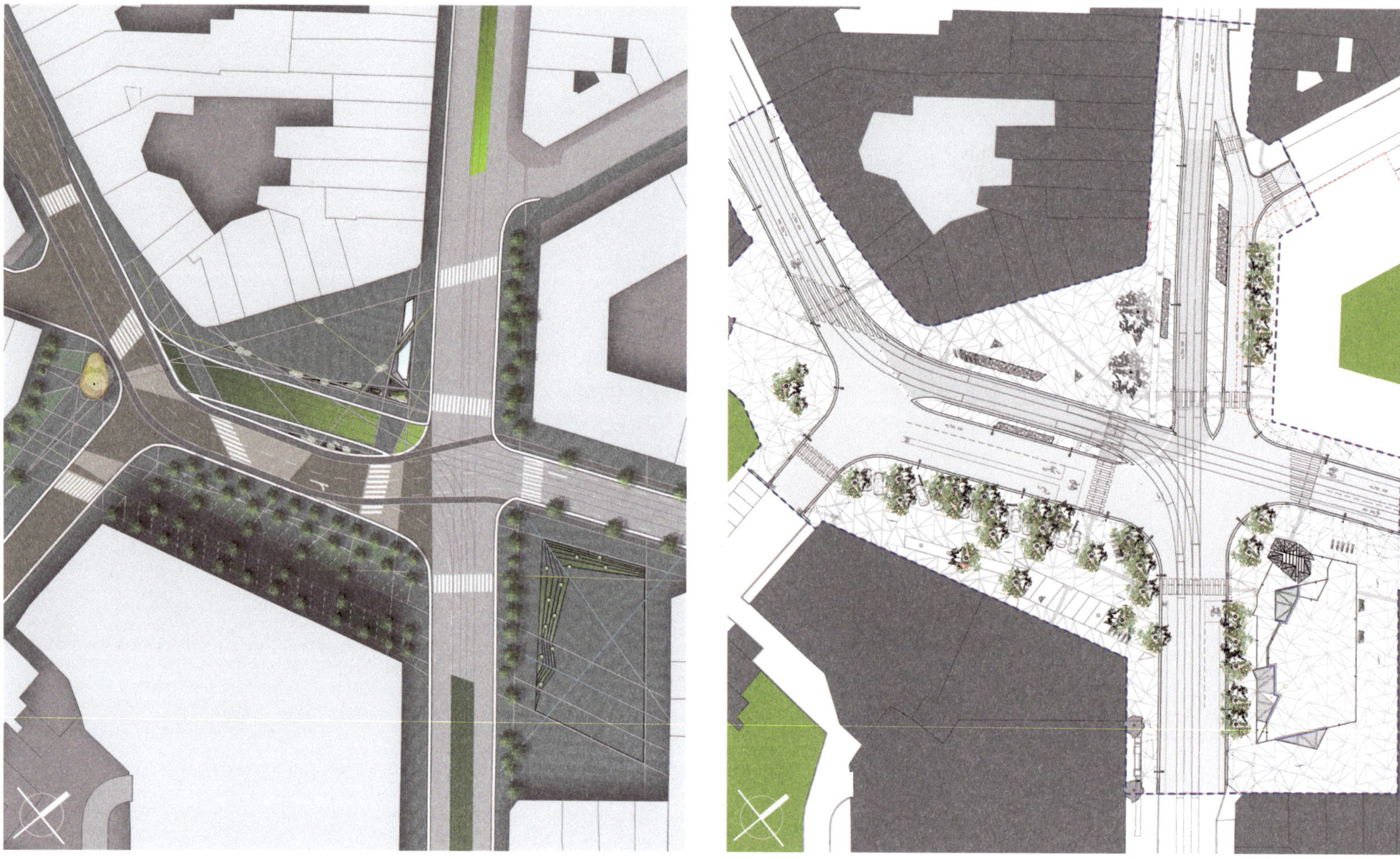

Master plan before and after participatory negotiations

ent ages were selected as test subjects in order to be able to respond specifically to the different requirements in the working groups. The architectural design and the further development of the technical details were tested with these test subjects, using mock-ups and simulations. With the help of the analogue simulation of the newly evolving public space it was possible to test behavioural patterns in order to discover day-to-day problems, such as a sense of inadequate safety and, at the same time, to create familiarity with the place. With the help of the constructed temporary prototypes, the proportions of the different planned architectural elements were tested within the ideas workshops. Thus it was possible to test whether the smaller and larger seats functioned in terms of form and material, and whether the stops and the pavilion worked as protective areas for people.

Once these different ideas workshops involving both young and older people had been carried out, our planning team was able to, once again, incorporate the results in the architectural details. The results of this were then used in the next step to check these new details for their usability in further workshops with working groups consisting of experts and actors. Following these workshops, which took place in the context of the conferences and district workshops, our interdisciplinary design and planning team was able to finally incorporate all concerns of the urban actors and stakeholders in the master plan, including the architectural details. At the end of this very focused participation process it turned out that, with all the dialogues, discussions, and idea findings, the entire participatory process that we had accomplished is comprehensive in the overall design of the Dr.-Schweitzer-Square.

BUILDINGS AND SUB-PROJECTS AS INITIATORS OF PARTICIPATION

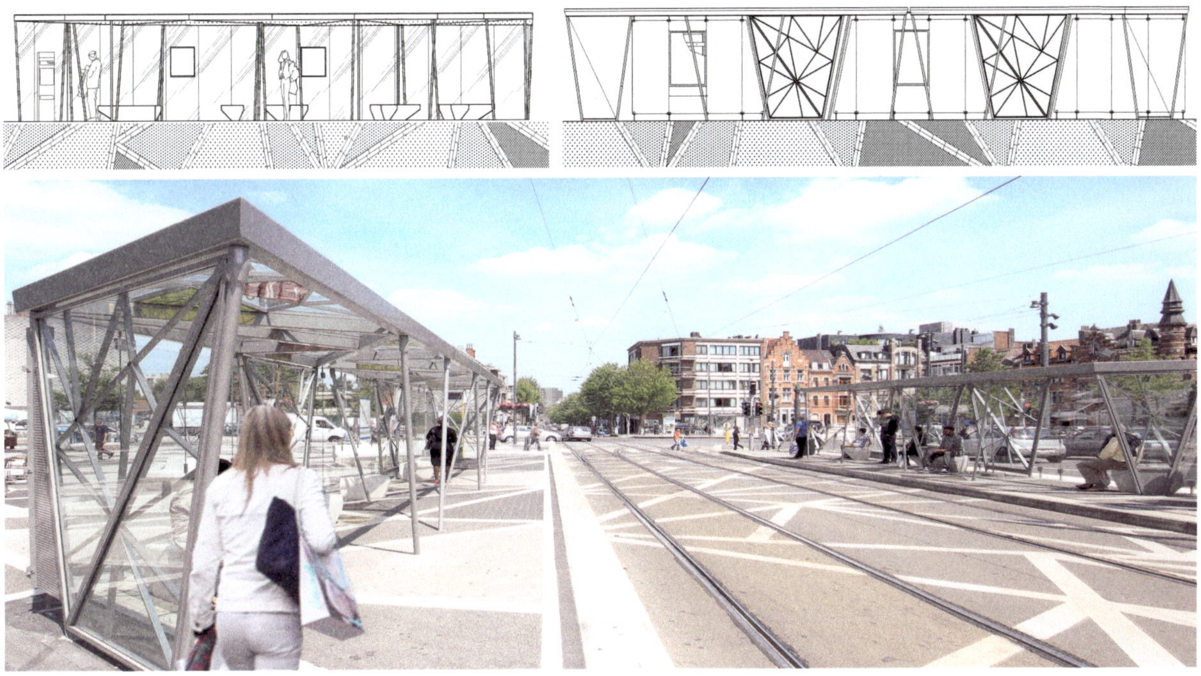

Urban elements: bus and tram stops

This chapter explains the detailed design and planning strategies with its description of the urban development participation principles, the individual architectural parameters are now set out within the planning process. Of special importance here is how built mock-up elements can function as initiators of participation. In many cases, affected parties may lack an adequate understanding of a planned urban project because there was no process of making the planning process and the planned designs tangibly comprehensible and visible. In larger urban development projects in particular, the population is mostly only presented with the plans of the finished design at a location that is far away from the actual place. Hence, it is not possible to achieve participation that promotes a process that leads to the best quality and potential development of the design. However, if the aim is to achieve open participation during which the involved groups can actually have an influence, it is imperative to prepare the process and design at an early stage so that it can be easily comprehended. In practice, this is mostly done with the help of visualisations; however, care must be taken to avoid idealising or beautifying the image of the planned proposal.

Very often the ability of participants and affected parties to understand the quality and atmosphere of urban development proposals depends on the detail. Not infrequently, items such as street furniture, pavilions, but also public works of art, which collectively account for this quality, are only devised or added at the very end of the development. In that case, the planned project development is already set out before and hence an effective and informed participative process can be established. So what happens when one reverses this process and produces prototypes, sub-projects, and details of the design at an early stage, and uses these actively for the purpose of illustration and as active tools of participation? In the best case, these tangible elements make it possible for the participants to form an objective idea at the location. The result would be that the size, quality, and materials of the design – as well as the atmosphere of the place – can be experienced and can thus be illustrated and conveyed in detail for the participatory processes. In the simplest form, these early efforts to show details can take the form of display cases in the case of residential developments, or three-dimensional details of facades such as is common practice in construction. As already mentioned, however, it is very important for the design process that these elements contribute to active participation at the location by providing areas of shared creation and development.

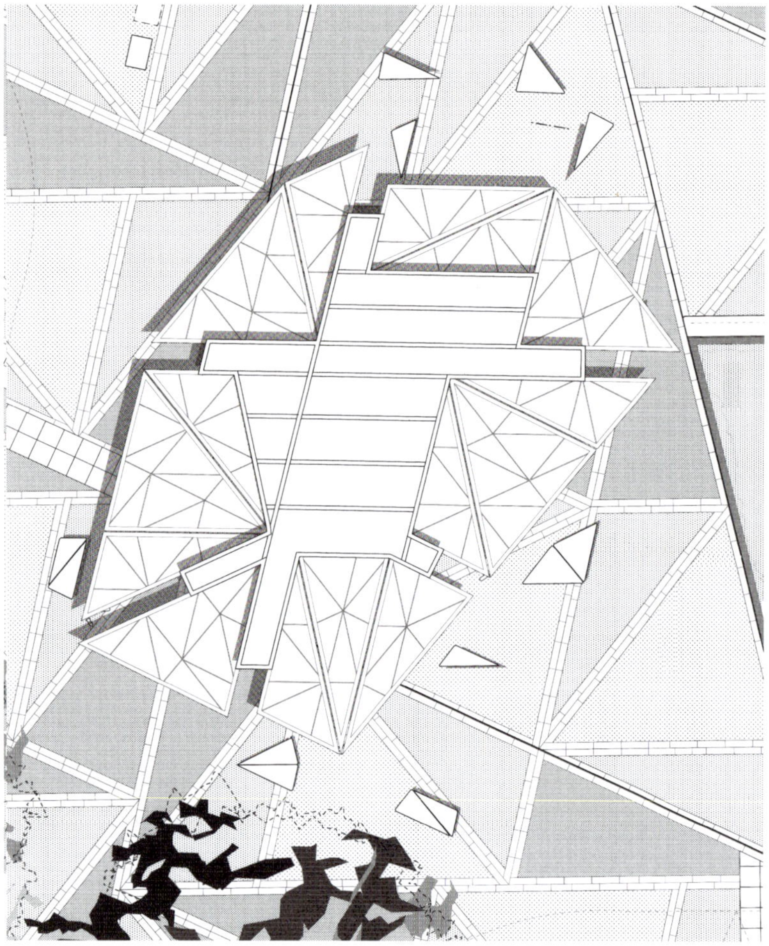

Paving pattern and participation pavilion

New avenues in project management

In such a way, the production of smaller elements of a design idea provides opportunities again and again, and at different times, to obtain suggestions for the modification and adjustment of the original plan design. This approach opens up new possibilities for project management: using actual examples, it is possible for groups and individuals – such as artists, associations, or interest groups, who in many cases are only involved at the end of the process – to take part in the decision-making during the ongoing process of a project and thereby to become stakeholders in the evolving plan. A special advantage of this approach is that these elements are created at an early stage in the planning process. This means that the project becomes more scaleable, and also that situations can be avoided where it is not clear whether a project will be implemented or not.

This is also evident in the design of the different plan levels of the entire Dr.-Schweitzer-Square, from the paving through to the pavilion. With the help of the principles mentioned it was possible to always retain local features and urban proportions, in spite of the new overall design pattern. The new street layout provides a framework for the different areas of the square, which are defined by their function as well as by their active and passive areas. Each of these areas provides space for leisure activities and local recreation. At the "La Plazza" area, a space for dwelling and resting has been created with the help of the urban furniture; similar to the tram stops, which are providing spaces for seating and are not just used as waiting areas. The design of the architectural shape of the public transport stops, as well as the lighting concept, is based on the Danzer pattern. The elements in the roof structure have been arranged in such a way that the sunlight shining through them during the day casts a pattern on the ground that exactly fits the triangular paving pattern. When it is dark this effect is also achieved with spotlights, which are arranged at the right angle to achieve this. This can clearly be seen in the renderings of the design and in the pictures taken after implementation. The seats at the public transport stops consist of concrete stools that are triangular in shape. The same stools can also be found in the other three areas, where they can either be freestanding or placed together to form a larger triangle. This again fits in with the pattern of the paving and forms a further triangle that is repeated in the street furniture. Each triangle is a piece of the puzzle in which each urban element increases in size, starting from the paving to the stools via the street furniture to the planters, and to the individual elements such as the pavilion and public transport stops.

Street furniture contributes to the character of the square

The Water Garden does not have any transport stops but features the participation pavilion, which was in use through the entire planning and construction process. The different levels comprise areas for resting, passing through, or to participate in activities. The flower beds encased in these levels provide spaces for sitting and observing or playing. With the help of the fabricated water elements such as pumps and seesaws, the flower beds can be supplied with water in a playful way. We hit on this idea after the client told us repeatedly that the municipality had scarcely any budget for the upkeep and maintenance of flower beds, i.e. no money for an irrigation system or maintenance staff such as gardeners or landscapers. In this way, the users of the square are invited to actively help with the irrigation by using these play elements. Overwatering of the plants is avoided because, at a certain degree of saturation, the water is directly drained back into the main system. The plant species have been selected to ensure that they flower in different seasons, thereby offering different colour combinations throughout the year. They match the colour combination used in the pavilion and, with this splendid colour scheme, create a visual experience that is subject to slow but constant change.

Great care was taken with the shape and size of the individual pieces of street furniture. The shape and size of the different seating modules was designed with the comfort of all types of users in mind and also to ensure that their arrangement within the different areas would invite people to rest a while. The same applies to the architectural elements. The largest element, the pavilion, has been designed to ensure that in its proportions it fits the overall spatial situation. The pattern in the roof structure of the pavilion replicates the overall pattern of the square at a reduced scale. This meant that the actors were able to "read" the future design of the square directly on site and at any time during the planning and construction process.

Water Garden, the area with water features

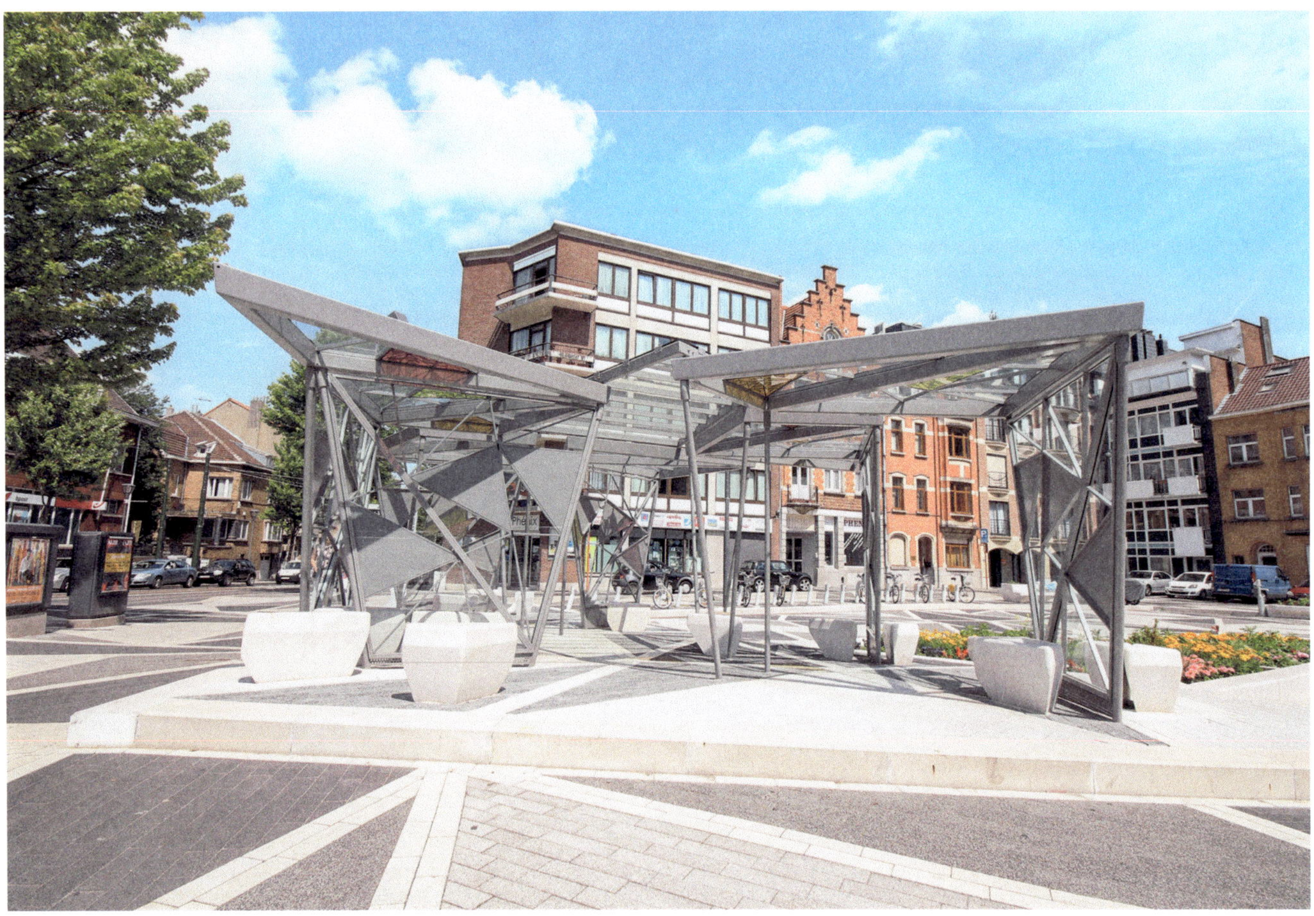

Water Garden, the area with the participation pavilion

THE AFTER-EFFECT – A SUMMARY

For this complex urban development project in Brussels at every level we prioritised open and intensive discussions with all actors and planning departments in order to drive an integrative process over a longer period. In this context, our planning group felt that it was especially important to convince the city and municipal authorities not to waste funds on public sculptures – which would not be usable by the residents in an active and participative way – as had been planned, but to use the money to create a participation pavilion which, from the beginning, would inform the population about the plans for the entire neighbourhood and what would be happening locally over the coming years.

In addition, we felt it was very important to integrate the different citizen groups – to consider them right from the start and ensure their participation on an equal footing, especially those groups that are frequently disadvantaged in the urban development process because of language barriers or other obstacles. With the help of the participation methods described above we managed to bring together and consistently involve different interest and focus groups from a wide range of social strata and age groups – including children and young people; pupils, apprentices, and students; employees primarily representing local businesses; and also older people who had not yet been involved in the planning process. During the workshops our team noted, with increasing frequency, that those participants with little experience of urban developments and participatory processes usually put forward much more interesting suggestions and more suitable proposals for the development of the square than we received from some professionals.

Creative ways of coming to decisions with the help of ideas workshops

The involvement of the focus groups in the creative decision-making processes within our ideas workshops was very helpful to us for developing the urban strategy, as well as for designing the architectural elements. This involvement process requires very intensive preparation and support at an early stage from the planning staff and moderators, but is an effective procedure for successfully driving the planning process. These participating groups are still very actively involved today in local matters. They organise get-togethers, such as neighbourhood parties and markets, and in this way maintain the communication and exchange of ideas that we initiated. In this context, the urban elements – such as the different areas, the street furniture and the participation pavilion that we designed and further developed with the local actors in the participation process – are used extensively.

What can we learn from the classic as well as the new, virtual participation methods to be able to pursue a comprehensive approach within the planning process with all participants in an analogue or digital setting? What tools exist or have to be developed to make this possible? At the present time it can be noted that in the virtual participatory online formats harbour similar obstacles, hurdles, and problems to those in the analogue formats: the challenge is to overcome them. How can underrepresented groups such as older people and children whose mother tongue is not French, Flemish, German, or English be involved in this process? How is it possible to prevent a situation in which it is always the same groups making themselves heard due to their privileged position or situation, whereas other groups don't have a say? Existing virtual communication platforms can manage the technical side of this, but there always has to be a moderator or mediator accompanying the process. Furthermore, it is imperative to collect background data and information to ensure that experts and laypeople can always be involved on an equal footing. This is another and extremely interesting field of research. The subject of virtual working methods is explored in greater detail in Chapter 2, "Learning from pedagogy and education", using the examples in which our participation methods were applied.

Continuing virtual or analogue participation of the actors in the planning process

It is important to note that, in spite of the intuitive approach of our planning team within the participation workshops, a comprehensive exchange has taken place, and that the ideas and suggestions of the participants were worked into the design process on an ongoing basis. At a later point, Katharina Simon and I undertook a scientific study to investigate these participatory and analytical methods and to systematically assign them to the different planning steps. They are illustrated in detail in the digram named "Urban development and participatory approaches in the planning process", which can be used by planning professionals and actors as reference material. It is important to note that the participatory processes are not only carried out in the classic way "on site", but also from a number of different, virtual platforms in an online dialogue. This was evident during the pandemic, but now also beyond this period. The method made it possible – over months – for all strata of the population to gain experience in exchanging information and acting on digital platforms; these findings can now be recorded, investigated, and examined, and then tested for their suitability in other projects.

The above participatory approaches with the various stakeholders in a range of workshops within the four planning phases involve terms that are common in the social sciences, primarily in use in countries such as Great Britain, the United States, Germany, and Austria. For example, in Germany my former colleague at the University of Wuppertal, sociologist Peter Dienel, is a pioneer in the field of participatory processes. He developed the planning cell as a consultation process for improving planning decisions as early as the 1970s.

This subject will be further investigated in a summary of participatory principles and methods within the urban development planning process and is set out in a kind of reference dictionary in Chapter 4 of this book. I developed these method maps with Katharina Simon and they were evaluated in a seminar on informal planning processes as part of the teaching process. Subsequently, the students used these revised urban development method maps directly in their designs in order to test them for their suitability in practical application; see the doctoral thesis (Simon, 2017).

The Dr.-Schweitzer-Square project clearly demonstrates that it is an important task of planners to negotiate with and involve all actors to end up with projects that not only achieve the smallest common denominator of the various ideas, but – via an integrative, stepwise process – achieve a result that goes beyond the original brief and expectations. Participation can no longer be viewed as an additional, inconvenient part of the planning work, but must be recognised as a creative, important contribution to a comprehensive process even though this approach involves considerable extra work and intensive effort.

URBAN DEVELOPMENT AND PARTICIPATORY APPROACHES IN THE PLANNING PROCESS

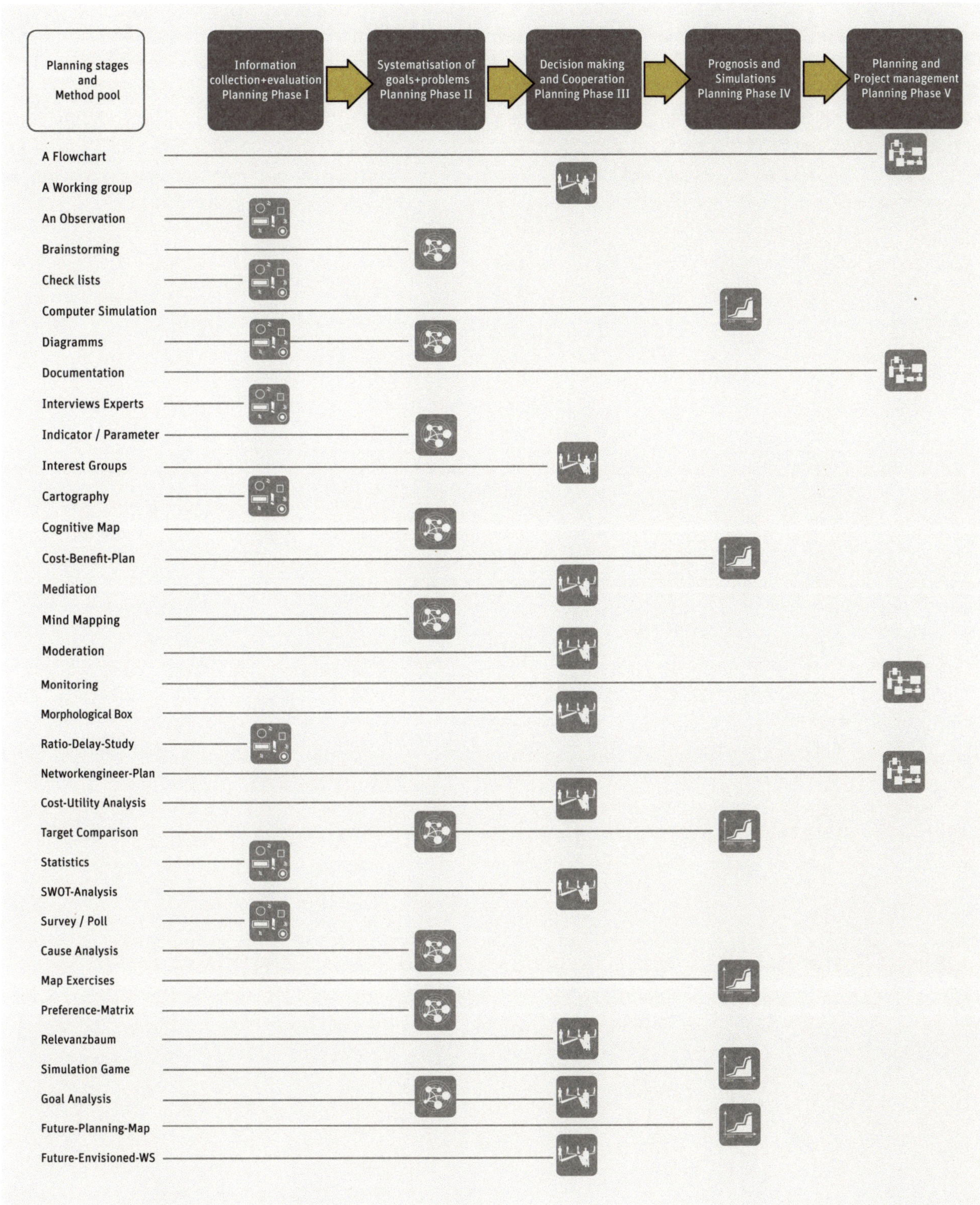

Allocation of urban development methods in the planning process

After our intuitive approach to the organisation and implementation of the workshops in the planning phases of the urban development project in Brussels, Katharina Simon and I discussed this subject with the students in the Master's seminar on experimental urban research and systematically defined the approaches taken. In the following section, urban development and participatory methods that can be applied in the various stages of the planning process are explained. The last chapter of the book contains a reference dictionary that explains the methods in detail and functions as a reference work for planning professionals. The urban development planning methods have been categorised in accordance with their systematic allocation to the different planning phases. See Figure "Allocation of urban development planning methods in the planning process" for an overview in diagrammatical form.

This defines which specific approaches are to be used in which planning phase. For example, in the first planning phase information will be gathered and evaluated. The second planning phase is focusing on structuring the objectives and the problems ad hand. When these are systemised various decisions can be made and can be finalised in the goals for the project. In the third phase, the participatory and collaborative processes are adopting these goals in the concept development process. In the fourth planning phase, prognoses and scenarios are developed, and will be tested with the help of analogue and digital simulations. The fifth planning phase is used to establish the principles of the planning and project management, and how to apply these.

APPLICATION OF THE METHODS DURING THE FOUR PLANNING-PHASES

Method Card "Observation"

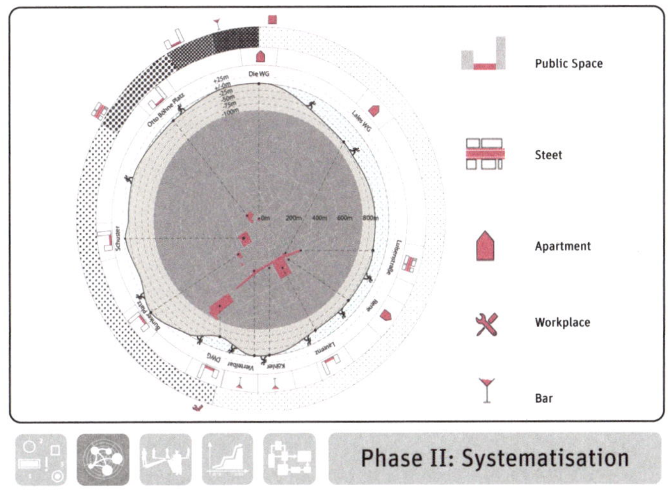

Method Card "Mental Mapping"

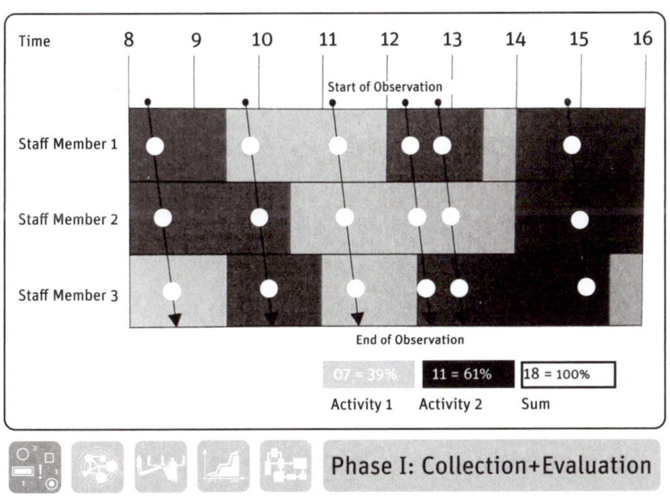

Method Card "Multi-Moment Analysis"

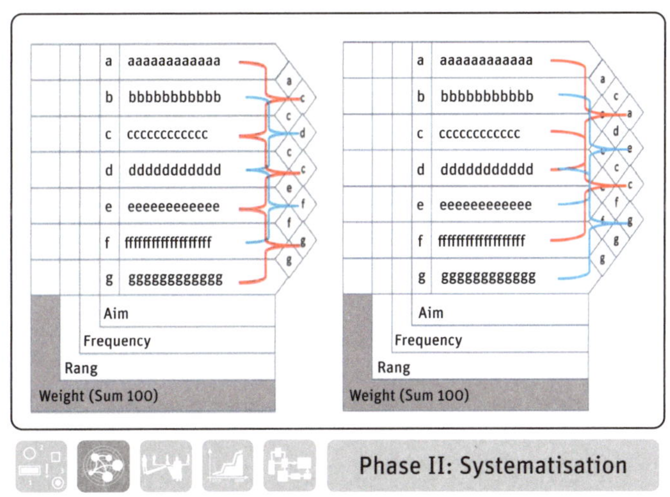

Method Card "Preference Matrix"

Planning phase I comprises the urban development analysis and its evaluation. In this phase, the existing situation of the place is recorded, and an assessment of the respective planning documents is carried out. The following four steps are carried out during the first planning phase. The first step of this phase involves observation of the situation. The following methods can be used: photo documentation, participatory or non-participatory observation, unguided interviews, and a tour around the site. In the second step, following on from the first, the gathered information is sorted and assessed. These urban development methods support the process with the help of statistical working methods, mapping methods, diagrammatical illustration, and multi-moment analysis. In the third step, the focus is on recognising the problem and isolating it from other current problems. This can be done using methods such as brainstorming, the preference matrix, a standardised guided interview, as well as surveys. In the last step, the problem is defined; this can be evaluated and described with the help of cooperation methods, moderation and mediation, as well as the analytical methods of target-actual comparison and relevance tree analysis.

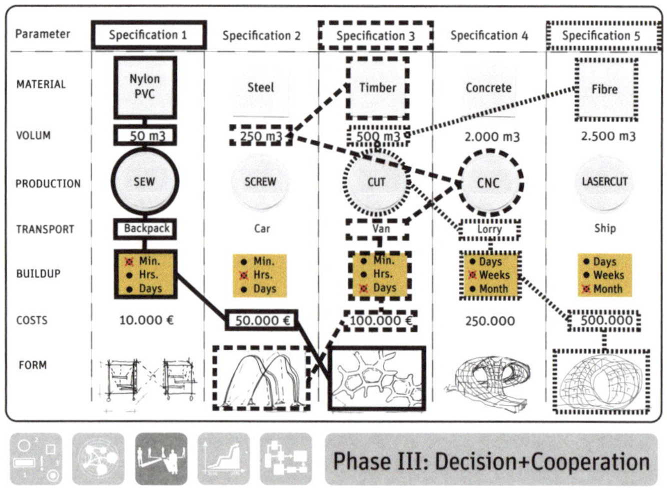

Method Card "Morphological Box"

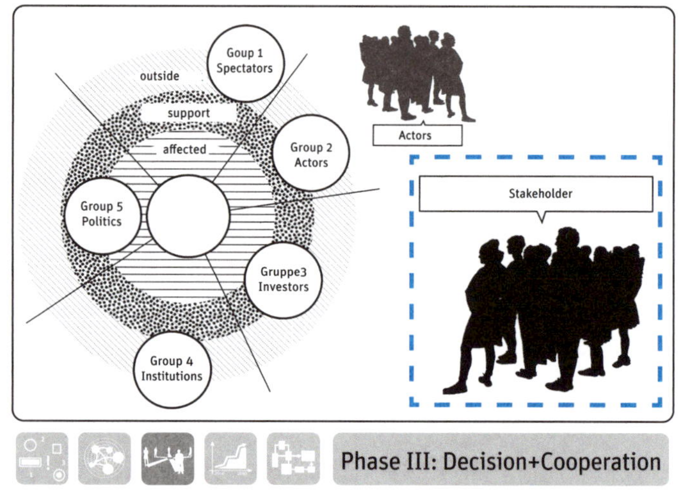

Method Card "Stakeholder Analysis"

Method Card "Cooperative Workshops"

Method Card "Strategy Table"

The objective- and problem-structuring phase

Planning phase II covers the description of the objective and a preliminary design of the actual urban development plan. It involves the following seven steps. In the first step, statistical data are collected. Furthermore, it is possible to conduct interviews with experts and surveys with selected groups of people, as well as to apply various mapping methods. In the second step the existing situation is recorded and analysed. This can be done using methods such as the checklist technique, photo documentation, mapping methods, as well as diagrammatical illustration. In the third step, a dialogue is held concerning the objectives of the draft plan. This is done in working groups with the help of different cooperation methods, such as workshops, and using moderation and mediation. This can be supported using social science and urban development planning methods such as mind mapping, relevance tree analysis and decision tree analysis, morphological box analysis, SWOT analysis, and target-actual comparison.

In the fourth step possible objectives are defined. This can be done with the help of workshops and social science and urban development methods, such as a target-actual comparison, an indicator formation, working groups, different cooperation methods, as well as moderation and mediation. After that, in the fifth step, different alternatives are presented in the context of the design or the strategy. Here it is also possible to use mapping methods and to carry out simulations, scenarios, and prognoses.

The decision and evaluations phase

In the sixth step that follows, these developed alternatives are evaluated with the help of clearly defined criteria. The following methods can be used for the analysis and evaluation: the Delphi method, weighted sum analysis and/or cost-benefit analysis, SWOT analysis, interaction analysis, profitability analysis, and ecological effects analysis. In the seventh and last step of the second planning phase, a decision is made in favour of one of the alternatives generated, or a new alternative is produced. The selected design and planning alternative can be confirmed with the help of the decision tree analysis, the relevance tree analysis, and the morphological box analysis; it can then be checked and tested in

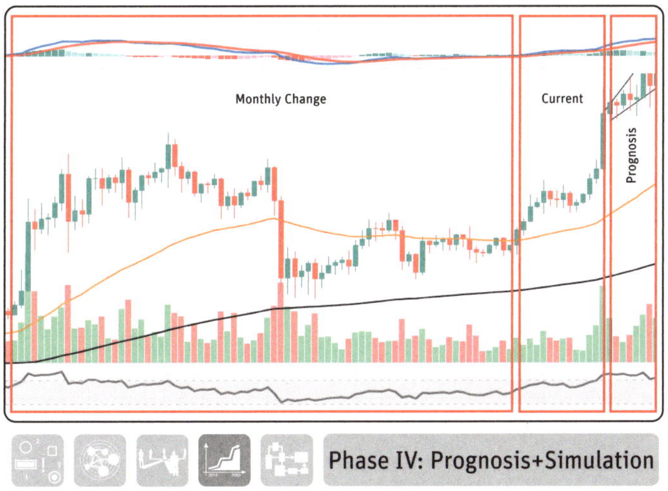

Method Card "Prognosis"

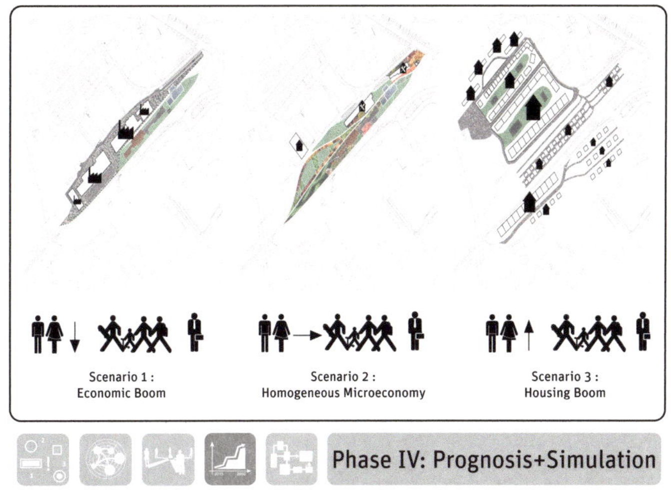

Method Card "Generating Scenarios"

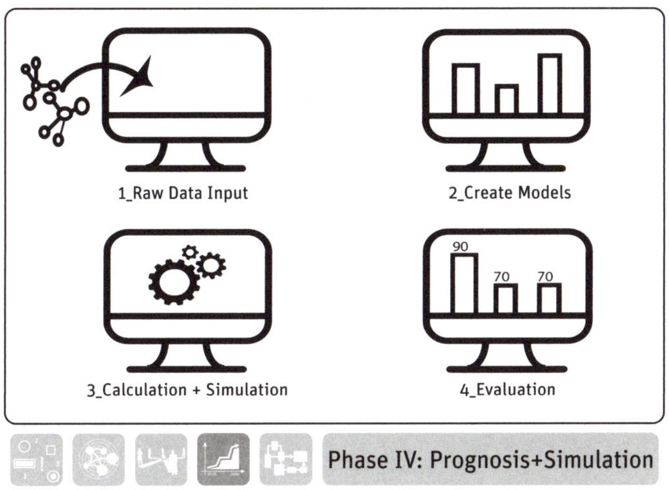

Method Card "Computer Simulation"

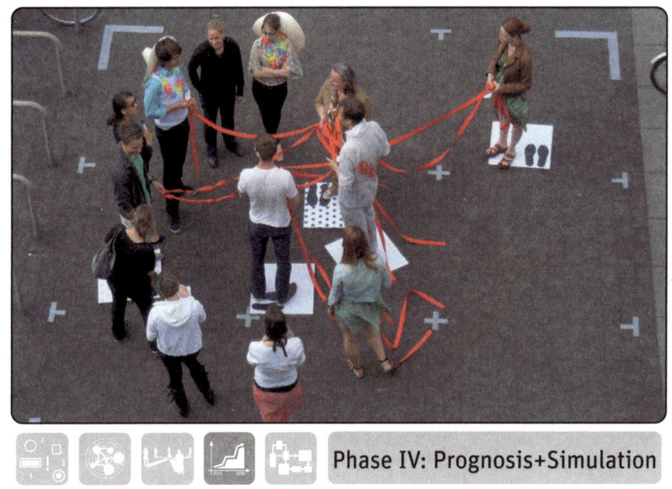

Method Card "Simulation Role Play"

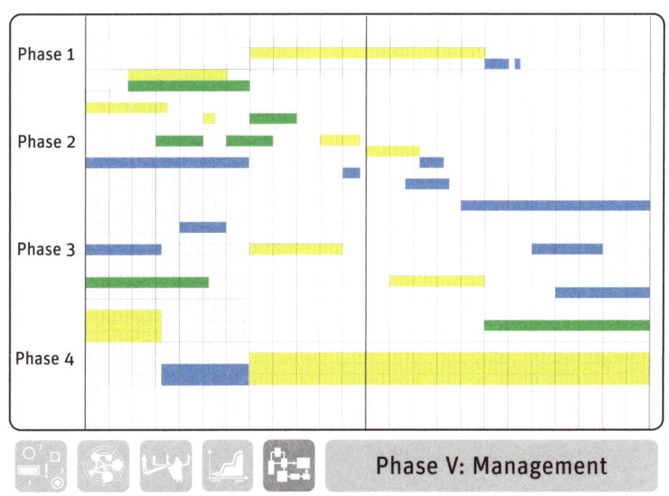

Method Card "Process Flow Diagram"

working groups using cooperative methods and tailored moderation and mediation.

The implementation phase

Planning phase III, also called the implementation phase, describes the outline and detailed development of the plan and focuses on the implementation of the urban strategy and/or the architectural design. In the first step, a catalogue of measures is compiled. Methods such as the process flow diagram, the network planning technique, and cooperation methods can be used here. In the next step, the proposed measures are actually implemented and, in the last step, from the beginning of the construction process to its end, support is provided using a range of cooperation methods.

Finally, in planning phase IV, the success and effect of the project is checked as part of the implementation phase. In the implementation phase, control methods such as monitoring can be used. Monitoring and checking the construction process, including an evaluation with the help of a comparison analysis, can lead to the proposal of appropriate improvement measures. The entire construction process is recorded in an extensive document.

For reference, a detailed listing of urban development and town planning methods and tools are included in the last Chapter in the "Dictionary".

2

LEARNING FROM PEDAGOGY AND EDUCATION

Wuppertal project profile

Project initiators and clients

Wuppertaler Tafel food bank in Barmen.
Wolfgang Nielsen, co-founder and director

Participating partners and institutions

BUW Chair of Urban Design – Urban Scape:
Elli Börgener, Tanja Siems, Katharina Simon
Food bank visitors and local district actors

Important data and facts

The Wuppertaler Tafel food bank was founded in 1995, received a new real estate grant in 2010, area: 8,700 square metres; area of the vacant building intended for redesign: 3,500 square metres

Project objectives and goals

Development of innovative adaptive reuse concepts for a building complex. These important research questions are related to design strategies: how to create affordable housing (problem of retirement poverty)? What does a dwelling or shelter look like that addresses addiction comprehensively (problem of gambling addiction)? Can a comprehensive functional programme counteract eating disorders, obesity, and malnutrition in children and adolescents?

Design project timeline

Analysis and development phase: investigation of the situation, proposal of urban design strategies and architectural concepts (0.5 years)
Construction phase: building remodelling (1.5 years)

Integrative adaptive reuse concepts
Wuppertaler Tafel food bank in Barmen

Site plan of Barmen, integration of the Wuppertaler Tafel in the district

In many projects, participation and cooperation are considered add-ons that either accompany or support the actual process. Typically, this is based on the assumption that the developmental process of projects is linear and homogeneous, often related to bureaucratic structures and long-term, static planning measures. Thus, many advancements and initiatives are overlooked. Situated in singular and isolated positions within existing structures, they do not possess the necessary political assertiveness in order to develop in an exponential manner. Correspondingly, their results lag behind their actual potential in terms of design-oriented and societal impact. In an increasingly networked world, it has become a central task of planners to detect and interlink precisely such initiatives and use them to develop projects that impact society in a sustainable and tangible way. This is necessary to address urgent tasks in the context of a changing social and natural environment, with broad support from the very beginning of a planning process.

The work of planners is, therefore, not limited to providing solutions to existing tasks. They also need to research which existing forces possess the potential for amalgamation, in order to develop outcomes that are greater than the sum of their parts. A necessary precondition for a sustainable impact of related initiatives is a broad understanding of their potential among planners in particular and society in general. Therefore, conveying and communicating this approach becomes an essential part of pedagogy as well as society-wide education.

The "Wuppertaler Tafel" food bank is a suitable example of how initiatives are combined. Within this project, a very diverse set of initiatives, social issues, and planning converged within creative projects that began to combine and advance ideas and approaches. The expanding scope of providing basic services to an increasingly diverse society against the background of increasing migration and resulting support mechanisms requires solutions. The same is true for the urgent question on the spatial expansion of urban structures, which requires answers that conventional approaches are incapable of providing. Only close collaboration between all actors involved allows the production of sustainable and creative approaches and, at the same time, broad social awareness of these issues.

The Wuppertaler Tafel food bank is a non-profit association. For nearly three decades, it has provided free daily meals to roughly 800 individuals. Across the years this has taken place successfully, based on a well-established local network including food producers. Food surpluses originating in large kitchens, cantinas, supermarkets, bakeries, hospitals, and hotels is collected and further processed. This is the only way for the association to supply individuals in need with breakfast, lunch, and dinner, seven days a week. The specifically instituted food charity for children is of particular note: it provides children and adolescents with a warm meal and offers them after-school supervision. This scope of services is complemented by the Wuppertaler Tafel with food, clothing, and book markets featuring items at discount rates. Further, the Wuppertaler Tafel operates a social department store, a children's boutique, and a sports centre offering shared cultural activities for children, adolescents, and seniors, located directly in their neighbourhood and open to residents of adjacent quarters. Assisted by the "Medimobile", a mobile clinic organised by the association, individuals in need receive a minimum of medical attention around the clock.

The association received a real estate grant that helped them expand their existing usable area by 3,500 square metres, offering room for further social services. The vacant nineteenth-century building is located in the immediate vicinity of the association and requires sustainable strategies for future adaptive reuse. For the urban design course, the students of our Bachelor programme had the opportunity to develop new and flexible concepts of use related to the particular construction type of the building and its structure, resembling a hall with tall ceilings. The design goal was for the students to search for new possible uses for a building in need of renovation, based on an intensive analytical deliberation on the district and the area the association was situated in and devise an urban and architectural strategy. Particular emphasis was placed on an integrative project approach in the context of expanding the Wuppertaler Tafel. Implementation strategies were formulated that support the intensive deliberation on highly topical and complex themes, including: poverty among older people; different types of addiction, most of all gambling addiction; and eating disorders, obesity, and malnutrition among adolescents, many of whom live in the city's Barmen district. The different concepts created by the students show that this particular location of the association in Wuppertal's Barmen district can be transformed in a sustainable manner.

ANALYTICAL APPROACHES FOR THE DEVELOPMENT OF SUSTAINABLE URBAN STRATEGIES

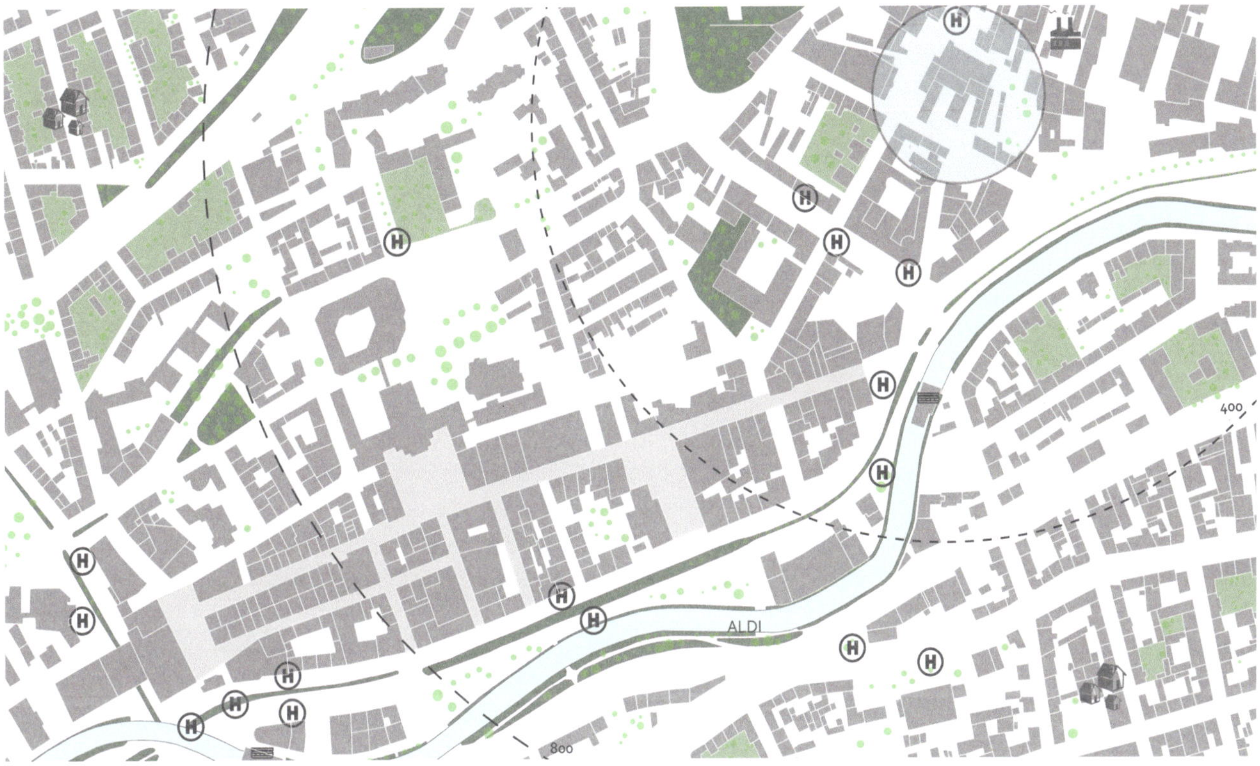

Mapping the superimposition of urban design functions

The goal of the assignment was to develop an urban design strategy and an architectural concept of use that correspond to the image of the Wuppertaler Tafel. Further, students were motivated to think within the boundaries of realistic framework conditions, allowing the creation of comprehensive designs for individuals in need, thus enabling the design projects to serve as serious sources of inspiration for the adaptive reuse strategy of the association.

We precisely defined the methodical approach for the individual design steps at the beginning of the assignment. Thus, it was identical for all students, allowing each group to proceed methodically as follows: during the analytical deliberation on the district, students attempt to record the existing conditions and atmosphere of the surroundings using various experimental methods. In doing so, they assume different perspectives and simultaneously attempt to think and work in the various required scales.

The goal of this approach within the urban design investigation is to specify the most urgent issues concerning the district and its residents and gather all relevant data and facts. Following that, the data and facts are filtered according to criteria determined beforehand, in order to illustrate them accurately within plans and maps for the further development of the urban strategy. The criteria of filtration are defined differently according to the selected theme, in order to corroborate the different design ideas. This contributes to the elaboration on different forms of mapping: the predefined area is mapped and the previously recorded data are integrated into the resulting map in an illustrative manner. Here, mapping most of all serves to visualise spatial phenomena that support the recognition of particular spatial structures.

Creating the related maps requires ensuring that they are legible and comprehensible to users and, at the same time, provide a correct image of the depicted reality. Prior to this step, students define questions of spatial relevance, the theme, and the scales of the space to be illustrated. The purpose of this approach is to support and identify generic and specific aspects of the structural and contextual conditions and display them in a suitable manner. In contrast to the step of preliminary mapping, the identified urban layers are analytically penetrated and illustrated within the successive weighted mapping, with a view to tackle the assigned task and to formulate a problem. Partly by employing different perspectives and spatial dimensions, this results in plans and diagrams which illustrate the contextual conditions and recorded situations as filtered by mapping in a way that is comprehensible to users, based on a diverse set of methods of representation.

Collection and visualisation of data

Students use the different types of mapping to precisely specify different urban layers, including the built structures, the technical and mobility infrastructure, the open spaces and green areas, as well as other phenomena, such as the demographic composition of residents and distribution of functions across the Barmen district of Wuppertal. On an architectural level, further important characteristics are illustrated and evaluated, such as the age of buildings, the degree of vacancies, and the status of renovations. The impeccable application of a map as a design tool is an important instrument for students. By employing it, they can precisely locate and assess insights gained, according to gathered and visualised data and facts, including the quantification and evaluation of social, economic, ecological, and historical aspects within final plans. This methodical approach illustrates the existing parameters of urban design. However, the genius loci, including the mood, atmosphere, and vivid character of a place, is not really represented by these means.

In order to capture the vivid character of a site, we provide the students with a further instrument: the method known as "dérive". Not only does it permit an alternative representation of the built elements and urban layers, but also the perceived, sensed, and felt situations and surroundings of a neighbourhood, quarter, or district. In order to understand this parallel and mutually inspiring approach within the analytical phase of the design process, it is prudent to offer a short overview of the dérive approach and to elaborate on the related difference between mapping methods.

The dérive can be understood as a form of strolling, drifting, promenading, or perambulating that serves as an investigative exploration of an urban environment. The important thing is to abstain during the observational stroll from personal habits. As a result, engaging in a dérive allows one to distance oneself from everything that is familiar, thereby permitting an emotional interplay with public space. The students strolling through the Barmen district can investigate and evaluate the impressions of the space. At its core, the dérive is about discovering something new or perceiving what is familiar as something unknown, thereby critically probing the environment of everyday life. A situation is constructed by the planned drift that establishes a unique collective experience, a structured intervention within a delineated area in the form of an impassioned play. The results are captured in mental maps that visualise the psychogeographic context of a place.

Methodical approach to developing functional programmes

The previously described design steps are intended for students to develop initial ideas for proposing new uses or new functional programmes for the building of the Wuppertaler Tafel. Thus, the students identified the existing physical and material spaces of the Barmen district of Wuppertal within the evaluation phase of the urban design investigation. Further, they mapped the atmospheric situations based on site visits and observations, interviews, photo documentation, and sensory perception and evaluated the gathered data using cartography and mental maps. In order to classify and categorise the structural, infrastructural, open space-related and atmospheric situations captured in these maps according to their urban design relevance, the next step comprised dérives of different kinds that were thematically designed and conducted in relation to the focus of the initial design idea. Students who discovered, for instance, by evaluating their maps, that barrier-free access was only available in partial areas or not at all in the district, conducted a dérive in the form of a simulation that allowed them to play the role of an older person. The limited capacity to perceive surroundings or restricted freedom of movement were, for instance, simulated using blindfolds or goggles that restrict vision, suits that feature weights distributed across the body, and walking aids, such as wheeled walkers or wheelchairs. These different types of equipment conveyed to young and active students, in a very immediate way, the situation of individuals who, due to these circumstances, can only conduct their daily activities to very limited degrees.

The illustration of the barrier-free dérive shows a collage indicating a fifteen-minute walking radius for individuals without restricted freedom of movement as defined for the investigation. After the dérive was conducted, the students recognised that, when weights were distributed across their bodies and while using wheeled walkers or wheelchairs, the time needed to travel certain distances increased many times over. Within the simulation, the students required up to two hours in order to directly access the relevant functions within the district as selected in the previous analytical step, in order to cover daily, weekly, and monthly needs.

In the barrier-free dérive collage, buildings for social, community, and healthcare infrastructure in the district are illustrated in grey. They are predominantly located beyond the radius of the area under investigation. Since these institutions are not located within the radius, based on the expe-

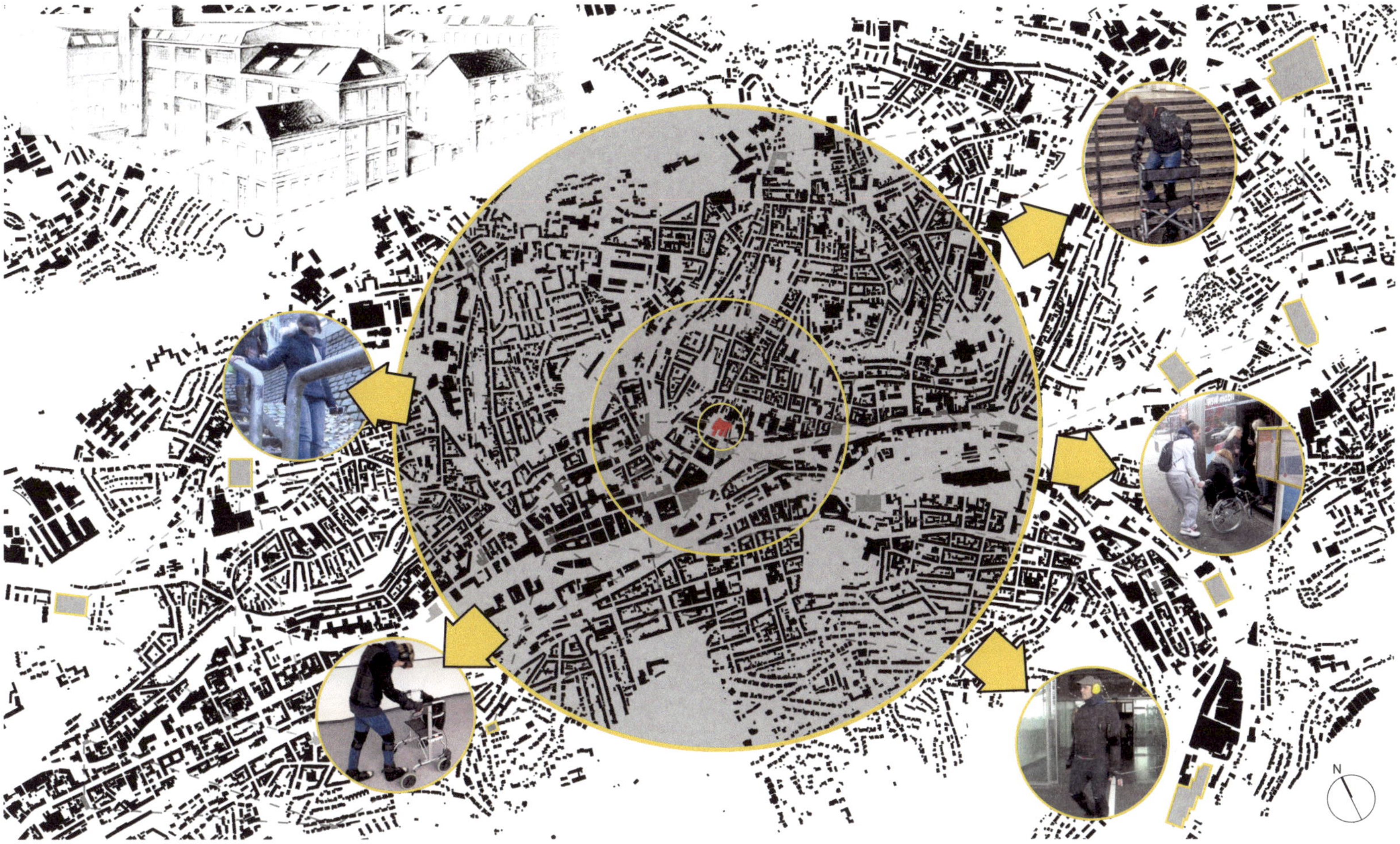

Collage of a barrier-free dérive

rience of the dérive accessing them would require more than two hours of travelling. The aim was to improve access by introducing public transport in the form of bus services or suspended railway lines. Further impaired mobility patterns related to crossing diverse types of barriers, for instance, elevation differences and distances from the kerb to the selected means of transport were analysed and addressed by the students. This experience influenced the further development of the urban strategy, as well as the architectural design, in a significant manner.

Based on the dérives conducted on site and captured by mapping, the previously created preliminary maps were revised by the students correspondingly. They offered additional important information to develop a comprehensive reuse scheme for the building of the Wuppertaler Tafel within the final architectural design. Some students developed housing typologies that were directly related and tailored to individuals of particular age groups. The experiences gained within the initial design steps and based on information from select case studies and best practice examples served to specify detailed measures for age-appropriate housing and develop innovative housing concepts.

At the beginning of a design process, our analytical approach results in the formulation of similar basic thoughts and ideas for developing new architectural functional programmes, and for the urban design-based regeneration of an area, quarter, or district. Here as well, the students proposed many similar solutions for reuse of the vacant building as a form of housing appropriate to older people, families, or multigenerational resident groups, based on the strategy drawn from the analysis.

This shows how important it is to repeatedly revisit the material developed in previous steps throughout the entire design process. In addition to the comprehensively filtered and evaluated data and facts, as well as the assertions captured by mapping on site, the perspective shifts towards further, large-scale social issues and challenges. These data and assertions offer an assistance in formulating related design questions for the individual project and can provide a sustainable impact on the entire architectural concept.

DEVELOPING COMPREHENSIVE DESIGN CONCEPTS

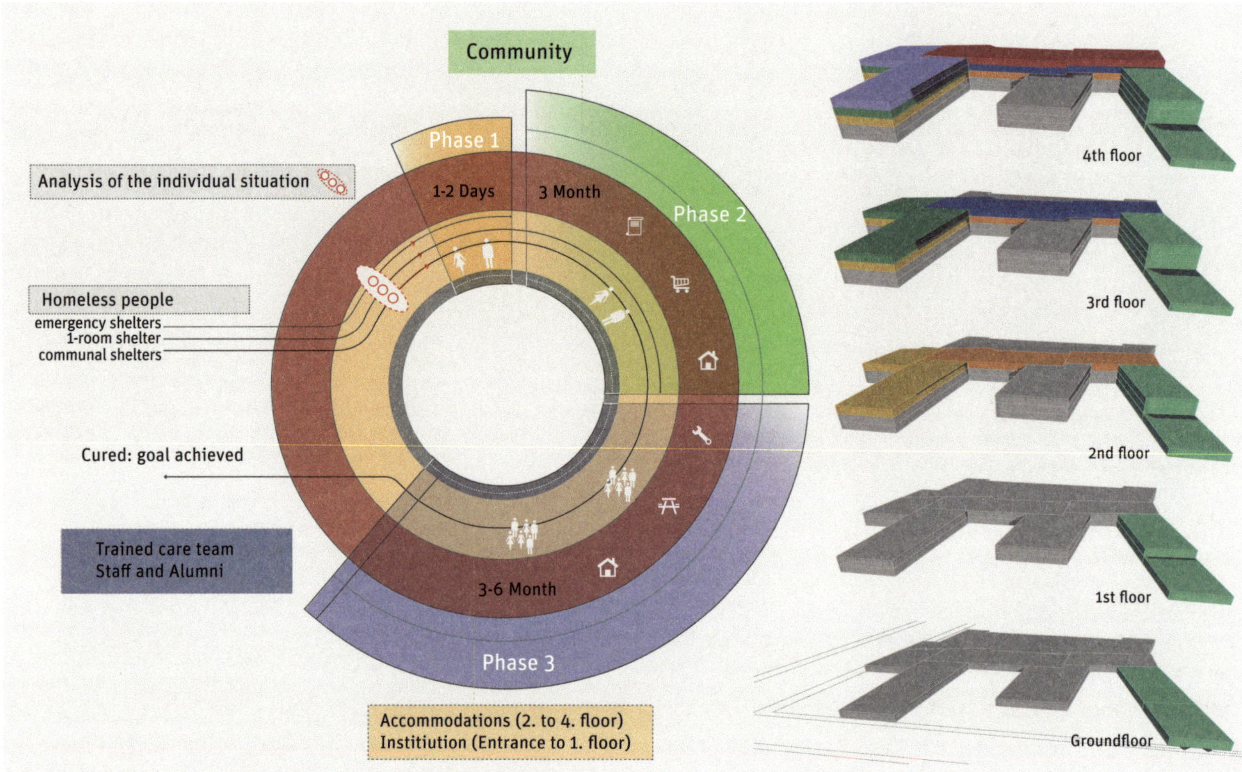

Organigram of the spatial and functional programme allocations

Within their further deliberations, students evaluated recent societal topics, such as poverty among older people, different types of addiction, as well as obesity, eating disorders, and malnutrition among children and adolescents. The group that deliberated on the topic of poverty among older people in depth, structured their respective design steps as follows: their search for innovative schemes for reusing the vacant building of the Wuppertaler Tafel and their investigation of the district led to specific insight. The students recognised that the building, due to its central site in the Valley, features excellent access to inner-city traffic connections and a diverse set of educational and cultural institutions. However, the entire district lacks an adequate mix of uses to cover daily and weekly needs, as well as high quality public spaces, flexibly designed green areas, and options for leisure and recreational activities – functions of particular relevance to a vivid neighbourhood. While researching poverty among older people, the students realised that many retirees only receive a low state pension and the major share of it is required to primarily cover costs for housing and food. A very large share of pensioners in Germany, following forty-five years of full-time employment, receive a net pension of less than one thousand euros, as recent statistics of the German Trade Union Confederation show. Other important physiological and social needs, for instance security and self-fulfilment, are quickly beyond reach. Everyday life leaves no room for options to meet friends and relatives, since many retirees need to focus on improving their income to secure their economic survival. The Wuppertaler Tafel offers some basic needs, such as free food and inexpensive clothing and furniture, to individuals impacted by this situation. A comprehensively structured design strategy and a functional programme drawn from it for an alternative co-housing scheme enable these needs to be addressed within the new spaces of the association.

Prior to the conclusion of the construction phase, different interviews took place in order to adapt the designed residential units of the co-housing scheme to the needs of older people. The residents further have the opportunity to work in

Architectural food alliance concept

the already existing facilities of the association, such as the nursery, the furniture workshop, or the shared apartments. The basis for this developed concept results from the prior comprehensive evaluation of organisations and associations located in close proximity, conducted within the urban design analysis phase. The inhabitants are therefore integrated into the diverse set of programmes which is provided (project team: Lukas Altreuther and Anika Pehl).

Design strategies for local youth

A further student group deliberated on the social problem of adolescents with eating disorders. During the analysis and evaluation phases, the students identified that a high percentage of children in the district of Barmen suffered from obesity (about 20 per cent) and from malnutrition (about 23 per cent). Most of these cases are related to eating disorders. Types of eating disorder were discerned, such as types comprising malnutrition in the context of excessive fast-food consumption.

The developed concept for a food alliance for the Wuppertaler Tafel is intended to increase individual awareness of the topic of nutrition and food consumption. The architectural strategy comprises distinguishing four steps towards achieving healthy and balanced nutrition that contributes to formulating related spatial concepts for growing food sources, food processing and preparation, as well as enjoying food and meals. The architectural concept is aimed at creating an appropriate mix of functions and housing for its inhabitants.

The design provides the building of the Wuppertaler Tafel with a generous foyer that offers room for information events on nutrition topics during different times of the day. The ground floor and the upper floors feature housing for adolescents and their caregivers, all of which include areas for cooking and dining that double as community spaces. The shared apartments provide sufficient room for up to four individuals and include bedrooms with bathrooms, as well as areas for eating and recreation, to be able to share the experiences surrounding nutrition and enable mutual learning and exchange. In order to create visual connections between the different areas, glazed elements are used to dampen noise while enabling views, thereby connecting different levels and floors. The size and location of the building complex of the Wuppertaler Tafel makes it perfectly suitable for this architectural concept of a food alliance. As a result, a vivid exchange is created between the programmes of the association, the residents of the district, and the entire city (project team: Matthias Lehner and Georgi Vlahov).

Design strategies for district residents in need

A further group developed a centre for individuals with addictions, based on the urban design analysis, the dérive conducted in the district, and a large-scale deliberation on local social problems. During the analysis phase, it became

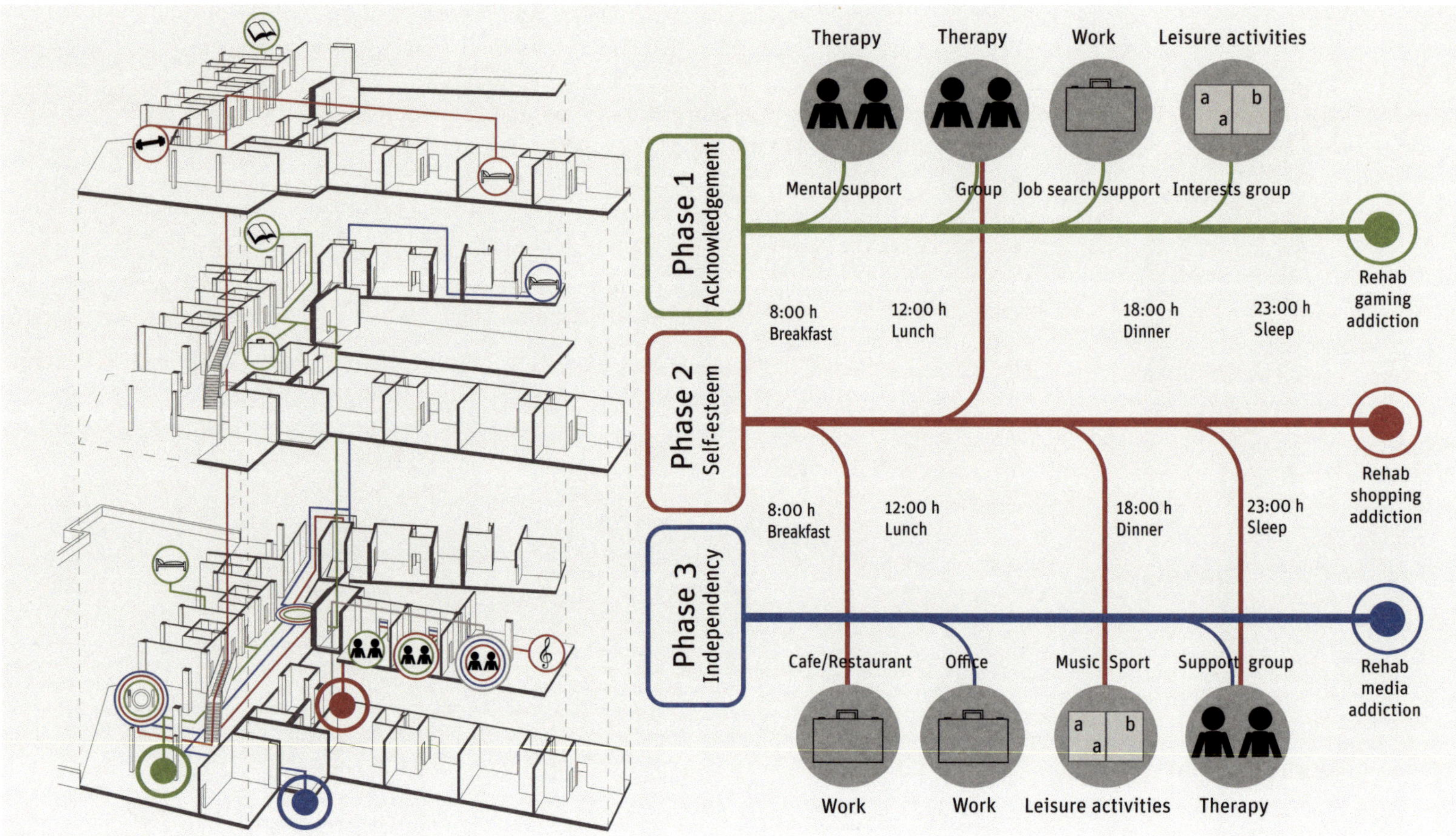

Diagram of the architectural addiction therapy concept

apparent that the topic of addiction, especially gambling addiction, is a distinct phenomenon present within the entire city of Wuppertal. The analysis of the existing facilities dealing with this issue revealed that the major share of services is predominantly or exclusively focused on addictions related to substance abuse. This raised the question of how to deal with the existing gambling addiction problem and other addictions to activities, in the future.

The architectural concept designed by the students integrates a care centre in the building of the Wuppertaler Tafel for individuals addicted to activities. On the one hand, it houses a point of contact for professional psychological counselling related to debt management or similar issues. On the other hand, it includes housing units that can serve as a temporary residence for people with addictions. The residential function results from the circumstance that residents can leave the context familiar to them in order to find a way to overcome their addiction, based on cooperation and located on neutral ground.

The concept aims at providing residents with caregivers who can assist them in managing and, if required, relearning everyday tasks and daily routines. The spatial concept offers areas for communicating strategies for conflict resolution and for empowerment, in order to regain a healthy sense of self-confidence beyond the addiction. The accommodation offered within the individual residential units is inspired by a stage model for treating addictions. The model is structured into three phases, each featuring a different treatment focus, facilitated and articulated by different housing situations. A step forward in overcoming addiction becomes spatially and physically identifiable within the process and serves to provide motivation and a sense of achievement to residents.

The community aspect is highly relevant within the architectural design concept. Aside from the residential units, large and open shared spaces are proposed that house dining areas and kitchenettes, as well as a roof terrace and a library for communication purposes. During the course of the day, residents are meant to meet each other repeatedly in the shared spaces, thereby communicating with each other and creating bonds. The comprehensive concept further includes spaces for individual therapy and group counselling, and for support groups and hobbies, such as arts or music groups, in the context of occupational therapy-related measures. These spaces can be adapted or merged as required based on flexible interior design, including sliding wall panels. Arranging these panels can lead to creating large rooms for lectures, events, or group meetings, as well as smaller, more private areas for individual counselling or therapy sessions. The aim of the urban strategy and the architectural concept for an addiction support centre is to prepare the residents – or rather, the clients – for an addiction-free life after leaving the centre. After conclusion of the therapy and living in the proposed centre, a network of counselling opportunities provided by psychologists, support groups, and contacts to other former addicts is intended to further help participants. They are supposed to be able to benefit from these opportunities at any time, should the risk of relapse arise (project team: Niclas Engelen and Richard Haverland).

A sustainable conclusion can be drawn from the results of the students' projects. Based on a realistic design task, we succeeded in inspiring students to collaborate both with the association, and later in the process involving the architectural office. We also succeeded in making the client feel enthusiastic about the various strategies and architectural concepts. Based on our comprehensive approach, we convinced them to adopt the concepts designed by the students within the implementation scheme for the Wuppertaler Tafel. This design project makes it very clear how important it is for students of architecture to present their conceptual ideas in public – thereby benefiting from including the input from experts and actors in the district into their design process.

Berlin project profile

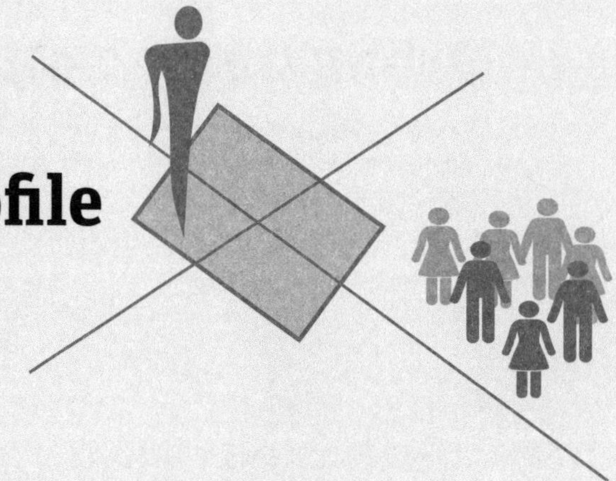

Project initiators and clients

The "Architekten- und Ingenieur-Verein zu Berlin e. V.", is an association that organises a sponsorship award, the "AIV-Schinkel-Wettbewerb", and has done so since 1852. The ideas competition is held annually in the categories of urban design, landscape architecture, architecture, structural and civil engineering, infrastructure planning, sustainability, historic preservation, and free art. Winners are awarded the Schinkel Prize.

Participating partners and institutions

BUW Chair of Urban Design – Urban Scape: Tanja Siems and Katharina Simon
In cooperation with Prof. Dr. Felix Huber, director of the Teaching and Research Area for Environmentally Friendly Infrastructure Planning and Urban Engineering of the Traffic Expertise Centre and students of the School of Architecture and Civil Engineering.

Important data and facts

Teltow was founded in 1265, as recorded in the land register, and is located on the southwestern urban fringe of Berlin, in the administrative district of Potsdam-Mittelmark, area: 21.54 square kilometres, population: 27,097 inhabitants (as of 2021), population density: 1,254 residents/square kilometre. Berlin-Zehlendorf originates in a linear settlement from approximately 1230 and was first mentioned in documents in 1299, area: 18.83 square kilometres, population: 54,328 (as of 2020), population density: 2,885 residents/square kilometre.

Project objectives and goals

The goal is to develop urban strategies that restructure the existing urban, commercial, and landscape fragments surrounding the Teltow Canal, while simultaneously reinforcing connections between the fragmented settlement spaces of Teltow and Zehlendorf. The design is intended to guide the long-term spatial development of the area and identify potential sites for urban development and redensification. The urban strategy is thus supposed to create an urban design- and infrastructure-based network and provide a basis for the design-related implementation of the further development of public space. One important research question for the interdisciplinary student teams in the development of their design schemes for Teltow is: how can a sustainably designed housing and work district promote the mobility transition?

Design project timeline

Analysis and development phase: investigation of the situation, proposal of urban design strategies, and architectural concepts (0.5 years)

Urban design strategies for the mobility transition
Berlin

The strategy development for the sustainable adaptive reuse of a building for the Wuppertaler Tafel offered room for deliberation on the theoretical and strategic approaches to a design process that includes the public. It is important to engage in a competition with other developed urban design projects, particularly in an interdisciplinary context. Competitions for students are especially suitable for this purpose. Given the range of options provided by the AIV Schinkel-Wettbewerb, we were able to successfully submit a diverse set of interdisciplinary concepts within the past ten years. Following the call for entries titled "Knowledge creates cities" for the Kreuzberg district of Berlin, the student team of Tim Hecker, Jan Philipp Heidenreich, Manuel Kramm, and Timon Nüsken won the Schinkel Award in 2019 for their "Urban Cluster" urban design strategy and the architectural concept derived from it. The submitted proposals featured a diverse set of urban design orientations and were supervised by our design studio team consisting of Alexia Radounikli, Julia Siedle and me.

In the previous chapter, structurally and socially critical themes were exemplarily communicated. In this chapter, design projects deal with the implementation of infrastructural strategies. The task outlined in the Schinkel Competition brief for the planning area of Berlin-Teltow offered suitable preconditions to deal with the topic of the mobility transition from a design viewpoint. To deliberate on this topic in an interdisciplinary context, the Chair of Urban Design – Urban Scape and our students of architecture cooperated with Prof. Dr. Felix Huber of the Traffic Expertise Centre and his students from the discipline of civil engineering throughout the entire design process.

To us, traffic does not only mean movement from A to B, but instead, a complex system in which not only infrastructure, but also principles and laws, items of societal value, as well as individual customs and sentiments play a role. To change this system, far-reaching processes of transformation are required to occur on all of the abovementioned levels. The mobility transition is intended to lead to a fundamental reconfiguration of the infrastructure system and a society-wide switch to environmentally friendly types of mobility. For this purpose, not only the energy systems of individual mobility types (motorised individual transport, public transport, cycling, walking) and built infrastructure are of importance, but also their overall share in the context of funding from the ecological mobility alliance. This refers to a comprehensive modal split of 20 per cent motorised individual transport use, 20 per cent public transport use, 20 per cent cycling, and 40 per cent walking. From this perspective, individual designs aim at reinforcing and expanding the ecological mobility alliance and its pedestrian, bicycle, and public transport components, based on urban design and infrastructure concepts and, by doing so, paying attention to the fair distribution of the available streetscape among the different actors.

In the context of the mobility transition, the transition to other modes of mobility is of particular relevance, since it emphasises avoiding and shifting traffic. Within their design projects, the students attempted to develop alternatives for this process and integrated them into a comprehensive concept. For instance, strategies aimed at a suitable provision of mixed-use and compact urban structures are intended to shorten distances residents are otherwise required to travel. This also included specifying concepts for coworking and home offices, to minimise commuting into the inner city. They were further detailed in the design process by using exemplary floor plans.

Model of plots, profiles, and typologies, 500 metre by 500 metre grid

DEVELOPMENT OF INFRASTRUCTURAL CONCEPTS IN COMBINATION WITH ARCHITECTURAL DESIGN PRINCIPLES

The design task was to advance the development of the Teltow district near Berlin. In terms of an intensive deliberation on infrastructural issues with regard to the expansion of the ecological mobility alliance, Teltow offers a fundamental precondition, due to its location and its infrastructural connection to the city centre of Berlin, that is highly interesting from an infrastructural viewpoint. Formulating principles for the development of alternative traffic modes played a particular role to us in this design project. Additional use of water transportation within the scope of public transport services and the realisation of a bicycle expressway against the background of the still provisional existing bicycle network were potentially of specific importance to the many commuters.

The area under investigation reaches from the Zehlendorf district of Berlin to the bordering municipality of Teltow. Unfortunately, during previous decades the development of the two communities predominantly occurred independently from one another. Teltow Canal, originally part of a super-regional waterway network, now constitutes a barrier. As of today, both settlement spaces are only connected by two bridges. The bordering landscapes reinforce this effect. The area under investigation is thus characterised by different fragmented settlement spaces and landscapes. It also included industrial and commercial sites as well as service centres, residential neighbourhoods, sites for allotment gardening, open spaces, and nature reserves. Remainders of the historical industrial and commercial uses still existed along Teltow Canal. Within the concepts under development, the residual urban and commercial sites and landscapes along Teltow Canal were supposed to be reorganised and, at the same time, fragments of settlement space in the Teltow and Zehlendorf districts were to be interconnected in a better way. Beyond that, the students identified potential sites for residential development and redensification, and this was proposed later on in their urban strategies.

To comprehend the distribution of structures and functions in the districts of Teltow, south of the canal, and Zehlendorf, north of the canal, the students created a profile and typological model in order to test the district structure, including residents and workforce, parallel to establishing maps. Specific plots that were considered representative of the entire planning area were selectively researched. The selected plots measured 500 metres by 500 metres and contained the structural typologies of residential, commercial, and service functions, while also featuring striking green and open spaces, making them suitable for an analytical comparison. The evaluated urban design criteria of the different plots were specified and illustrated in a legible manner for purposes of demonstration and possible comparison within profile maps. The selected criteria and parameters for comparison indicated the distribution of built-up areas in contrast to the entire plot, as well as residential, production, and retail functions and spaces used by restaurants, administration, and associations, according to individual typologies and age distribution among the population. As a result, precise statements could be made regarding differences and commonalities, deficiencies and qualities of the selected plots of the district. Consequently, these characteristics could be integrated into the urban design scheme and embedded conceptually.

Overview of urban design parameters

In the selected Zehlendorf plot, predominantly comprised of linear slab buildings, association housing defines the character of the district. At first, following the Second World War, very small apartments were realised within this specific housing typology. Fifty years later, the same apartments were subject to extensive renovation measures. Setback rooftop additions and new extensions to the lateral building sides supported the creation of larger apartments, including tenant gardens, and the transformation of the structures into high-quality, low-energy buildings. In parallel, the selected Teltow plot predominantly features linear slab housing types realised as a "new residential city", similar to the association housing buildings in Zehlendorf in 1962. The apartments and facilities for everyday household needs in the centre of the area include childcare institutions. Following German reunification, the linear slab buildings were redensified by creating rooftop additions and additional smaller building units. The two selected plots intended for comparing nodal building typologies were planned and built for single-family or multi-family residential use, both in Teltow and in Zehlendorf. The difference between the two is the degree of densification of the urban structure. In Zehlendorf, the 500 metre by 500 metre plot features 12,000 square metres of built-up area. In comparison, Teltow comprises only 1,000 square

The "Re-Cycle" concept creates a fundamentally new design of pathways

metres of built-up area featuring the same residential typology. The structure of commercial uses in the same plots in Teltow and Zehlendorf is similar in terms of function and densification of the built-up area. However, businesses display significant differences in terms of the number of employees and the degree of internationality, as well as the different typologies of commercial buildings. The businesses in Teltow comprise only about 4,500 employees on site, yet have 300 branch offices worldwide. In comparison, 18,000 employees work on site in Zehlendorf and more than 2,000 branch offices exist worldwide. The question of how to deal with the development of commercial and service functions in both districts is relevant to the design process. The comparison between the different plots in Zehlendorf and Teltow, with their existing urban structure and typological diversity comprising housing and work functions, reveals similar urban design developments, despite independent regulatory urban planning policies in both German states at the time.

Following the analysis phase, the design concepts developed by the students were all based on a balanced interweaving of the Teltow and Zehlendorf districts, with the aim of designing them to become more attractive and innovatively interconnected. The new road network balances the deficient infrastructural connections between the urban districts and creates an alternative traffic route. Different from the predominant urban planning schemes that give priority to the automobile, the different designs allow the creation of new infrastructure specifically aimed at cyclists and pedestrians. Based on this infrastructure network, diverse neighbourhoods can develop in the district and a new quality of built structures can emerge within the existing urban fabric.

"Re-Cycle" an infrastructural design concept

Since the natural patterns of movement of a cyclist or a pedestrian differ greatly from those of a motorised vehicle, a natural form of networked roads is desirable. By its design, the "Re-Cycle" concept developed by the students creates fundamentally new ways of circulation in the context of a lack of infrastructural connections. The design of a bicycle path network is based on an algorithm that makes use of the statistical method of kernel density estimation for a nearly optimal distribution of nodes along routes and, as a result, calculates a direct connection between them. Consequently, the many interlinked nodes can, in sum, lead to the creation of a minimalist route network. Based on its organic form, this algorithm-generated infrastructure is the best option for

Infrastructural strategy for the Teltow district

optimising cycling or walking as forms of mobility. The generated routes serve as links between the formerly divided districts and are the basis for the urban design scheme.

A non-motorised form of mobility requires effort and is often thus considered unattractive. The new quarter offers optimised infrastructure to counteract this problem. The important points of contact within the urban fabric of the bordering districts constitute the initial input parameters. Since the residents of the district want to get from one place to any other place as quickly as possible, students begin with a direct connection between all places. Correspondingly, the related routes are divided into as many nodes as possible. The density distribution of the nodes surrounding a particular kernel is calculated using kernel density estimation. The surrounding nodes approximate the particular kernel, while the directions are defined by the tendency of the system to achieve maximum density. Each successive calculation results in an increasingly optimal distribution that leads to creating centres and merging individual connections into joint links. It is important to propose different levels of hierarchy within the pathway network. A system comprised of primary and secondary routes can produce an optimal infrastructure network for cyclists and, at the same time, for pedestrians as well. This infrastructural network is not supposed to be interrupted by the barrier constituted by the Teltow Canal. For this purpose, the routes transform into pedestrian and bicycle bridges at the related nodes.

In the centre of the area under development, the existing urban design structure is integrated into the plan. The configuration of the planned buildings and the pathway network comprise an axis that directs the bicycle and pedestrian infrastructure towards bridges crossing the Teltow Canal. A main focus of the design is the open and public spaces, since community facilities are hardly available in the surrounding urban area. The spaces are located centrally in the area and offer functions for the public realm that are easily accessible by bicycle or by walking. The community and the interactions of individuals of different age groups receive particular support within the design scheme. The students considered their concept as a phased development scheme for the entire district that partitions the planning area according to different construction phases. The building typologies include individual townhouses and multi-family terraced houses. The proposed building forms and their flexible floor plans and ramp-like facade designs enable compact living across multiple levels, including small businesses on the ground floor, as well as family-friendly and barrier-free housing. The core of the design is the bicycle. The floor plans of the individual

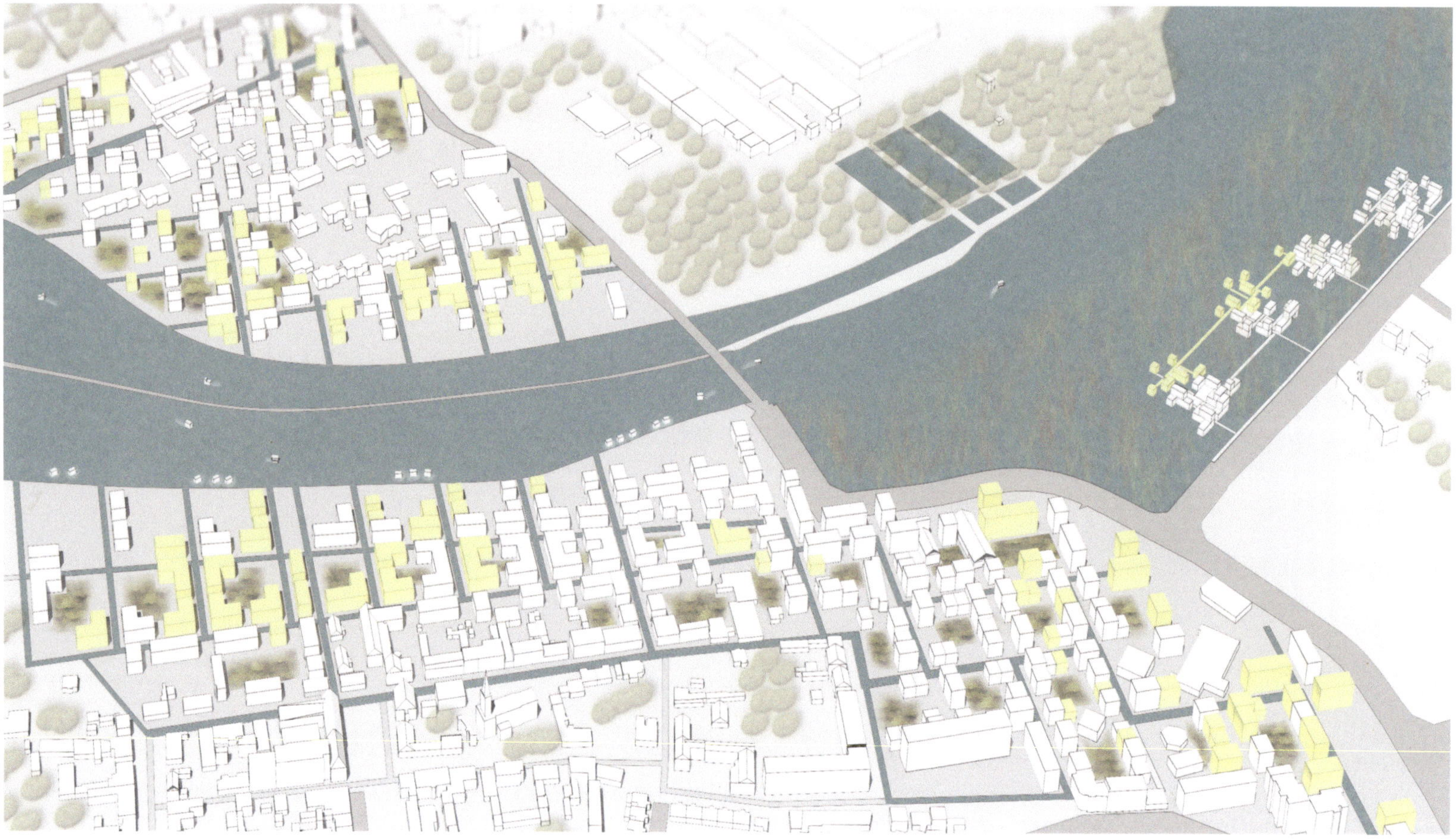

Urban design strategy and architectural concept

apartments are focused on it. The opportunity exists to take the bicycle along as an exclusive means of transport, all the way to the apartment door.

To support removing motorised individual transport and other motorised vehicles from the entire district, a sustainable energy concept was proposed that enables transforming the newly planned routes into intelligent, energy efficient pathways. This is based on expanding the public transport system by creating further bus lines, in addition to large taxis, thereby supporting the mobility alliance. A new, vacuum-based waste management system is supposed to additionally lead to a reduction of motorised vehicles in the district. The students suggested complementing the energy sourced from waste with a solar road in order to generate power. Based on their robustness and low cost, amorphous solar cells in the form of rollable mats are intended as surface cover for the main bicycle pathways of the design. Despite the low yield in comparison to crystalline solar cells, the 75,000 square metres of planned pathway surface can cover nearly the entire demand of planned electric buses. In the concept, the remaining energy demands are covered by solar collectors on the rooftops of houses, while heating energy is supplied by wastewater heat pumps. The deliberation on the entire district as a comprehensive infrastructural energy cycle enables the creation of a homogeneous plus energy district while still providing buildings that permit flexible floor plan design and different types of facade surfaces. The "Re-Cycle" concept not only benefits the residents of the new quarter, but the surrounding districts as well (project team: Jacoba Istel, Kimberley Müller, Nadine Uiberall).

Living and working by the water urban strategy

Another student group deliberated on their urban strategy by asking how additional modes of mobility could be activated for the mobility alliance. The Teltow Canal plays a particular role within this strategy. As a structural and infrastructural border between the two districts of Zehlendorf and Teltow, the canal offers the potential of optimally interweaving the waterway network of Berlin and its surroundings. Since German reunification, these two regions exist, for the most part, independently of one another. There are only two bridges across the Teltow Canal and it is also extremely overburdened in terms of traffic. Thus, traffic jams occur on both sides of the canal in the respective districts. Further, only a single bus line connects Teltow and Zehlendorf. Teltow is one of the few municipalities that displays growth and vivid public life, while population growth is foreseeably strong. This perspective offers an optimal basis for the design, with the aim of creating an innovative and new residential and work quarter. Commuter traffic and motorised individual transport are very distinct, also due to the fact that Berlin-Mitte is only fifteen kilometres away from Teltow and many residents work in the city centre. By evaluating the traffic systems and the related dust loads, the students detected that driving from the district to the centre of Berlin by motorised individual transport takes triple the amount of time required for travelling along the waterways by, for instance, water taxi. This finding offers one of the key criteria for the design and explains why the development of the strategy and the concept focuses on the use of the canal as a means of transport.

Breaking up the artificial borders created by the canal generates new and unique areas that can be used more intensively, in urban design terms, in the future, thus creating space for new and alternative architectural housing concepts. The newly developed canal system that traverses all parts of the district enables shifting the mobility of individuals and goods to small boats capable of responding flexibly to demands. Beyond that, the omnipresence and proximity of water creates spaces for high-quality dwelling and work within the architectural design. The water-sensitive concept allows the existing side roads to be transformed into canals and a new electric bus line for the entire area to be introduced, since the traffic concept proposes a ban on cars in the area. The aim is to generate more ecologically friendly infrastructure systems and to interweave them sustainably in the future. The provision of neighbouring natural areas for recreation turns the individual places for housing and work into green and breathing living spaces for the residents. A comprehensive approach to water management on this level supports the water-sensitive concept through rainwater collection and its use as greywater for outdoor plants, as well as for indoor sanitary installations.

For the processual implementation of the concept, the students proposed different construction phases that are interdependent in temporal and spatial terms. The entire planning area is zoned in a manner that allows individual project profiles for each zone to be established. Here, it becomes important to create identities and develop related flexible typologies, to enable future residents to live and work there in the long term and establish sustained neighbourhood ties.

Within their urban design scheme, the students developed a grid-based block system that connects the districts of Teltow and Zehlendorf and newly structures them. The structural arrangement of the built-up block border areas facing the streets suggests high-density buildings that house residential and work functions. On the block interior, a mix of different types of spaces for dwelling and work are developed, while the height and density of buildings decrease, compared with the block border. The proposed urban design grid, the developed canal system, and the traffic infrastructure are zoned according to different construction phases. The development of all water-relevant areas and systems receives priority and is intended to support the formation of an identity for the quarter based on its accessibility and attractiveness. Redensifying the urban structure at a later point is possible, as required. The developed urban grid and its building typologies continually provide for homogeneous structures and a balanced urban fabric (project team: Maximilian Berg, Carlos Camp, Sophia Leipert).

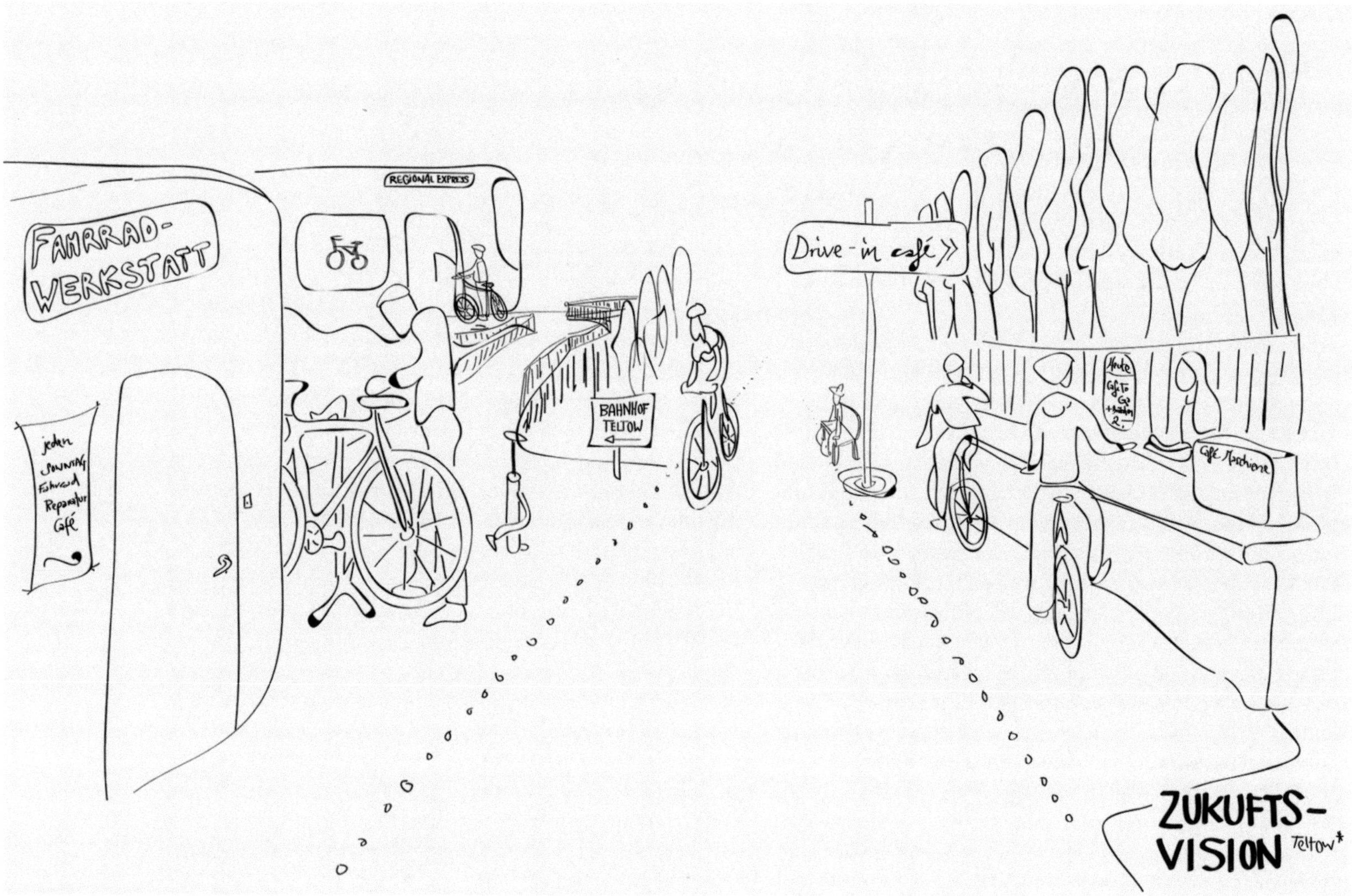

Illustrating the vision for Teltow

DISCOURSE ON EXPANDING THE MOBILITY ALLIANCE: CRAFTING A LINE OF ARGUMENTATION USING URBAN DESIGN METHOD MAPS

Within the two previously described concepts, the mobility alliance plays an important role, due to the provision of new public transport and bicycle services within the urban strategy and the architectural design. The need for this was clearly specified by the students within the urban design analysis and the successive investigation and was integrated into the design concepts. To further substantiate this in methodical and argumentative terms, a student group used urban design method maps to initiate a discourse, in addition to the analytical examination of the district. The question was raised whether it was possible to sustainably change commuter traffic by creating an improved bicycle path network with additional bicycle expressways. For this purpose, the students employed different methods, including surveys, working groups with residents and experts, as well as evaluation analyses. Based on the evaluated analyses, the students discovered that Teltow is a prosperous commuter suburb of Berlin, where rents have remained highly affordable. The infrastructural separation between Teltow and Berlin-Zehlendorf due to the Teltow Canal is only seldom bridged within the traffic system. The result is traffic jams, due to commuter traffic, which pose a significant problem since the public transport system offers no suitable alternatives.

Investigative steps from observation on site to visualisation

The investigative procedure includes the following steps: the exploration begins with an observation of the situation on site, to advance the gathering of information beyond statistics and secondary data. The major share of commuters from the regions of Teltow, Kleinmachnow, and Stahnsdorf commute to Berlin. The inadequate provision of local public transport services stimulates motorised individual transport. Altogether, nearly twice as many employed taxpayers commute from the region to Berlin than the other way round. The population growth predicted by the statistics will lead to an even greater traffic volume. Information gathered and observations made on site were compiled for a visually appealing impulse lecture and presented to the entire group. The individual topics were filtered by using diagrams, visualisation techniques, and a brainstorming map. This supported formulating the following research question: can a bicycle expressway increase the attractiveness of Teltow as a commuter town and simultaneously lead to reducing pressure on motorised personal transport?

Evaluation of gathered information

In a successive step and while evaluating information, individual sets of data were condensed into planning information. Already at this stage, the students considered alternatives to motorised individual transport, to minimise the traffic jams caused by commuter traffic that occur in the vicinity of the two bridges. Due to the existing street widths, the provision of public transport services, for instance via new bus lines or express bus lanes, is incapable of improving the situation. Thus, it is necessary to emphasise new concepts for bicycle services. Based on the research question and the resulting topical focus on bicycles as a commuting alternative to cars, all gathered materials were once more reviewed, with a focus on infrastructure. Correspondingly, the students once more developed a line of argumentation, to demonstrate that the provision of a bicycle express lane could change the behavioural patterns of commuter traffic participants. Beyond this, the provision of a bicycle expressway offers the opportunity to attract new residents to Teltow. For this purpose, the site factors of Teltow were tested again, in relation to the central urban area of Berlin, and further newspaper articles were reviewed, including statements made in the *Tagesspiegel*: "The main railway line could be expanded into a bicycle expressway."

Documentation of gathered information and evaluation

A photo documentation is a suitable point of origin to approximate the topic defined by the research question. Photos of Teltow that include depictions of already existing bicycle paths, their quality and composition, as well as the successive indication of traffic jam situations can offer further ar-

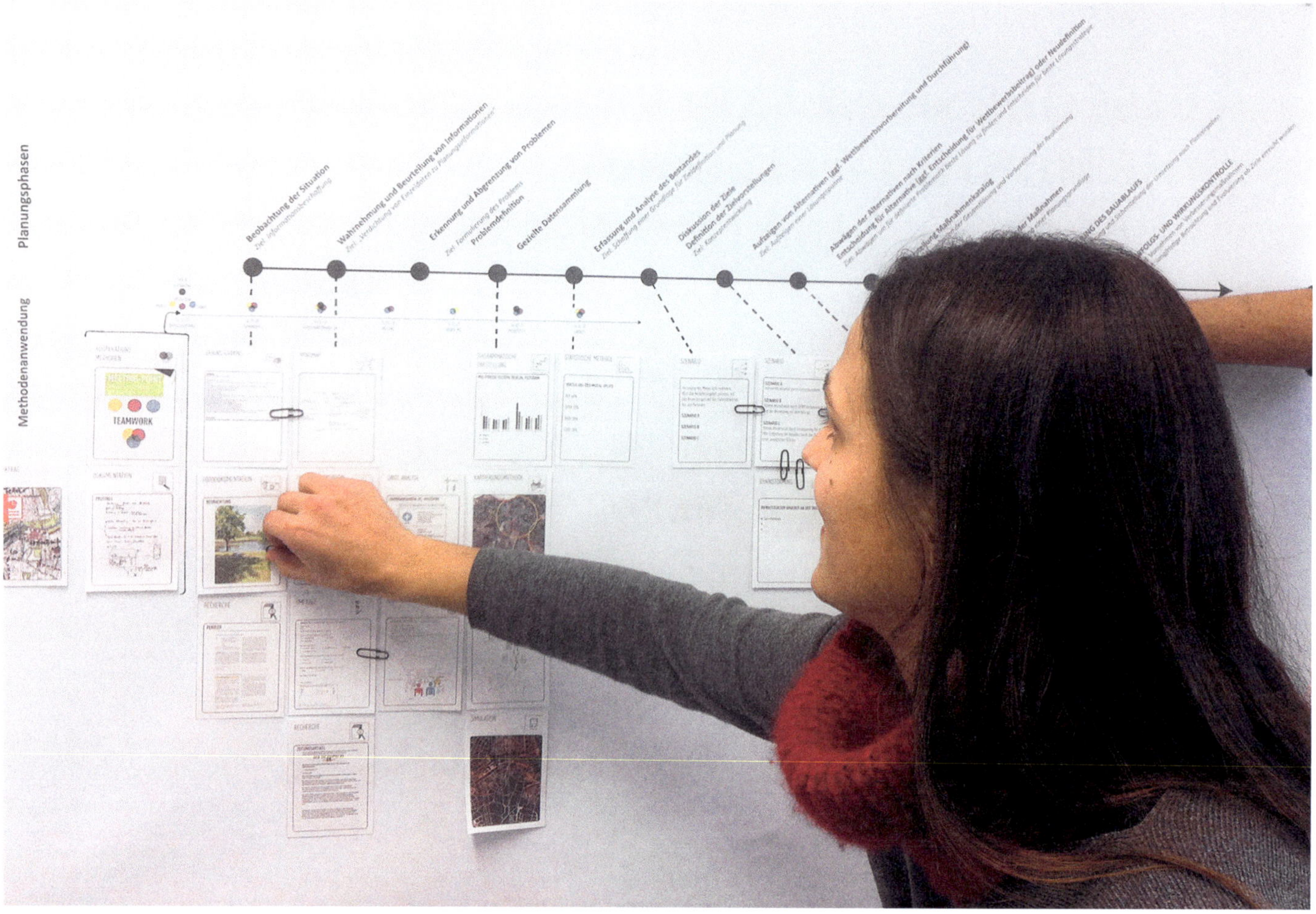

Discussion of the urban strategy, matrix of urban design methods

guments for the evaluation of the proposed theory. In parallel, traffic networks are mapped, to illustrate the relation between streets for motorised traffic and bicycle pathways, the catchment areas of the public transport stops, as well as the distance and time required for different modes of mobility to reach certain destinations. In addition to maps, students developed a survey intended to access public interest in riding bicycles to work. The results show that nearly half of all commuters who live in Teltow are willing to consider switching from motorised individual transport to bicycles. In a third step, to propose concrete identification and delineation of problems, and thus their definition, students conducted a SWOT analysis. It shows strengths, weaknesses, chances, and risks of the project and, therefore, demonstrates why cycling as a mode of mobility poses advantages, as opposed to motorised individual transport or local public transport.

Integrating the public in a creative process

After completion of the analytical procedures preceding each of the first three steps, the proposed measures were tested with regard to individual acceptance. The students initiated a working group to evaluate specific ideas for a bicycle expressway and discuss them in public. The working group as a platform for discussion worked very well and accompanied the entire design process to follow. To test the data collection and initial conceptual ideas in a targeted manner, simulations of traffic flows in the existing and planned street network were undertaken. The bridges crossing the Teltow Canal once more proved to be areas that are prone to traffic jams. For the current commuter flows to Berlin, these bridges neither exist in sufficient numbers, nor are they dimensioned sufficiently. Within this step, the commuter flows to Berlin and Potsdam were analysed in a targeted manner. Distances and travel time of different modes of transport were illustrated using diagrams. The results of the simulation and the verification of the infrastructural concepts derived from it were supported by using a preference matrix and a cost-benefit analysis (project team: Vassilissa Airaudo, Daniel Branchereau, Moritz Scharwächter).

A sustainable effect resulted from the use of method maps within the individual design steps: prior to the design, the supervisor team selected method maps from the diverse set of scientific methods and pre-emptively assigned them to the individual phases within the planning and design process, in order to allow students to test and evaluate them

Method toolbox as argumentative aid for the development of an urban design strategy

within a case study. As a result of this case study, urban design methods including mapping, photo documentation, brainstorming, working groups, scenarios, and simulations proved to be essential and particularly productive. Further methods for generating and substantiating the urban strategy include flow diagrams, preference matrices, target-actual comparisons, cost-benefit and cause-effect analyses, as well as the use of mental maps.

The research questions developed within dialogues were further refined within this process and, as a result, were allowed to develop further in the urban design strategies. They are conclusively specified by the individual groups within a catalogue of measures relevant to the design and presented in a detailed manner within the architectural design concept.

This procedure demonstrates how a comprehensive urban design analysis serves to generate a research question and, as a result, elaborate an individually formulated task and an individual functional programme. What needs to be considered is that a targeted retrieval of urban design methods should not lead to neglecting an individual and mostly intuitive approach that would otherwise lead to decision-making without relying on the method catalogue. For this purpose, it is important to draw some inspiration from the method toolbox, while not becoming overwhelmed by it.

Düsseldorf project profile

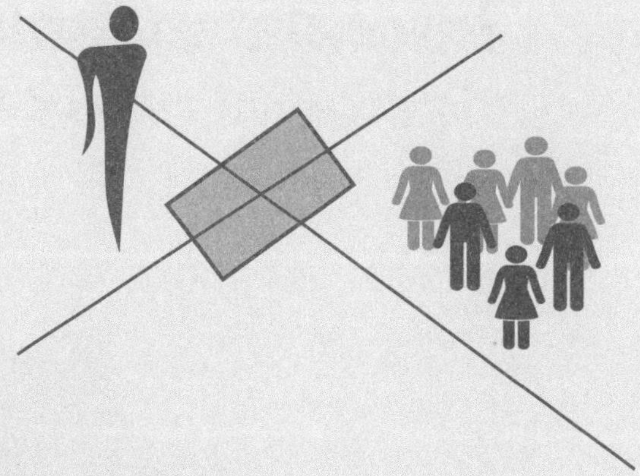

Project initiators and clients
BUW Chair of Urban Design – Urban Scape: Prof. Dr. Tanja Siems
BUW Institute of Civil Protection and Disaster Relief: Dr. Tim Lukas

Important data and facts
The main station district covers 1.16 square kilometres and comprises 30,000 residents who live or work in the district. A total of 9,107 apartments are located in a block border-type buildings erected between 1949 and 1969 including commercially used interior courtyards. The population density of 12,000 residents per square kilometre is exceeded by far during the day, due to the local daytime workforce. In comparison, Düsseldorf comprises an overall population density of 2,769 residents per square kilometre. The main station district displays an unusually high degree of fluctuation: nearly 25 per cent of the population experiences turnover, due to high degrees of in- and outmigration per year. In the city of Düsseldorf overall, this figure is merely 8 per cent. The number of employed taxpayers is 5,100 which is 52 per cent. The unemployment rate of nearly 13 per cent almost matches the citywide average
(source: https://dmitte.de/das-quartier-in-zahlen/ retrieved 12.10.2021).

Participating partners and institutions
Studio team: Elli Börgener, Mohamed Fezazi, Alexandra Radounikli, Julia Siedle, Hedda Vorwohlt
Project cooperation: Dr. Tim Lukas and Prof. Dr. Frank Fiedrich, Faculty of Mechanical and Safety Engineering, Bergische University Wuppertal.

Project objectives and goals
Sustainable urban design scheme for the centre of Düsseldorf. Integration of the local population in the development process for the redesign of the entire district surrounding Düsseldorf Main Station. Urban design strategies are to be developed that prevent the displacement of long-term residents from their accustomed socio-spatial context neighbouring the main station against the background of increasing pressure for valorisation within district development.
The research questions important to the design process are as follows: how do we deal with limited housing spaces in the main station district? How do we maintain social structures in the district? How do we create new affordable housing?

Design project timeline
Analysis and development phase: investigation of the situation, proposal of urban design strategies and architectural concepts (0.5 years)

Informal planning in the urban design process "Act not react"
Düsseldorf

CONTRIBUTION IN COOPERATION WITH ALEXANDRA RADOUNIKLI

Within design projects, our intention is to develop comprehensive strategies and concepts in cooperation with the students. In doing so, we often ask ourselves how guiding images and urban development concepts can contribute to formulating sustainable planning tasks. To us, guiding images comprise urban design solutions that have already proven their merit as basic ordering principles. Often, they possess a prototypical character and serve to advance the goals within the discipline of urban design. Guiding images represent ideal conceptions, and thus basic opportunities to exert sustainable influence on the future development of cities. Guiding images also describe future goals and fields of action, as well as possible projects. They are, therefore, extremely relevant when promoting participative processes in the context of urban planning. Guiding images that have proven reliable in planning practice are included within building codes. Rigid and inflexible rulebooks correspond less and less to the vivid processes and behaviours of a continually changing urban society. Due to this circumstance, cities and municipalities no longer develop guiding images of general validity within strategic initiatives for sustainable urban development. They have been replaced by integrated urban development concepts (ISEK) that are collaboratively established by urban institutions, professional planning firms, and the citizens.

Within the urban design course for the redesign of the main station district of Düsseldorf, we evaluated and scrutinised the principles of the Leipzig Charter in a corresponding manner and in particular in the context of the current discussion on the Düsseldorf Declaration and its demands. The following overview of the Düsseldorf Declaration on Urban Design Legislation (Düsseldorfer Erklärung zum Städtebaurecht) of the German Institute for the Art of Urban Design (Deutsches Institut für Stadtbaukunst) and the related appeal of the Association of Town, Regional, and State Planning (Vereinigung für Stadt-, Regional- und Landesplanung, SRL) to decision-makers within federal, state, and municipal tiers of government to critically review the Düsseldorf Declaration indicates the importance of re-evaluating urban design regulations originating in the Leipzig Charter, not least in the context of urban design- and architecture-related developments against the background of the COVID-19 pandemic.

The Düsseldorf Declaration sets the following goal: "In order to be able to develop socially and functionally diverse urban districts with adequate urban density and beautiful urban spaces, it is necessary to fundamentally change some of the laws, for instance the Federal Land Use Ordinance (Baunutzungsverordnung, BauNVO) and the Technical Instructions on Noise Abatement (TA-Lärm)." In the Leipzig Charter on Sustainable European Cities, European state ministers responsible for urban development declared in 2007 that cities should be strengthened according to the guiding image of the European city. According to the Düsseldorf Declaration, as the many diverse neighbourhoods of European cities demonstrate, the following preconditions exist for successful urban design: a clear separation of public and private spaces (1), good and enduring design of houses, streets, and urban spaces (2), the creation of functional diversity (3), social diversity (4), and urban density (5). The designs for urban districts of our time often lack these preconditions which are prevalent in the districts of European cities and facilitative of the development of beautiful and viable cities. There are many reasons for this. One decisive reason is rooted in the legal provisions for urban design, such as the Federal Land Use Ordinance and its functional catalogues and density limits and the provisions of the Technical Instructions on Noise Abatement, which counteract the demands of the Leipzig Charter, because they inhibit functional diversity. Therefore the time has come to support the Leipzig Charter through legislation and implement it accordingly. Only in this way can the five preconditions related to urban space and functions aimed at the beauty and viability of cities be fulfilled in the manner demanded by the Leipzig Charter and specified by the Düsseldorf conferences of the German Institute of the Art of Urban Design during the past ten years.

The comprehensive commentary on the Düsseldorf Declaration issued by the Association of Town, Regional, and State Planning indicates certain problems, briefly summarised in the following: one main demand of the Düsseldorf Declaration consists in abolishing the density limits as determined by §17 of the Federal Land Use Ordinance. This deregulation of density would lead to enormous consequences for real estate business. Real estate speculation and property values would immediately increase dramatically than ever before.

Municipalities would, at the same time, lose a fundamental basis for negotiation. As a result, property owners would be rewarded with non-productive assets, while the public sector would have to invest in the adaptation of infrastructure and public services on its own. The lifting of urban design-related density limits without corresponding adaptation of land policy instruments would equal far-reaching deregulation of the real estate market and a loss of municipal control. The Düsseldorf Declaration is a metropolitan strategy. It reflects the perspective and problems of a few select metropolises that experience development pressure. It forgets that planning legislation is in force throughout Germany. As a result, it must also address the needs of suburbs, small towns, and rural areas. Planning legislation must demonstrate value-neutrality for all structural spaces and building typologies. It must also do justice to the diversity of lifestyles and housing needs of people. A professional review of the Düsseldorf Declaration also reveals that numerous demands have already been met in the context of the recent Federal Land Use Ordinance.

INTEGRATED URBAN DESIGN STUDIO FOR THE MAIN STATION DISTRICT OF DÜSSELDORF

Large-scale model of Düsseldorf with individual drop-in models created in the architectural design studio

For the redesign of the main station district of Düsseldorf, we as supervisors selected a site southwest of the railway embankment, to apply the criteria formulated in the catalogue of measures derived from the students' urban design analysis to the urban strategy and the architectural design. The existing land use plan and the initial competition contributions for the site in the district propose an exceptionally high degree of densification. However, this is strongly reminiscent of the deregulation aims pointed out in the review of the Düsseldorf Declaration by the Association of Town, Regional, and State Planning: "The demand for the annulment of density limits is a call for deregulation and intensifies current real estate speculation. In the current situation, we require regulatory instruments more than ever, to bring calm to the land and housing markets that have gone completely off the rails."

Against this background and prior to the urban design analysis, the students deliberated on the criteria of the Leipzig Charter and the resulting debate on the annulment of density limits. In their designs, they attempted to balance the degree of density specified by the land use plan and the building height restrictions.

The following urban design projects created by the students show that it is possible to adhere to sustainability principles with an appropriate degree of density in the urban district when choosing a balanced mode of building, including: fair use by overlapping criteria in terms of ecological and social issues, as well as stable rentability by effectively interweaving ecology, economy, and equitable growth through the combination of social and economic principles. Based on this approach, the students developed a diverse set of strategies for a balanced deliberation on the genius loci, the urban elements, the residents, and the new urban and building structure under consideration. The inclusion of the existing population, the preservation of the local social infrastructure, the creation of affordable housing, and a diligent orientation on the ecological development of urban space and its mode of construction were of particular importance for the new urban quarter.

Design studio discourse: the relevance of informal planning within the creative process

Communicating the importance and particular effectiveness of informal planning instruments is a focus of our pedagogy. The necessity of conveying these productive, yet also

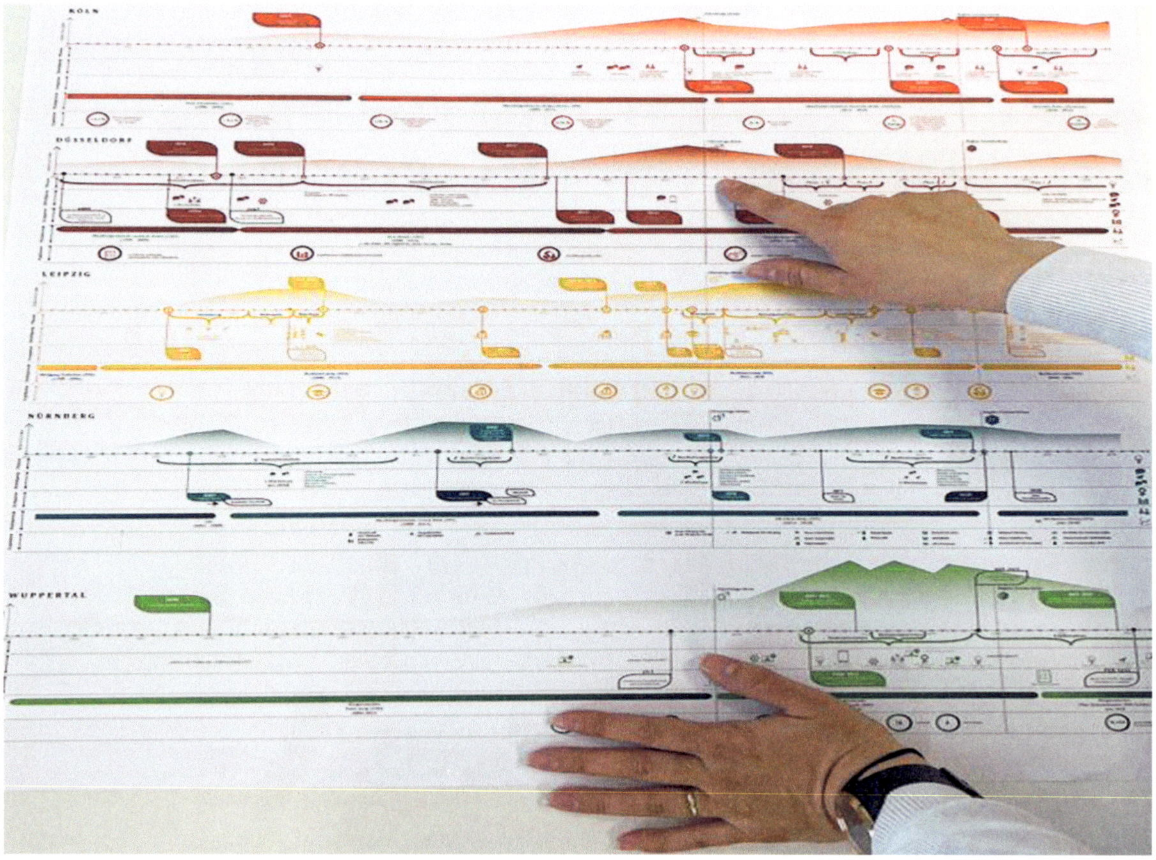

Evaluation matrix of informal planning processes in German cities

experimental instruments is confirmed repeatedly by examples from practice. Further, this is particularly apparent in the individual teaching modules, such as lectures, seminars, exercises, and design studios, structured differently in relation to methods.

Informal instruments are not only sensible in the context of generating urban planning concepts, but also in the formulation of a design concept. The development of strategies for the main station district in Düsseldorf demonstrates this clarity. The related issues are communicated through design assignments and specifically within the analytical approach to formulating a concept. Observation and analysis of the current planning situation and planning trends are immanent to our teaching methods. They also demonstrate the timeliness of our teaching topics. A diverse set of urban development concepts reflects the range of possible formats and implementations. They differ significantly in terms of quality and quantity. Analysing this situation comprises a substantial part of teaching the potential of informal planning.

The approaches offered by the various methods include the comprehensive observation and explanation of formal and informal instruments in the overall context of urban design-related planning processes. Understanding the thematic levels of impact as an interactive system – meaning social and cultural issues, energy and infrastructure, economy and ecology, and all participating actors within federal, state, and municipal tiers of government, of the economy, and of civil society, as well as involved institutions and applicable laws – forms the basis of a critical examination of applied procedures in the arena of urban design. Formal planning guidelines agreed upon decades ago and requiring strict adherence and safeguarding throughout the planning permit process comprise an initial contest and challenge to planners. Students are required to recognise them as such. These necessities and their rationale are analysed in the context of their historic origins, in juxtaposition to new social requirements. Setback calculations, site occupancy index, and floor area ratio decisively determine the way our cities look. Due to the manifest legal power of these measurements, short-term responses to new needs in the context of social change are hardly possible.

In contrast to the strict rules of formal planning, informal planning comprises a multitude of options. Its levels of impact are not legally binding and thus are considered "soft". However, in terms of diversity and potential, they are more far reaching and flexible and, as a result, more sustainable in the context of qualitative implementation. One far-reaching aspect of informal planning is participation within the planning process. The participation of the public or of citizens and users of a city is precisely defined by §3 of the German federal building code: "(1) The public shall be informed as early as possible and shall receive an opportunity for expression and discussion." The way the paragraph is formulated affords sufficient flexibility to the design of the public's participation, either in a very restrictive or a very extensive manner. Merely a form of "education" is provided for and can be omitted under certain circumstances, as stated in section 2. The quality of participation in planning processes strongly varies in relation to the involved municipality. The evaluation of such participatory processes, aside from the communication of basic knowledge, is also a core topic of our pedagogy.

Evaluation of existing and ongoing processes of urban development

In the past fifteen years the number of completed urban design concepts has strongly increased. As a pioneer of participative processes, Berlin has already embedded them very strongly within related processes. Other municipalities and cities have eventually followed this lead and invested in elaborate participation and planning procedures aimed at involving the public. The published results of these procedures become part of the broad range of urban design development concepts and the spatial guiding image of a municipality. In particular, urban development concepts (STEK) are illustrating how a municipality envisions their future urban development. An integrated urban development concept (INSEK) in addition intends to involve as many of the key actors of urban and municipal society as possible within a process and at its very beginning.

The evaluation matrix cooperatively developed by the students enables an analysis of individual participation processes according to the different parameters which were set. For this purpose, the results published in the STEK and the INSEK processes and related documentation could be reviewed and evaluated in a neutral manner. For the objective evaluation of processes, further sources and publications were also reviewed. The research yields further datasets that comprise detailed and specific information: radius and intensity of information flow on project endeavours addressing the public, active and passive opportunities for participation, or actual feedback influence of participants within the planning endeavour are only a few aspects related to parameters under review. The elaborate research on the implementation of participation also included the long-term observation of project realisation, in order to evaluate the actual influence of the public on the planning.

Discussion on participation quality of actors within teaching modules

Decisions on the degree of influence exerted by the public offer a new basis for repeated and continuous discussion in pedagogy. The following questions are asked: how does democracy express itself in urban design-related planning? How much participation of unqualified citizens is reasonable? Attempting to find a neutral answer to this question is already rendered moot by the fact that it is planners who are asking. Nevertheless, it can inspire a discussion on methods in pedagogy that allow students to recognise their responsibility within the related process.

The experimental deliberation on such questions on the quality of participation encompasses the teaching subjects of the Master's programme seminars. Deriving newly developed strategies and concepts from this deliberation on the implementation of participative methods constitutes the students' field of experimentation. The intentionally experimental debate and the freedom afforded by the assignment in this field support conveying core topics of informal planning. The character of the space of participation, the format of an event, the implementation schedule, and the final product of participatory planning are only a few of many analysed criteria of an innovative participation process. Design assignments are formulated in a manner that implies a necessary examination of valid formal planning instruments, such as preparatory and binding land use plans. Only by clarifying the relevance of the levels of impact of formal planning can the potential of an informal planning process be understood, in particular with a view on social sustainability and dealing with rapidly changing social aspects and needs.

Against this background, a tool was designed in cooperation with the students, intended to simplify the organisation of participative processes for municipalities and cities. The tool comprises an app that considers all abovementioned and further criteria of decision-making processes in planning and the implementation of public participation. Users are guided through an intelligent questionnaire, after which the app generates a suggestion for a recommended participation format, taking into account the framework of conditions embedded in the questions.

Information on the size of the municipality and planning themes that receive priority, such as green spaces, housing, mobility, energy, economy, or investment volume are only a few specifications among many that the users are supposed to submit. All the data required in order to generate the intelligent questionnaire for the app was compiled and filtered by the students. This database is composed of examinations of source materials, interview results, and elaborate research conducted by the students. In doing so, various sources were reviewed to test the sound character of the data and evaluate them in an objective manner. Regardless of the content-based evaluation, transdisciplinary competence is required. Here, students have the opportunity to freely select the mode of collecting information and design it creatively.

For the creation of the app, aside from professional urban design-related content, economic and business-related aspects were relevant as well. For the design of the app, the students had to play the role of product designers who use methods of product development to establish the final purpose of the product: who are the clients? What do they need? How can the product address this demand? Is the result of my automated evaluation valuable and sensible?

The transdisciplinary approach allows students to learn how to design the intensive analysis phase in a focused and

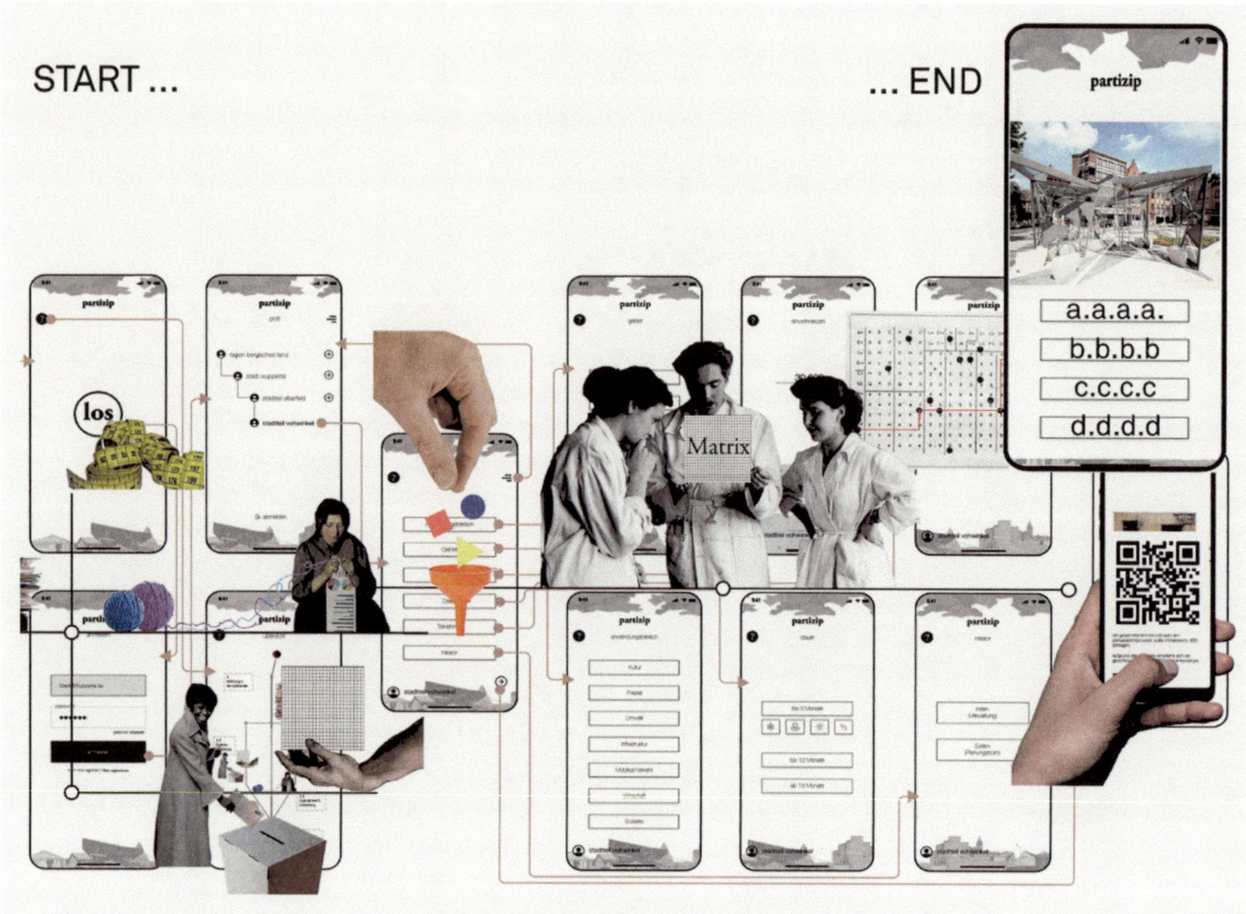

Participation app, support for decision-making processes in the context of urban design-related planning

goal-oriented manner. Based on this methodical approach, the extensive beginnings of information collection can quickly facilitate a goal-oriented gathering of data and lead to useful results within the limited time available in a semester. Beyond that, the relevance of employing new digital teaching methods during the pandemic became particularly apparent in this seminar, considering the pedagogic aim of creating a virtual platform for participatory processes. The design of an app for the communication of content relevant to the students' work indicates the necessity of a general redesign of communication pathways, given the limitations also experienced during the pandemic period. Online meetings have become everyday practice in the business realm, as well as for teaching courses. Lectures, counselling, and even examinations can be conducted spontaneously and without requiring physical presence in virtual space. Given that a field of study such as architecture is particularly shaped by presentation, communication, and interaction formats, students adopted the new task of elaborating the "final result" of their work within a digital presentation that was also suitable for use after the fact.

THE DELIBERATION ON INFORMAL PROCESSES WITHIN A CREATIVE DESIGN PROCESS

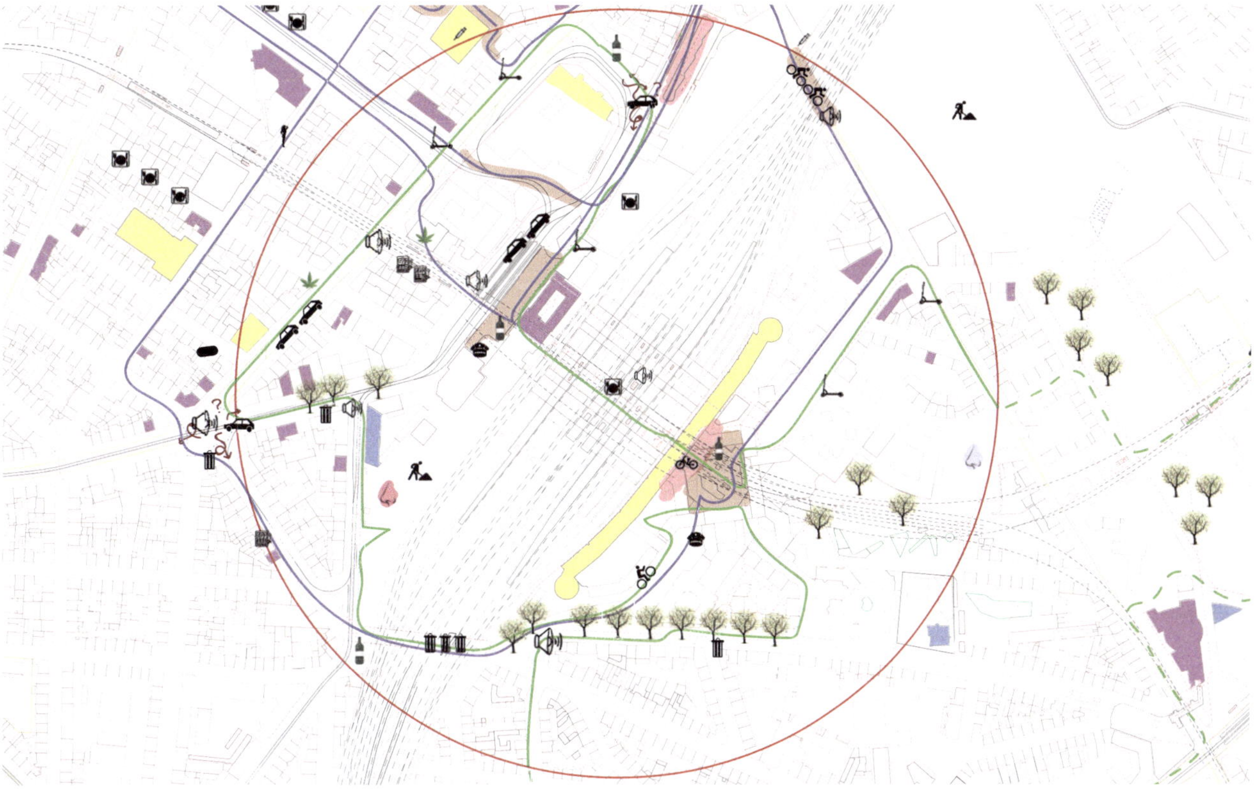

Evaluated characteristics of the train station district

The urban design-related centrality of train stations and a general trend towards living in the city turn train station districts into contemporary urban places that are equally attractive to municipalities and their residents, as well as real estate investors and developers. In the proximity of main train stations, new neighbourhoods for living and working are under development which are leading to a valorisation of the structure of districts that have developed over the course of decades of urban planning. For the urban design assignment in cooperation with Tim Lukas in the context of his research project on security in train station districts, we inquired on the degree to which more attractive and secure housing could be realised for new residents in environments considered centres of criminal activity. How could urban design strategies prevent the existing population of train station districts from being displaced from their accustomed socio-spatial context, due to increasing valorisation pressure?

To propose a comprehensive neighbourhood development concept in the vicinity of Düsseldorf Main Station, the students were required to examine and evaluate a diverse set of urban development-related criteria. This included an intensive analytical deliberation on the area surrounding the station and the bordering urban neighbourhoods, as well as a comprehensive evaluation of the urban design-related examination, in order to generate an urban and architectural concept. Within the urban design assignment, the reorganisation of the social and traffic-related infrastructure can sustainably improve the characteristics and qualities of the urban spaces and their local interrelations across the entire district. In recent years, many municipalities and cities attempted to upgrade central locations adjacent to train stations through retail and residential functions. Such urban design-related developments often cause new problems and potential for conflicts as for example the gentrification of the

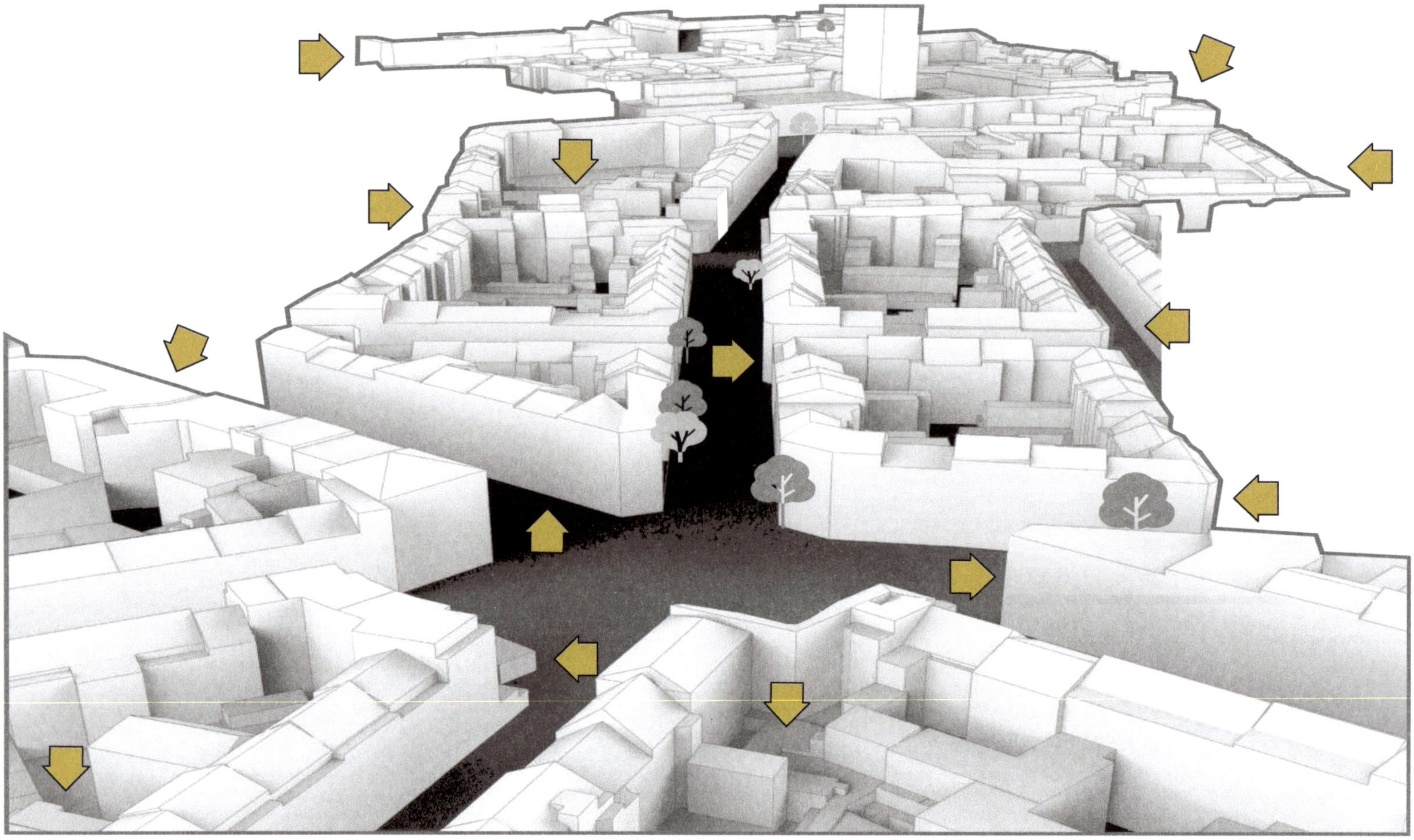

The train station surroundings and social spaces

inhabited area of homeless individuals and for long-term residents of train station districts alike.

In the context of the hierarchical structure of urban districts and neighbourhoods, the Düsseldorf train station district does not constitute a distinct spatial entity. Corresponding to the socio-spatial structure of the city of Düsseldorf, the area under observation consists altogether of five distinct social spaces that cover roughly 1.7 square kilometres surrounding the main station, and thus about 0.8 per cent of the entire area of the city. The predetermined social spaces are located in the direct vicinity of the train station and, in spatial terms, border Mintropplatz and the Handelszentrum commercial centre. While the train station districts in other cities are often characterised by retail functions and their immediate proximity to inner-city cores, a specific characteristic of the Düsseldorf train station district is its mixed-use structure that encompasses a significant number of residential units in the train station surroundings. About 30,000 people live in the Düsseldorf train station district. In comparison with the entire city, this indicates a very high population density. Settlement density is particularly high in the social space Am Bahndamm, comprising multi-storey slab housing. In contrast, the social space "train station and commercial centre", due to generous green spaces and extensive office and hotel complexes, displays the lowest population density of the district. In the south and north of Düsseldorf Main Station, the development of new residential quarters is being planned. The intent is to offer housing in the middle range price segment. The construction tasks are supposed to create surroundings that connect mobility with retail and residential functions and valorise the train station district as the city's first address. The design assignment poses the question of how to improve the quality of the district, while preserving the existing social infrastructure and the availability of affordable housing. The design goal was to generate urban design-related measures and concepts for action that identify the specific characteristics of the urban spaces in the train station district and the existing actors on site, to sensitively integrate them into the urban and architectural design concepts.

GENERATING SUSTAINABLE DENSIFICATION WHILE SIMULTANEOUSLY STRENGTHENING SOCIAL INFRASTRUCTURE

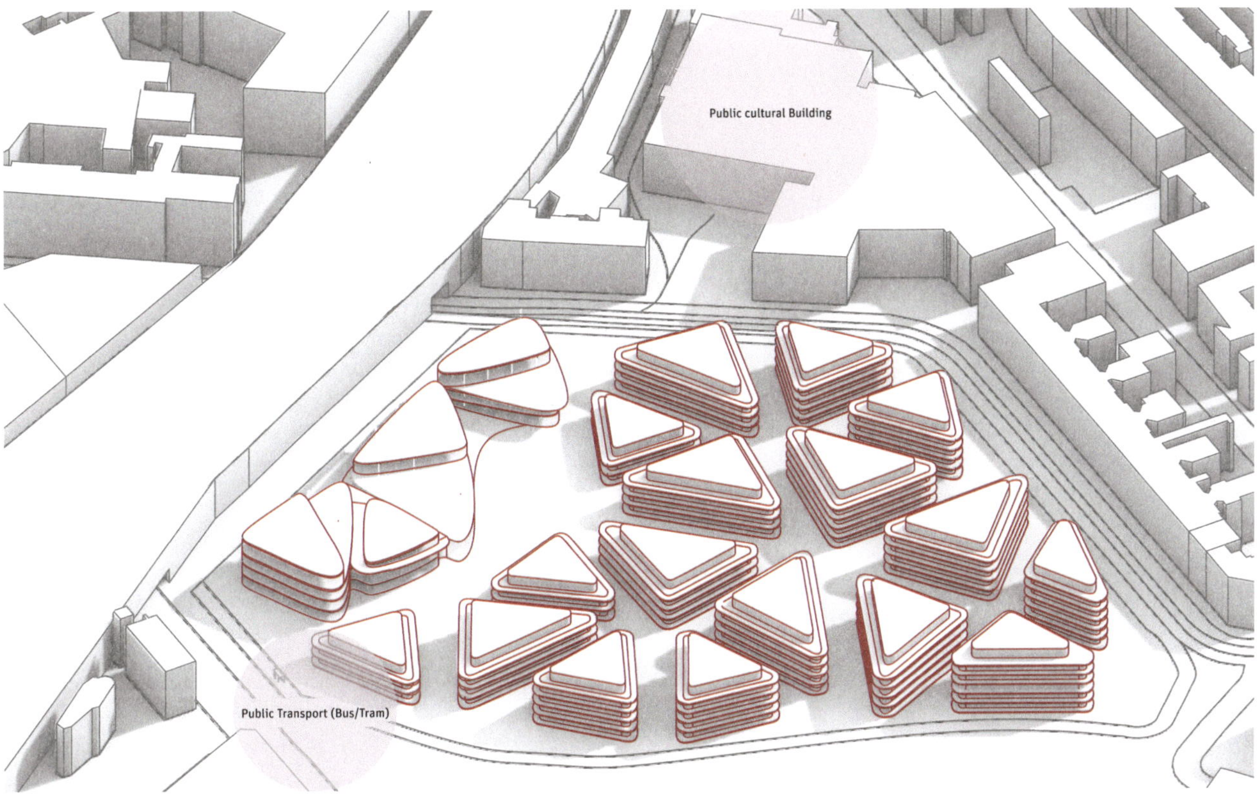

"Corpus Urbis" urban design strategy

The planning area is located near Düsseldorf Main Station and thus immediately next to an infrastructural hub relevant to the entire urban fabric. The degree of fluctuation near the train station and the fast pace of urban life is, as expected, very high. The high number of individuals who depart, change trains, or arrive and immediately move on to their workplaces in the inner city, to their homes, or to socialise, or to briefly stay at the train station, characterise this urban space. The districts in the centre of Düsseldorf and at the direct border to the train station are defined by a high degree of unemployment and are a place of refuge for many homeless individuals, as well as those addicted to drugs and alcohol. For most parts, these individuals are living on the street. As a result, the train station district in Düsseldorf features numerous social services and a good infrastructure for people with addictions. The following design concept's aim is to integrate them better into urban life.

Located in the area northeast of the train station, the "Maghreb quarter" features Arabic restaurants, grocery stores, hairdressing salons, and other services. It thus offers cultural diversity that benefits the entire quarter. The building structure and the relation between building height and street width create public spaces that permit active communication and familiar exchange between residents. The urban strategies devised by the students reinforce local communities within design concepts oriented on urban space. By doing so, the existing degree of interaction is supported and establishing new contacts is simplified.

Against the background of ongoing social change in the train station district, one student group designed a diverse set of cultural services in the ground-floor areas, aimed at balancing mixed uses within the building configuration. For their urban design concept "Corpus Urbis", the students designed a market hall for the planning area southeast of the train station. It is intended to serve the existing and new residents of the newly developed residential and work quarter as a place of communication, based on flexible and open floor plans. As a new urban typology, the market hall functions, for one, as a noise barrier for the residential areas oriented towards the train tracks. Further, it is a place of communication and exchange.

The market hall houses further functions for the district, such as a café that can be turned into a dining hall in the evening, to serve additional food for an individually defined price. The concept embraces different service proposals for the new quarter that particularly address homeless individuals. In addition to serving them free meals in the market hall, the ground-floor areas of the planned buildings feature areas for social workers to support them, and also where they can get bureaucratic assistance and support. Further, mailboxes are installed for homeless individuals to have a postal address, thus creating a starting point for their renewed integration into society.

According to the guiding theme of "all roads lead to the market", the students proposed a dynamic pathway network that is predominantly oriented towards pedestrians and cyclists, with primary and secondary pathways leading through the planned quarter and the surrounding districts. To create affordable housing in the new quarter, apartments were planned and reserved as social housing. Contrary to existing patterns, they comprise variable floor plan designs, to generate larger and smaller apartments as required, and thus permit quick-use conversion of residential spaces. Within the design, the building structure and its facade and floor plans were configured in a manner that allows communication between public and private spaces to remain possible at all times.

For this purpose, the students conducted a comprehensive examination of their urban design-related analysis that served to derive principles for an optimised configuration of the street cross-section in relation to the buildings. These principles are clearly illustrated in profile maps and are successfully employed within the design. Based on these articulated criteria the design achieves a balanced social mix in the quarter in its urban and infrastructural related design and creates therefore a suitable interrelation between the new quarter and the train station district (project team: Sayneb Abbas, Farah Alnihawi, Anna Ußler, Zhiyuan Wang).

Urban design strategy and architectural concept "Lungs of the City"

A further group emphasised the necessity for a socio-ecological orientation of their design, in addition to addressing the societal conditions and resulting social problems in the quarter. Based on its urban design-related measures and a correspondingly adapted architectural design concept, the design "Lungs of the City" achieves an improvement of both the train station district's micro-climate and the entire urban climate.

The urban design micro-analysis revealed problems, as recognised by the other design groups as well, with regard to the traffic infrastructure in the train station district. Most of all, it identified the existing narrow streets, without clear separation between areas for pedestrians, bicycles, and car traffic, as a problem source, as well as strong degrees of air and noise pollution in the quarter and in the area where emissions were measured. Noise and traffic jams not only affect the residents of the train station district during the day, but at night as well, in certain areas. Beyond that, the urban quarter is characterised particularly by its rapid pace, shortage of places to go to for leisure or recreation, bad lighting, and the prevalence of fast-food franchise restaurants and gambling halls open 24 hours a day. The quarter is hardly an inviting place to stay for longer than necessary, neither for residents nor for tourists.

In a follow-up step comprising the macro-analysis, the students selected a larger scale for the area under observation to provide statements on climate circumstances, in addition to the urban design-related and infrastructural conditions. For this purpose, the large-scale impact of thermal conditions, precipitation, and air flow as well as traffic infrastructure were analysed and evaluated in order to draw conclusions for the train station district subject to observation. Large degrees of thermal stress were measured in the area, caused by narrow street profiles. On the planning site, three different wind corridors intersect, which adequate planning could use to improve the urban climate in the area. In addition, the large degree of coverage and insufficient green spaces lead to repeated flooding in the quarter, caused by heavy rainfall. These insights impact the urban design-related and infrastructural organisation within the design, as well as the orientation and placement of planned buildings.

The students proposed elevated buildings in their architectural design concept. This leads to creating clear separations between public and private spaces and at the same time enabling improved ventilation throughout the site. The raised residential complexes consist of different timber modules that permit rapid construction and expansion as required. Using timber module systems shows a sustainable design approach also in terms of the manufacturing process or supports demolition, if necessary, of unused building structures. Raising the buildings creates covered ground-floor areas that provide sufficient space for public functions in small-scale building units, such as restaurants, kindergartens, shops for daily and weekly needs, commercial units, and the planned Museum of Photography for Düsseldorf, all of which can enliven the quarter. Residents can escape everyday life in the urban jungle, based on a green lung that increases the residential quality of the quarter. By combining micro- and macro-analysis and interweaving their results, many redensification potentials were identified and sustainably implemented within the urban strategy and the architectural concept (project team: Filip Daust, Luna Emembolu, Tugba Kaya).

Creation of an urban natural space through raised buildings

Infrastructural and urban strategy "The LINK"

A further group attempted to address sustainable densification of the planned building structure based on the topics of mobility, fast-paced urban life, and speed within their design "The LINK". The train station district in Düsseldorf thrives on high velocity that defines the movements of travellers, commuters, consumers, and temporary workers through the quarter, in addition to the residents. Velocity defines this place, and thus the area under development. Therefore, areas for rapid transit intersecting the quarter are generated by using direct and straight pathways and with twists and curves for slow movement which allow space for interactions. The planned plazas, bridges, and rooftop surfaces are areas for intentional communication. They create visual interrelations and connect the buildings with their users and inhabitants.

The building form results from the developed pathway system and the evaluated visual connections. The curvature of the building facades directs the movement of visitors and residents throughout the quarter. The ground-floor areas house public functions and offer room for a neighbourhood meeting point, shops for daily needs or sports and cultural facilities. These areas are completely integrated into the design of the curved building structure. The upper floors are mainly used as residential living. However, they can also be combined with coworking spaces or other small-scale cultural facilities. The upper floors are accessed by a staircase core leading to interior access balconies. The access balcony system serves as an additional space of encounter. The site of the building defines the distribution of residential, work, and leisure functions. The location of the northwestern buildings, which contain residential spaces, art studios, and spaces for small exhibitions and storage, indicates a spatial relation between them and the cultural uses of the Capitol Theater and the dance theatre called "Tanzhaus".

The roof surfaces are used for urban gardening projects or for sports. Due to their orientation, they offer additional room for solar power units. The buildings featuring public ground-floor areas include a walkable interior courtyard. The upper floors and the rooftop are accessed by a semi-public staircase core in the building interior. This staircase core is connected to bridges that lead to the other buildings.

The different terraces and heights of the building result from the surrounding built context. To indicate pathways and the wanted related velocities through the buildings, the students developed a model consisting of physical strings as a test object for the design process. Depending on the way in

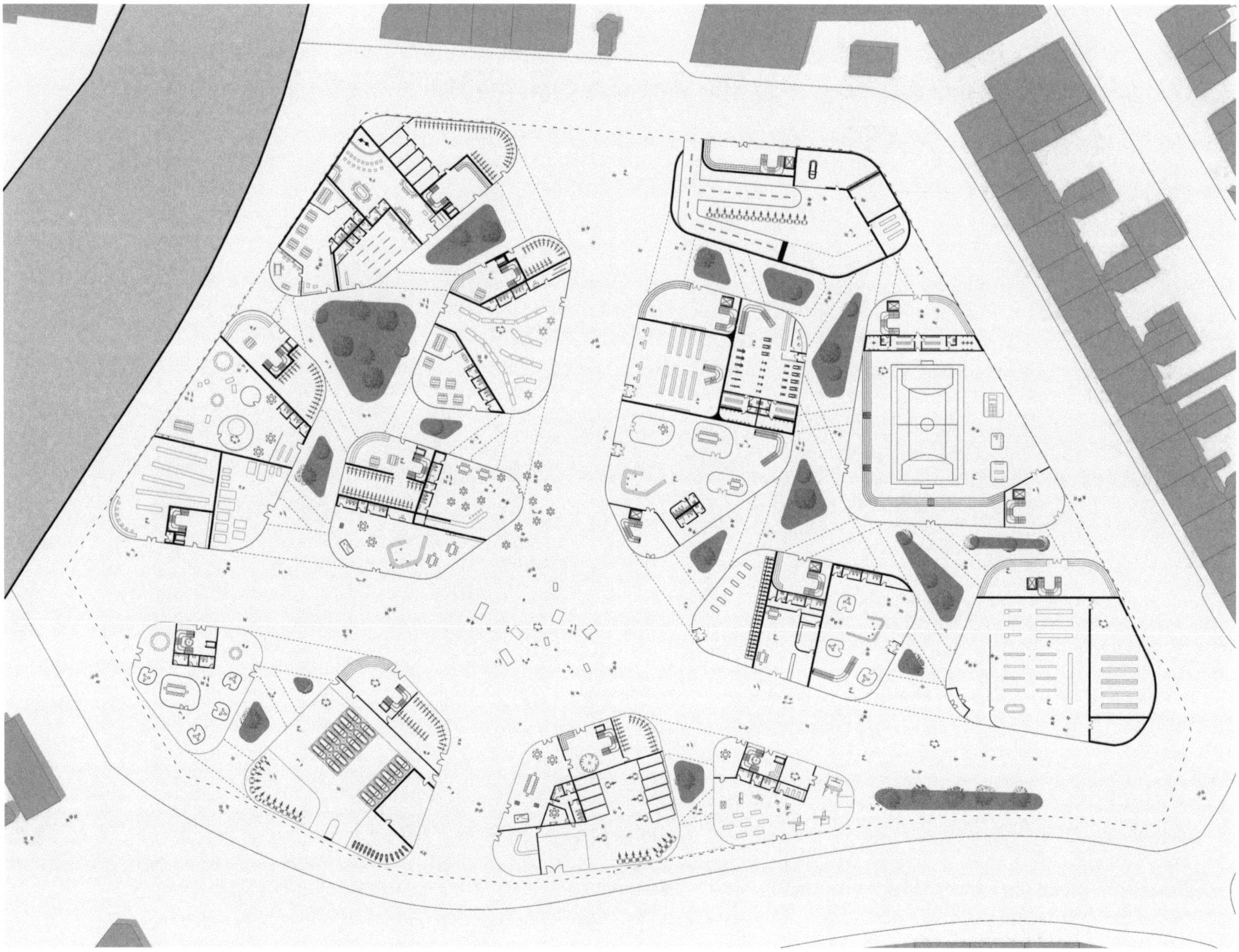

Site plan and ground-floor area with functional programme

which strings are fixed or wrapped, the outcome is a horizontal facade configuration that defines density in relation to the area of specific velocity. Calm areas feature horizontal strings fixed to a specific node per storey. Supported by post-beam facade construction along the upper storeys, the vertical organisation becomes visible and merges horizontally. The concept of wrapping allows individual buildings to be connecting and interwoven into clusters. The bridges and air spaces above the public plazas also result from this process of wrapping.

The students proposed a car-free quarter to create a space for movement without dominant motorised individual traffic, as particularly in the city centre, it is no longer necessary to own a car. Low-cost car-sharing opportunities increasingly find acknowledgement and usage from inhabitants and support from the government. As a result, parking spaces required for vehicles are reduced and expenses for individual cars can be spared. To simplify the transition into a new urban transport concept, mobility hubs for rental cars, cargo bikes and bus stops are located in the north and south areas of the site. Also bicycle parking areas are available on the ground floor, either for personal or for rentable bicycles. The created mix of residential and work functions in the quarter, combined with leisure and recreational opportunities and business areas on site, keeps distances short and supports the sustainability approach for the development of the train station district. The selected urban and infrastructural design approach creates a new train station district as a shared space for the surrounding neighbourhoods, for residents, commuters, and travellers alike (project team: Domenico Alberta, Finn Gundermann, Annika Porschen).

SYSTEMATIC DESIGN PHASES AND STEPS: AN EXPLANATION

For us as supervisors, teaching design strategies and how they relate to practice is the most important task. In addition, it is also very important to us that students are confronted with the processes of planning and construction. In the context of developing and advancing concepts for the Wuppertaler Tafel, the students had the opportunity to continue participating in the planning process, together with the client and the involved architectural office. By doing so, they were able to provide their input into the design process and witness the actual construction process in its entirety. For other design assignments and within urban design and architectural competitions, the students were able to present their theoretical ideas and concepts to the broad public, enter into discussions with experts from different disciplines, and test their work with regard to its applicability in practice. In the following, in order to describe a set of phases and steps within the design process as a decisive procedure for planners, students, and supervisors within its overall context, the individual phases and steps will be explained in detail and visualised using examples from different student design courses.

The analytical approaches and technical illustration types were introduced in the preceding chapters, according to the particular design course examples for Wuppertal-Barmen, the Düsseldorf Main Station district, and Berlin. These three presented case studies show how urgently necessary it is to conduct a comprehensive analysis (1) and evaluation (2) phase at the beginning of the design process: a preceding examination can support the development of an extensive urban programme based on functions and related structures that have been evaluated within the urban design analysis. This substantive approach to programming can lead to formulating site-specific strategies (3) for an entire neighbourhood, quarter, or district. In the phase to follow, students can use this urban strategy to develop various concepts for a detailed architectural design (4). The urban fabric is a complex system subject to ongoing processes of change. These ongoing processes of change comprise urban transformation procedures of continuous construction, conversion, expansion, and demolition of urban structures. Within the planning process and especially within a design assignment, it becomes clear that the diverse range of possibilities of manifestation and spaces of effectuation of built structures as hard factors and physically involved actors as soft factors possess multi-layered character.

Hard and soft analytical factors

Hard factors include distinct facts, data, and numbers, as well as topographical and geographical conditions, the type of mix and density of uses, or areas required for vehicular access systems, stationary traffic, or parking. It is important to observe the configuration, orientation, and elevation of built structures, the organisation of plots, and the interrelation between built-up and open space, as well as public and private space, and integrate observations into the design concept. The character of a neighbourhood, quarter, or district also plays a role and is defined by streetscapes, building structure, and facade design. The interrelation between buildings, streets, and open spaces is of particular relevance, as is their quality. The physical form of a city always results from social processes: planners integrate this interdependency into their investigation of built, structural, and infrastructural layers.

Soft factors tend to be indicators, parameters, or criteria gathered in an open, intuitive, spontaneous, and instinctive manner. They relate, for instance, to the composition of a district social structure, the residential population comprised of employed individuals and stakeholders, their social and cultural mix, as well as the atmosphere, mood, and attractiveness of and within a certain area.

A layer analysis is based on the assumption that former and recent processes of everyday life can be interpreted by observing the urban structure. For the examination of settlement space, its culture and identity, it is particularly important to consider this assumption against the background of structural change, and thus adopt economic, societal, and technical aspects. The layers of an urban system reveal themselves within urban design structures, according to the manifest and non-manifest character of the urban fabric. Within the analysis phase of the design, they are illustrated and captured with graphic methods in the form of different types of mapping. This type of illustration serves to display the built-up and open spaces, while giving consideration to phenomena such as vegetation, hydrological systems, or infrastructures of traffic and technology as part of the urban layers.

Historical references of illustration types

This complex type of illustration is not a new invention, but rather a method developed over the centuries by various planners across Europe. In 1748 the engineer and architect Giovanni Battista Nolli was the world's first cartographer who did not orient his "great plan of Rome" eastwards, as had been customary. Instead, he oriented his plan towards the north, in order to show how open spaces were shaded by surrounding buildings. Beyond that, in this urban plan, a typical figure-ground plan of its era, he made a distinction between urban structure, roads, and pathways – and in particular, private and public areas – by graphic means. As a result, it was possible to use this map as a planning basis for the future development of Rome.

A century later in 1854, Dr. John Snow created a list of cholera-related disease cases in London's Broad Street within an urban map. By integrating medical information into an urban map of Soho that displayed technical infrastructure, he was able to ascertain that the disease was not transmitted by respiratory infection, but by the water supply and contaminated local urban water pumps. This targeted superimposition of gathered information on the disease patterns, in combination with cartography, allowed John Snow to make a statement on a medical problem by using an urban design method. In this way, he was able to propose a technical approach to solving the problem that influenced the entire future planning of the city.

Maps as analytical tools

In the same era, in the year 1869 Charles Joseph Minard presented his map of Napoleon's failed 1812/13 invasion of Russia. With this method, he attempted to show the reasons why the campaign had resulted in such an extreme loss of life. Of the 423,000 soldiers who had joined the campaign in June 1812 at the river Niemen, only one thousand returned one year later. In his map illustration, Minard not only showed the spatial and topographic situation of the campaign, but also the size of the army, its marching directions, and its respective location in terms of longitude and latitude and how this was related to time and temperature. He was able to explain that the loss of the army did not occur due to strategic or technical advantages of the Russian army, or due to unfavourable geographical conditions. The majority of soldiers were killed because of the fact that prevalent temperatures measured nearly minus 30 degrees centigrade and that extreme cold had led to the extreme reduction of the army and the failure of the campaign. The graphic methods Minard selected are very close to a contemporary "diagrammatical" means of illustration. By creating a map in this manner, he was able to relate existing data and facts of the army to the geographical and natural conditions, thereby correlating them. He fundamentally changed the cartographic approach to illustrating plans.

During the same era, the engineer Louis-Léger Vauthier used the mathematical method of illustration offered by topographic contour maps to show the population numbers of Paris in 1874. This geographical means of illustration was further developed by Vauthier in a manner that no longer showed geographical conditions by using contour lines, but instead, visualised purely statistical data. As a result, planners gained the opportunity to compare population numbers, not only in numerical, but also in graphic terms, and correlate them.

Visualisation of data and facts

In his 1930 atlas on *Society and Economy*, Otto Neurath used graphic means to bundle different data on population development, international trade relations, and the global accessibility of resources, and through his illustrative methods, correlated them. In one hundred diagrammatical illustrations, the atlas shows the means of production, and the types of societies, cultures, and lifestyles of the early twentieth century: "This seminal work of visual statistics titled *Society and Economy* represents the first attempt to systematically visualise a colourful image of contemporary human civilisation and its development on the basis of diligent processing and linking of existing data and all manners of combination thereof."

In the 1960s Kevin Lynch went even further than the previously mentioned, purely analytical plan illustrations of urban design layers and their basic elements in his theoretical work on *The Image of the City*. In his maps, he captured spatial structural elements of cities and correlated them with the perceptions of individuals, thereby displaying the connections between human perception and the type and quality of the city's physical form. The city can, therefore, be understood as more than merely a built manifest structure with its infrastructures related to construction, traffic, technology, and open spaces. Instead, it permits illustration as a far-reaching space of perception. These types of mapping are described as mental maps: they comprise cognitive charts that present a mental image of the city and its atmospheres. This type of cartography allowed Lynch to directly include the citizens and their perception of the city into planning processes.

Further theories of the 1970s and 1980s deal with participative strategies and democratic planning processes. The motto of "the citizens build the city" guides an initiative to construct imaginary buildings for freedom and equality. They are connected to existing urban structures, to reconcile tradition and utopia. To display them in an effective manner, the utopian designs are implemented using a diverse set of illustration methods. A suitable method of illustration includes montage or collage techniques, in order to visualise planning ideas or design constructs and their utopian appeal in an easily accessible manner. Beyond that, building tangible models and testing planning ideas by using related models gained increasing importance during this era, also as a scientific approach. For instance, Constant Nieuwenhuys experimented with collages, models, drawings, and paintings in the course of his development of a visionary city model.

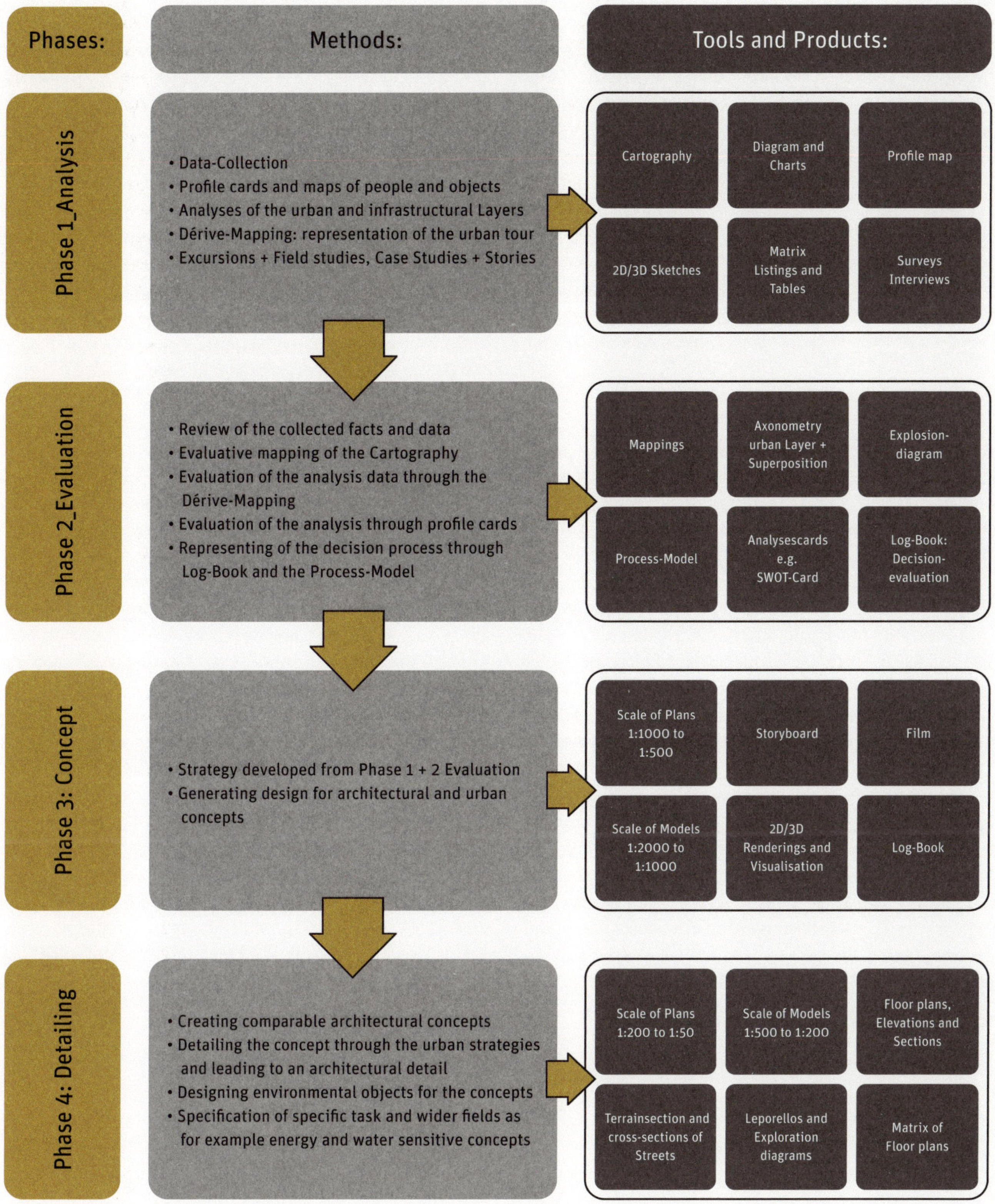

Diagram of "Steps and instruments of the design process"

Within different test sequences spanning two decades he attempted to evaluate his urban future strategy "New Babylon" by using these illustrative techniques and further develop it in a sustainable manner.

The urban model of "New Babylon" describes a city without borders that can expand in all directions and, at the same time, offer its citizens free and flexible options for self-expression. In an interview with Hans Ulrich Obrist, Constant Nieuwenhuys described his urban model on the occasion of the exhibition of his strategy concept during the Documenta 11 in 2002 as follows: "New Babylon was, from the bottom up and to the level of details, planned as a flexible living environment. It was supposed to be an open city without borders that can expand in all directions, similar to a liquid. The idea was to understand New Babylon as a place that had transcended common understandings of cities as places of identity. New Babylon is not an urban planning project, but rather, a mode of thought, of imagination, a perspective of things and life. New Babylon is home to homo ludens, it is the world of playful humans. It is a kind of societal pattern that includes thinking about permanent change and transformation." It becomes clear that these different types of illustration allow planning disciplines to employ their principles as critical instruments aimed against a planning culture fixated on standardisation and uniformity in urban design.

Mapping: Generating maps

In the 1990s, James Corner developed the approaches of "mapping" and "layering". They are of specific importance to our pedagogy in the context of design processes. According to James Corner, urban design- and infrastructure-related layers can be specified beyond purely drafted, traced, or computer-aided visualisations by using the method of superimposition. This allows data to be generated on the individual layers of the urban fabric and, as a result, the identified facts can be used as the basis for a conceptual strategy of the design. According to Corner, mapping is distinguished by its evaluating, analytical illustration of existing urban elements. As a result, capturing an urban element by using graphic methods in all cases means to evaluate the selection it is based on and its illustration to follow. In contrast to mapping, the method of layering, according to Corner, describes the superimposition of the individual, displayed urban layers that, through their superimposition, generate and organise new information.

"Data-scaping" is a further method aimed at understanding and capturing the city and its urban layers. This approach views the city as a kind of data landscape: based on rational data processing, aesthetic and subjective observations are put on hold. By using objective documentation and the quantification of criteria and parameters, the designers attempt to auto-generate forms. Within this automated process, aesthetic bias is suppressed, to allow the creation of something unknown and new. Data-scaping can lead to the creation of visualisations of statistical or technical data that, in return, can be integrated into the design concept. As a result, the use of computer-aided technologies allows the generation of potential urban landscapes developed by computer algorithms within a complex data analysis. This computer-aided procedure, in principle, sustainably supports the generation of forms. In sum, we can ascertain that it is possible, based on these gathered datasets, to generate architectural and urban design structures in real time.

Overview of individual design phases and steps

The following diagrammatical overview of the individual phases and steps within a design process, compared with applied methods and tools, clearly reflects a necessarily systematic approach, the use of which allows a comprehensive urban and architectural concept to be developed: by using analytical, evaluative, and design-related methods, the physical and geographical conditions of a neighbourhood, quarter, or district under examination can be evaluated. It is further possible to conduct cognitive investigations through observation, conversation, and interviews directly on-site. Further, the dérive as a scientific form of exploration has the potential to reveal urban situations and to allow people to perceive the "feeling" of a place, which can be filtered and represented by graphic methods in a comprehensible manner within the design assignment. This allows people to see the city not as a product, but as a system that experiences a process. In the following chapters, the individual steps of the design process are explained in detail and illustrated using graphic representations.

ANALYSIS PHASE: APPLICATION OF URBAN DESIGN METHODS AND TOOLS

In the final chapter of this book, planning methods will be presented in the systematic form of a dictionary. This chapter deals with expanding these methods in the context of pedagogy. In return, we can use these expansions and alternatives to demonstrate the potential for further development in practice. Based on this, further methods and applicable instruments are presented in the following chapters and assigned to the different phases of a design process.

A comprehensive urban planning and design process always begins with a detailed analysis of a city. In order to create an informed and robust framework for successive steps within the planning and design process, a methodical procedure comprising distinct steps is required. The first step within the planning-related creative process is defined by a phase of analysis and systematisation, as well as an initial evaluation phase. In this phase, the basis is created for the project approach and orientation. Its dimensions and expanse are specified, measured, and precisely delineated.

At the very beginning of the design process, planning data are researched, elicited, collected, and displayed within an urban design analysis. Extensive research aimed at gathering data can take place with the aid of analogue or virtual aerial photography, city guides, historic maps, topographical illustrations, and preparatory and binding land use plans. Beyond that, further planning data can be retrieved and collected for design purposes using geoportals, apps, or GPS equipment. The graphic illustration of built structures and infrastructure takes place after data gathering and collection. The raw data from statistics and tables are transformed into graphic charts and plans. These raw data are further processed by graphic means within figure-ground plans and zoning plans, as well as maps featuring precise depictions of streets, open spaces, and green systems. Open-source programmes such as "openstreetmap" can find use as a basis for generating these types of maps by employing existing vector data.

These data and facts are further elaborated within the mapping of zoning plans or different information on residential and work-related structures. They are included in figure-ground plans in colour-coded form. For instance, they can display the zoning structure of ground-floor or upper-floor areas in comprehensible plans. Or, they can show the typology of housing construction and commercial uses in block border, linear slab, or nodal structures. Further, they can distinguish between residential functions in relation to single family or multi-family housing. Further approaches to mapping can produce insight on cultural or social infrastructure according to facilities for healthcare, education or services, and trade and production.

Mapping for infrastructural or landscape-planning purposes can assume specific forms, as follows: traffic-related functions are displayed on a route map, to differentiate between primary and secondary streets, pavements, bicycle lanes, dedicated bus lanes, or tram and train lines, or to precisely depict areas for stationary traffic and parking. Public and private green spaces are not displayed on route plans, but instead, on regional maps, which can also show vacant or unused areas reserved for possible later use. Related maps can show tree and plant stock in greater detail and different formations.

It is important that a notion of neutrality guides mapping in the first step of the design process. The aim is to display a precise image of the existing urban design situation, without evaluating the situation. This evaluation takes place in the second step of the design process, within the evaluation phase, in which other methodical approaches are employed.

Visualisation of data and facts in diagrams and profile maps

The basis of all methodical steps within the analysis phase is to gather as many data and facts as possible and enable their easy access. Gathered data and facts are catalogued according to different and precisely contoured criteria and compiled for evaluation. The catalogue of criteria enables planners to systematically evaluate requirements and situations of the circumstances under observation based on the gathered data and facts. Targeted means of illustration can help to clearly define the evaluated topics within the different plans. They are applied within the urban design concept phase, where defined criteria and established parameters serve to develop a comprehensive urban strategy.

In this design step, in addition to gathering and visualising data and facts, profile maps are generated for the superimposition of urban layers. Different issues are under consideration here: the examination of different profiles that depict the development of individuals and objects is an important component of the data to be surveyed, in order to permit an objective processing, despite their multi-layered character. A diagrammatic visualisation of data can serve to demonstrate the population density, the age distribution, the

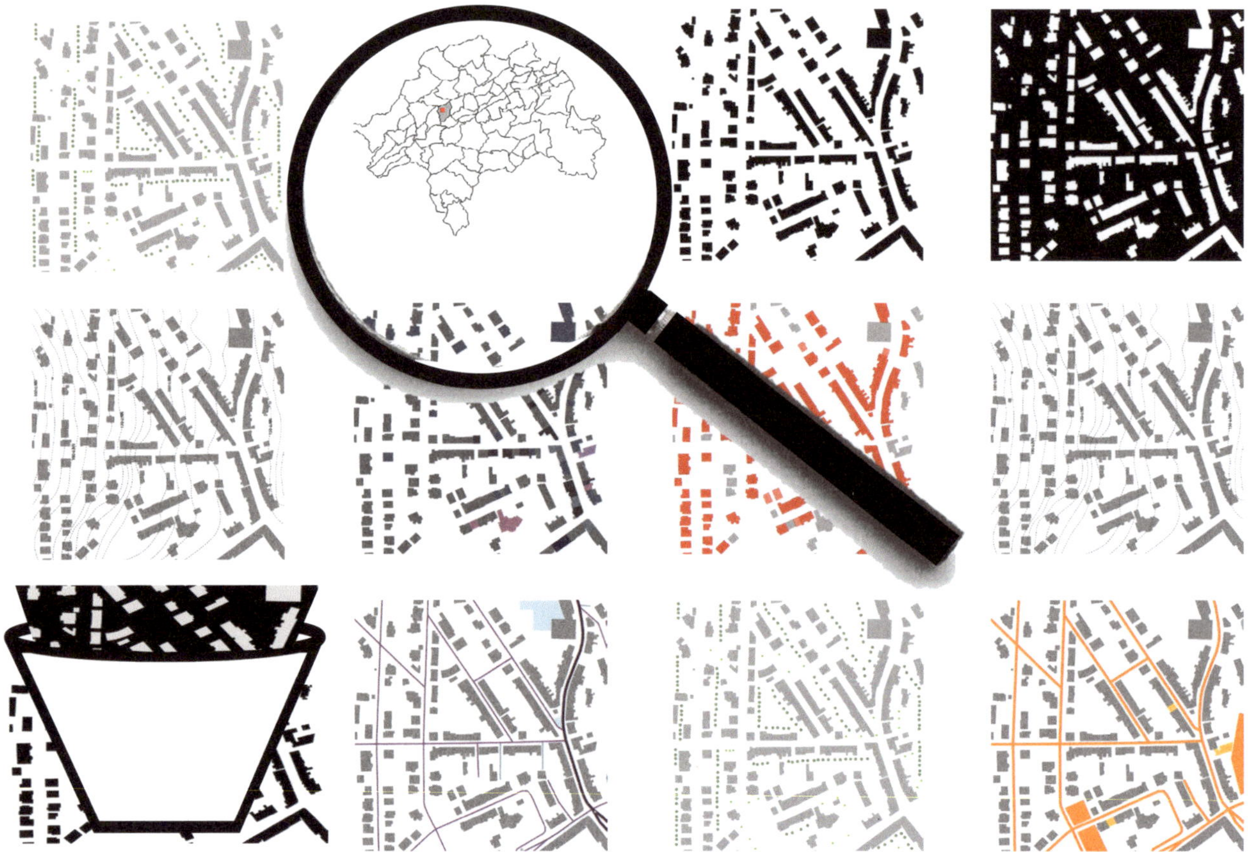

Overview of different mapping types

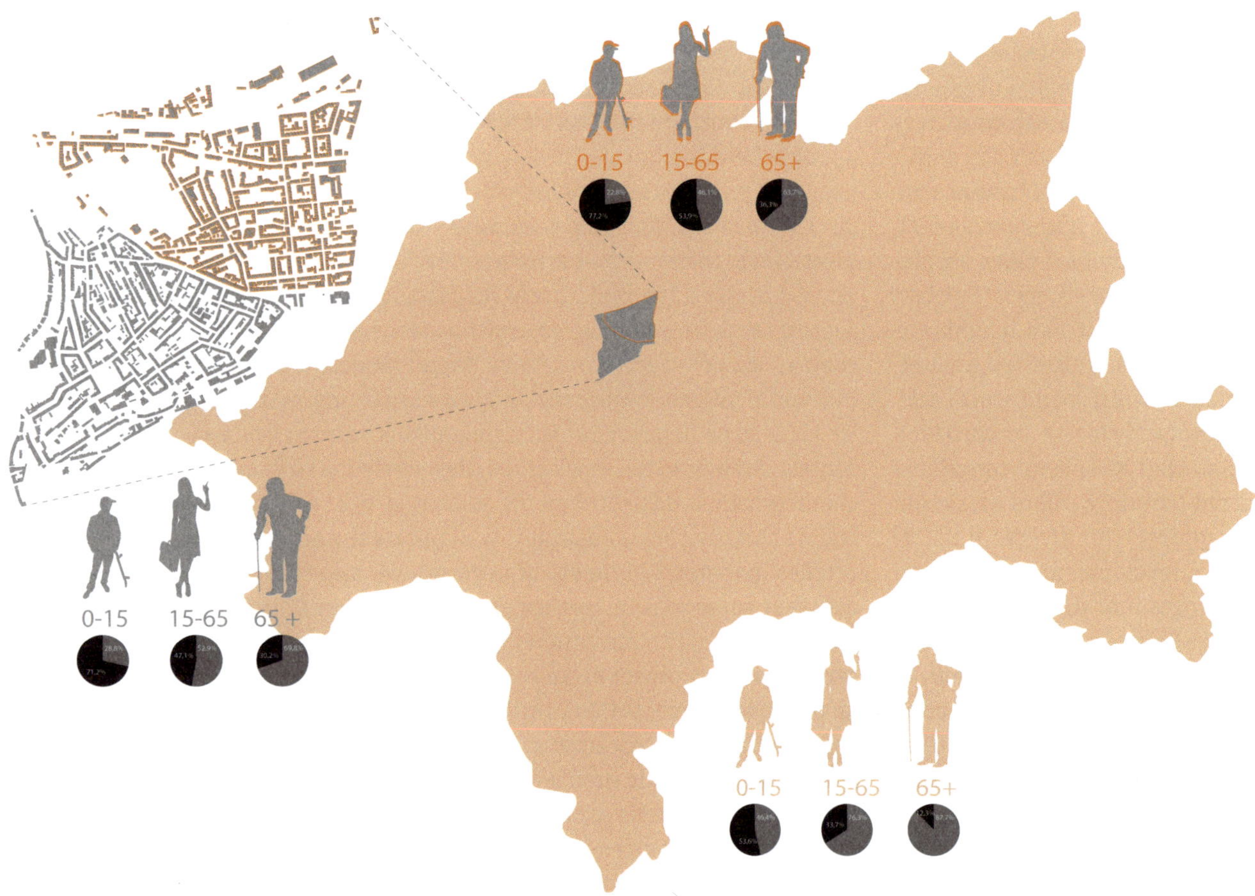

"Age distribution in Wuppertal". Visualisation of data and facts

Diagrams for supporting an urban design analysis

employment structure, the share of job applicants on site, or other characteristics. The urban living environment with its built and social aspects can be depicted by using urban design functions, such as living, working, mobility, or recreation. Residential functions can be displayed using graphic illustrations within plans or structural maps, for instance, in terms of existing housing models or types and specific residential functions, such as accommodation for older people, multi-generational housing, or student dormitories. Further important criteria for the analysis of an urban neighbourhood, quarter, or district are commercial functions, including services; facilities for social, cultural, healthcare, and education purposes; trade, manufacturing or production; gastronomy and restaurants; as well as special functions, such as sports facilities or sacred buildings. All of these can be suitably represented by mapping. The diverse illustrations can serve as a basis for the development of a comprehensive functional and spatial programme in the next phase of the design.

To correlate a systematic as well as a dynamic content, it is necessary to illustrate this in a clear and differentiated manner. Diagrams or profile maps serve this purpose. Diagrams are visualisations that depict interrelations between different data and facts, while enabling viewers to draw new conclusions from them and evaluate them. The underlying data can assume a variety of formats, from statistical lists and scientific calculations to map and text-based materials. The aim of diagrams is to communicate the multi-layered diversity of information as simply and comprehensibly as possible. Within an urban design investigation, diagrams are used as a "translation tool" between the different involved actors and users. Thus, they decisively contribute to communication throughout the entire process. Based on this, diagrams are also an important tool for displaying goals within a design assignment and the resulting concept in terms of a comparison between "actual" and "target" conditions.

Profile maps allow details and facts regarding a particular issue to be displayed in a homogeneous manner and in context. Similar to the index cards, they determine issues as characteristics and requirements as criteria, thus enabling a legible comparison. Comparability supports the analysis of profiles in terms of individual categories, yet also correlates different categories. A further decisive function of profile maps is to display information in a summary manner and to serve as an instrument to connect and separate other instruments and documents that contain far-reaching and detailed data and facts. For instance, symbols included within maps or illustrations within profile maps allow data and facts to be ascribed to topics relevant to the design. In return, these can refer to detailed sources and information.

Profile cards: Showing analytical details e.g. strength and weaknesses of the urban fabric

Development of different analytical mapping methods

Mapping serves to specify the individual aspects under examination in the area under deliberation and visualise them within maps. For this purpose, several common analytical mapping methods are available. The common types of illustration include figure-ground plans, zoning plans, infrastructure or green open-space maps, as well as maps showing demographic characteristics or traffic emissions. Further and ever new criteria and types of illustration can be developed that are tailored to specific tasks. The intention of maps is to display information in an impartial manner. As such, they do not produce qualitative or quantitative statements. Instead, their purpose is to make urban specificities and peculiarities evident and communicate which of them will be subject to detailed analysis and evaluation in a following step. Within this design phase, suitable scales, depending on the size of a neighbourhood, quarter, or district, range from 1:50,000 to 1:5,000 or from 1:10,000 to 1:2,000.

In the context of the mapping method, physical and geographical situations, such as structure, infrastructure, and open-space design are first captured by graphic means. These large-scale phenomena can be complemented by depicting more specific categories and themes within maps, such as the identity of place, vacancies, building classes, need for or degree of renovation, or empty plots.

When open spaces and green spaces are mapped, they are depicted as active or passive regions according to private, semi-public, and public areas. Plant and animal life can also be visualised with graphic means, in relation to temporal changes, by illustrating plant and animal species, depending on the processual and operational phases. For the most part, diagrammatic illustrations serve this purpose, as well as mapping techniques originating in landscape planning. In the context of traffic infrastructure, mobility networks can be displayed within urban design plans as line drawings for different mobility types, as well as different travel distances between public transport stops, stationary parking, and bicycle parking. This can also include traffic-related emissions, such as traffic noise levels, featuring corresponding decibel ranges that can be displayed comparatively.

Mapping the existing flat roof structures in an urban quarter may not be particularly relevant in the first phase. However, within the concept phase it can offer a suitable basis for strategic deliberation. Related maps can, for instance, serve as a basis for argumentation within a sustainable structural densification strategy: they provide the opportunity to determine areas for redensification within a district that are suitable for rooftop additions. In addition, flat-roof structures can be assigned as areas for green roofs to provide space for balanced plant and animal life. This makes it possible to counteract urban heat island effects within existing heat areas and improve the urban climate in its entirety by means of planning. This is only one example, but it shows how maps that are set aside at an early stage can become relevant during a successive stage in the design process.

Distribution of functions for the development of an urban functional programme

Mapping infrastructure to generate sustainable traffic systems

Green open-space map for the evaluation of recreational areas

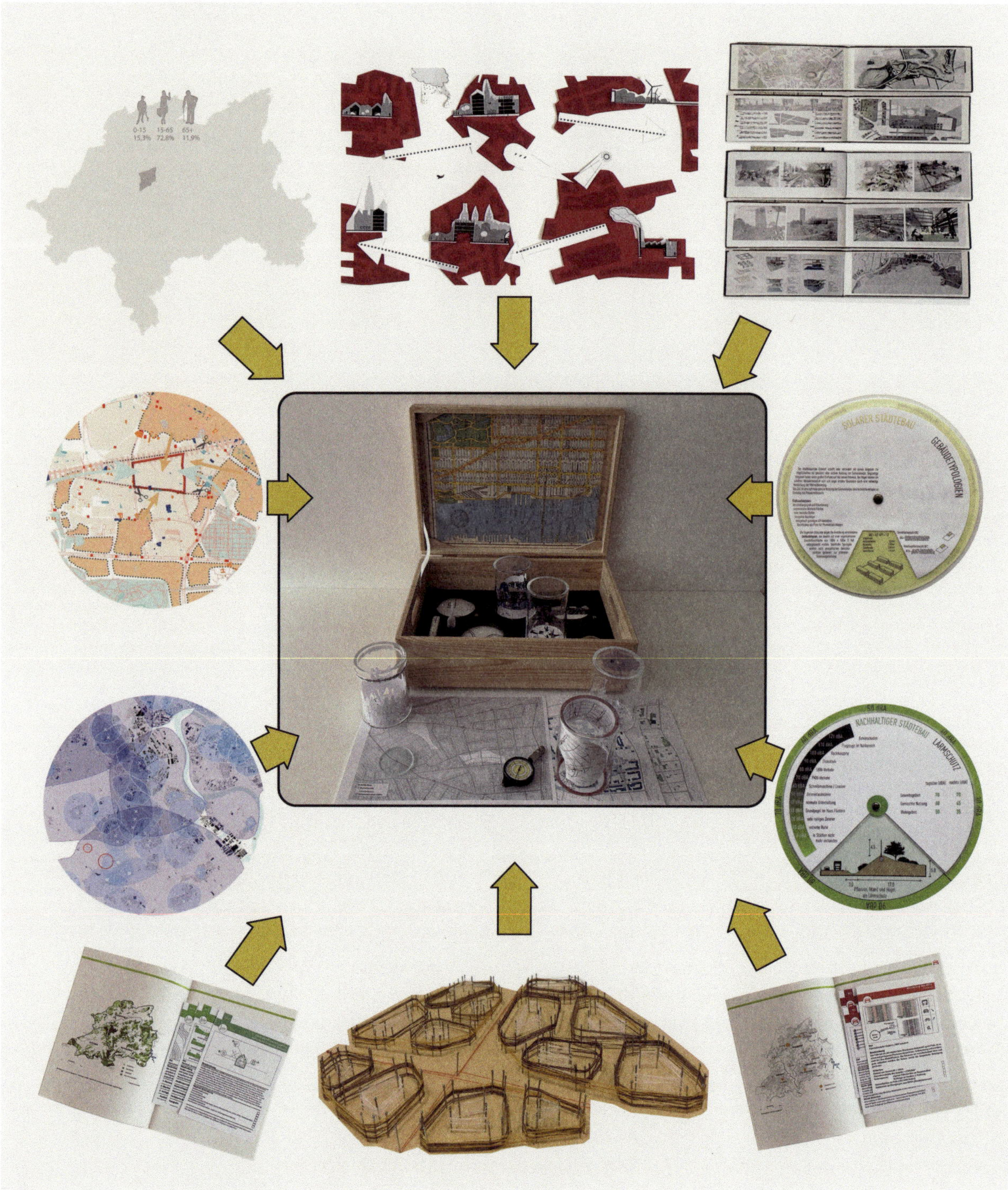

Toolbox for the urban design analysis

Instruments for the investigation phase

In the context of the analysis phase, in addition to the scientific approach guided by the motto "get out of the lab!", we conduct field trips to the planning area, in order to undertake real-life field studies on site, beyond an exclusive remote analysis of data. In this way, the previously achieved results from the urban design analysis can be directly tested and new characteristics or situations on site can be elicited. During a field trip, it is sensible to look at other architectural and urban design projects beyond the planning area. Following field research, a renewed evaluation of the gathered information takes place, as well as a review of the catalogue of criteria regarding their suitability as possible design parameters.

In the application of the different analytical methods within the investigation phase, a set of tools is relevant for successive steps and the development of results. As previously mentioned, these include typical mapping methods, two- and three-dimensional sketches, diagrams, or tables. In

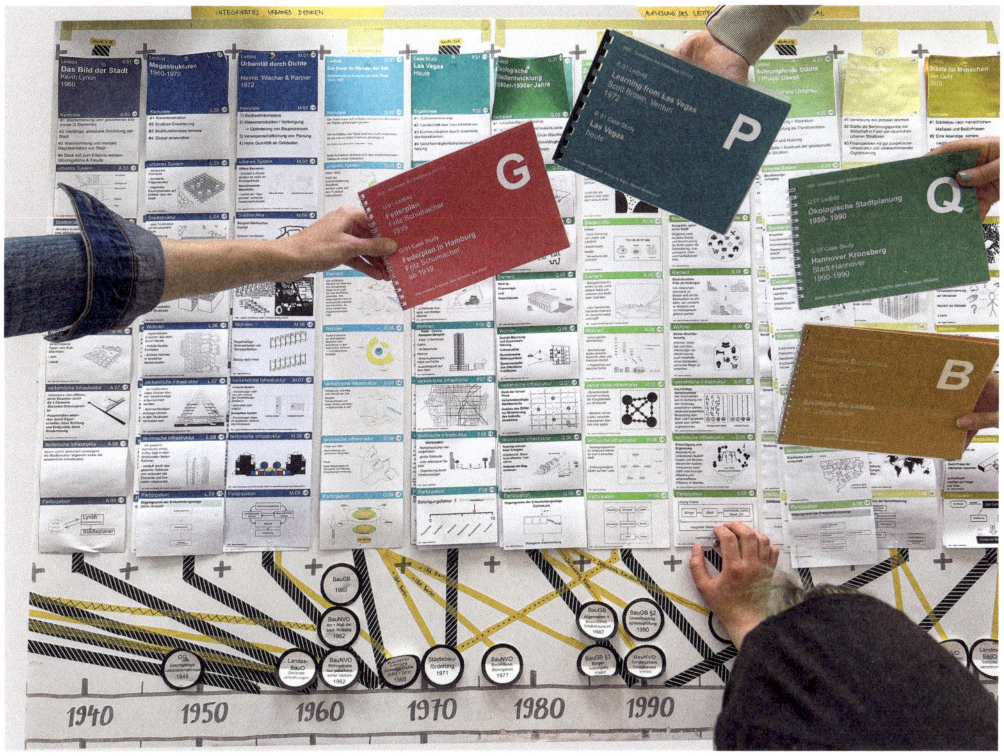

Matrix of urban design basics studies, including depiction of guiding principals and their realisation.

this phase, generating a matrix, compiling profile maps, or conducting surveys or interviews are also appropriate.

A matrix as a systematic support for design

Simple lists or tables are often the basis for the representation of data and facts. For the most part, they serve to capture, sort, clearly display, and categorise data and information. The displayed content can be depicted by different types of media and contains text, numbers, and symbols, as well as drawings and diagrams. Different from a table, a matrix juxtaposes content sorted according to specific categories with additional categories. By expanding a table accordingly, interrelations between individual elements can be created and analysed.

A functional matrix permits conclusions from these interrelations to be drawn, which can become important to the evaluation. In an urban design context, for instance, a matrix is used in the examination of ratios of sizes and functions. This allows different functions and the area they require to be compared. Based on their ratios, differences and discrepancies can become visible and support the drawing of conclusions for the existing demand and the efficiency or feasibility of measures.

Aside from the systematic mode of illustration, the analysis phase also includes dynamic tools, such as two- or three-dimensional sketches. Sketches are understood very intuitively, and thus can visualise ideas in an unfiltered manner. The depicted content can, in an urban context, be highly multi-faceted and encompass the analysis of social situations and the illustration of objects or technical processes. In this way, sketches become an integral part of the investigation process and the related conversation: a sketch is not intended to be a permanent or precise representation, but instead serves to inspire argumentation and enable a continuous development within a specific discourse. The immediate flexibility and spontaneity of illustrations are the basic preconditions for a sketch. However, sketches are required to fulfil a purpose, regardless of whether they are created by using a pencil on paper, as objects resembling models, or as computer-generated prototypes.

Testing design assumptions with surveys and interviews

Surveys and interviews are further important instruments used to retrieve and record dynamic data on public opinion and involved actors. Surveys are intended to gather statistical, quantitative, or qualitative data. They are used to research the dissemination of particular aspects, key figures, or characteristics, which opinions are prevalent, or how public opinion changes over time. Interviews go beyond a survey or questionnaire on public opinion. They serve to ask targeted questions to help elicit individual answers that are honest in terms of the content. The results can be evaluated and qualified within selected frameworks. Questions can be precisely formulated within a research or design assignment by using an interview guideline. Based on this, an interview can be open-ended or closed and highly structured. In an open-ended interview the interviewees offer spontaneous answers, for instance in an intuitive, conversational interview conducted in a public space. In a closed, fixed-response interview, mostly employed by professionals and experts, the interviewer shows the interviewee the guideline and topics beforehand and explains them in order for the interviewee to be able to prepare answers to the questions.

Generating additional data by interlinking the content

Aside from the depiction of different profiles, an illustration of structural characteristics in the area under deliberation is an important component of the analysis phase, in the context of developments of urban history, as well as their superimposition. Using this tool, planners can acquire, filter, and evaluate the information relevant to the design at the beginning of the design process. In particular data protection regulations are a limitation to comprehensively collecting data and facts within the analysis phase.

Data privacy legislation prohibits publishing certain data, even if they are included in statistics or tables. Therefore, basic information required for further investigation of an area under development is often unobtainable. In such cases, the possibility exists to independently derive such information, based on an evaluation-driven approach and by interlinking other, publicly accessible planning documents or datasets. In such cases, assumptions are made that permit verification based on multi-layered, existing information that supports systematic comparison and analytical evaluation.

On some occasions, it may be impossible to collect all necessary information for the compilation of specific maps. In this context, it is sensible to apply creative alternative approaches to produce a meaningful map. A good example of how to independently elicit information is the creation of a vacancy map. In many cases, due to reasons of data protection, cities or municipalities abstain from making public statements on the vacancy of specific buildings, either in ground-floor areas or on upper floors. Under certain circumstances, statistics or databanks exist that refer to related plots or larger building complexes, yet never regarding individual buildings or apartments. During an urban design assignment, this information is important to propose a meaningful urban design scenario or strategy. When compiling a vacancy map, an initial step comprises gathering data on power, gas, or water supply. However, as experience shows, suppliers do not release this information. Using a "doorbell plate analysis", information on possible vacancies in building complexes or individual structures can be gathered that permits statements within a map on the use of private or commercial areas to be made.

Repeated site visits and direct building observation during daytime or at night can serve to identify how many individuals live in a building. The observation of lit apartments or floors at night and capturing this by drawing information onto city maps can, beyond the doorbell plate method, support data collection and the creation of a vacancy map. However, when engaging in this course of action, it is of extreme importance to inform residents beforehand of this approach, using different media. Only in this way is it possible to use this method of observation and inquiry in a neighbourhood, quarter, or district in an immediate manner to gather further information on the urban surroundings and their residents. Therefore data and facts that are often publicly inaccessible can additionally take place by using the interlinking method, which in a certain way refers to "reading between the lines".

These are only a few suggestions on how planners and designers can gather additional data. As mentioned previously, during the compilation phase for the creation of different maps, all important built situations and circumstances require representation within these graphic maps and plans. The selection, and thus the evaluation of maps required for the urban strategy or concept, can only occur in the following step, after all maps and plans have been created.

EVALUATION PHASE:
SYSTEMATIC PROCEDURE

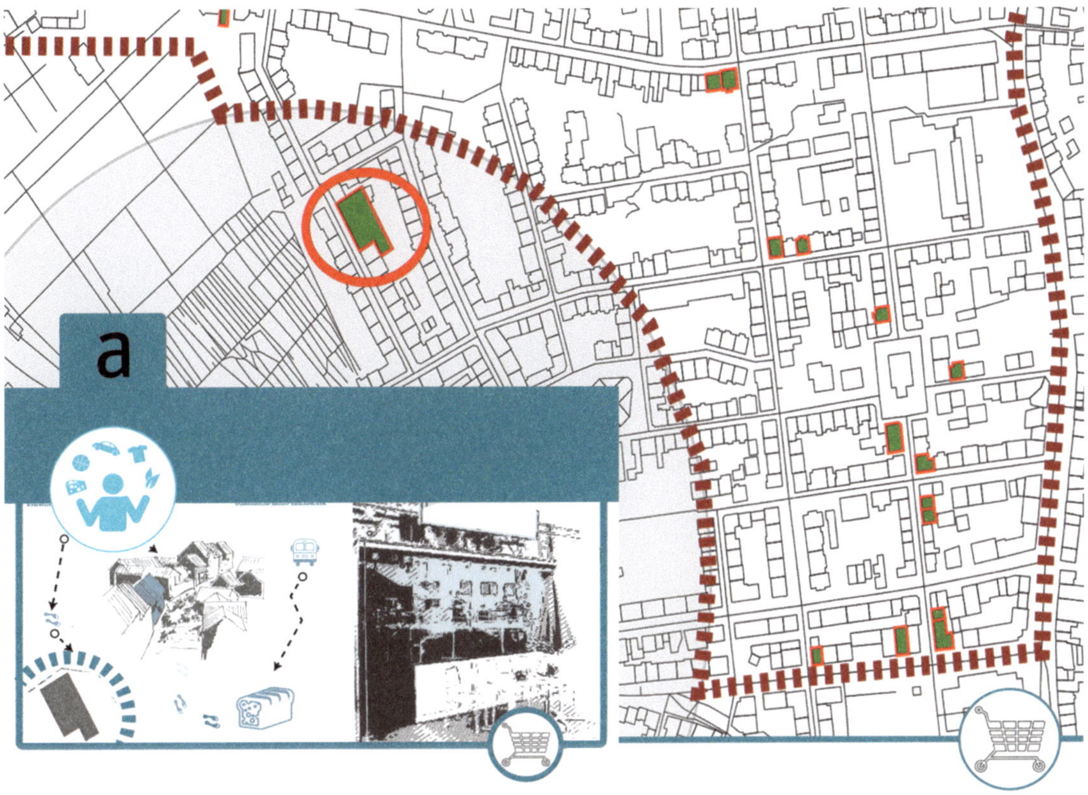

Evaluation map showing the access to daily functions e.g. retail

The following phase of the design process comprises evaluation or assessment. In this phase, the established materials from the analysis phase are tested and revised by using the tools discussed in the following. This scientific and, at the same time, creative approach is supported by different experimental methods of representation, which enable a precise evaluation of the previously generated products and materials.

Within the first phase, maps are compiled that are based on different analytical steps. They are detailed and elaborated in the evaluation phase by including further systemising methods of representation. At the beginning of the evaluation, index cards or evaluation maps, for instance SWOT maps, can support the evaluation of relevant data and facts. Evaluation maps display the existing situations, as well as phenomena established on the basis of data. These can, for instance, include daily, weekly, or monthly needs according to specific categories that are compared with the actual situation, and thus substantiate a need for action based on visible differences. SWOT maps, comparable to SWOT analyses, display strengths, weaknesses, opportunities, and threats by means of map-based graphic illustrations. Such maps emphasise the internal advantages and disadvantages of an area under planning. They also serve to show which external factors or trends can influence the process, either in a positive or negative manner. As a result, they allow the visualisation of how these factors are interrelated, cancel each other out, or prevail.

During the evaluation phase, the analytical maps from the analysis phase are tested and replaced by evaluating maps. The application of mapping as a method of representation allows the established results within new maps and plans to be reorganised, summarised by means of graphic illustration.

Mapping as an element of evaluation allows phenomena to be displayed by using graphic illustration. Content represented within maps and plans is newly evaluated based on goals and frameworks. Mapping can thus visualise whether content is evaluated in a positive or negative manner, in relation to the established criteria. The aim of mapping is to

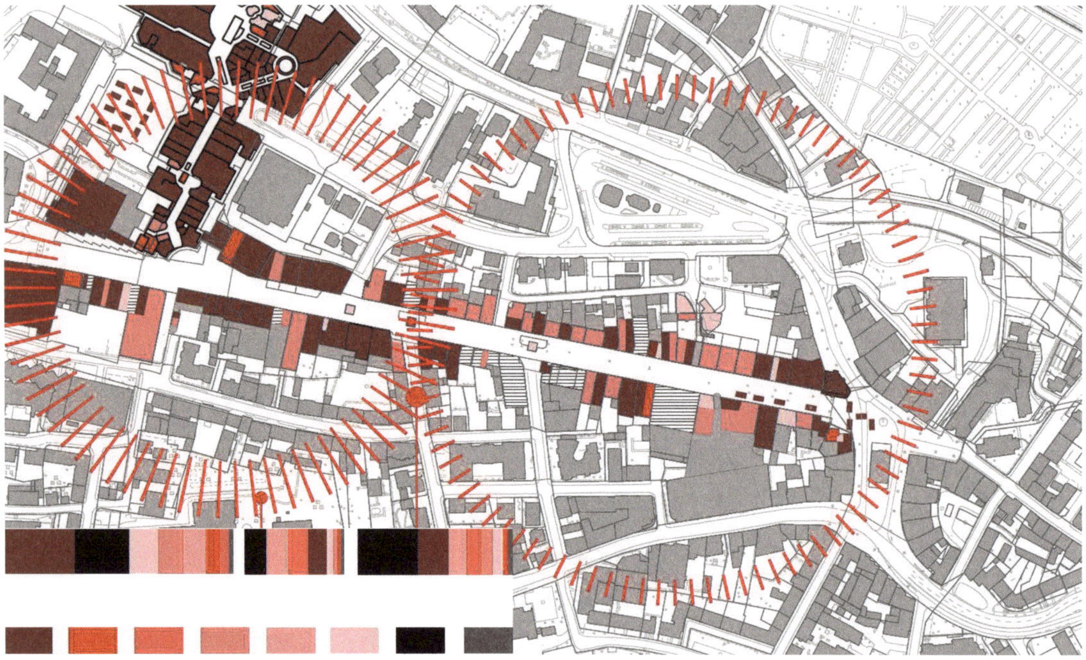

Bar codes as method for compiling evaluation maps

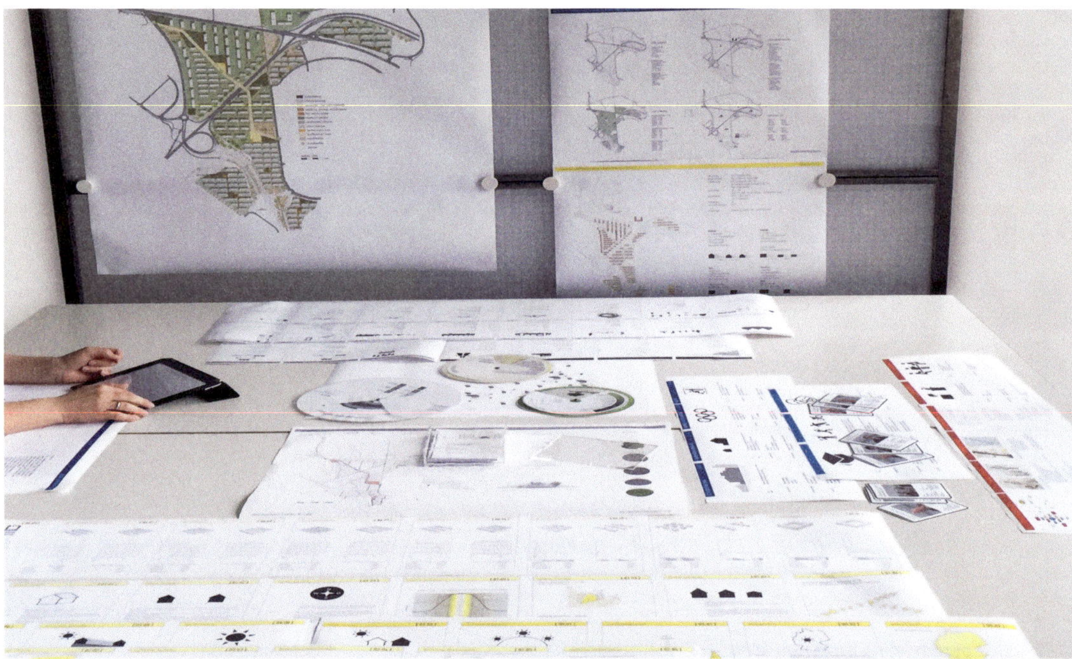

Evaluation maps as supplementary master plan information

Mapping as a method of illustration for evaluation purposes

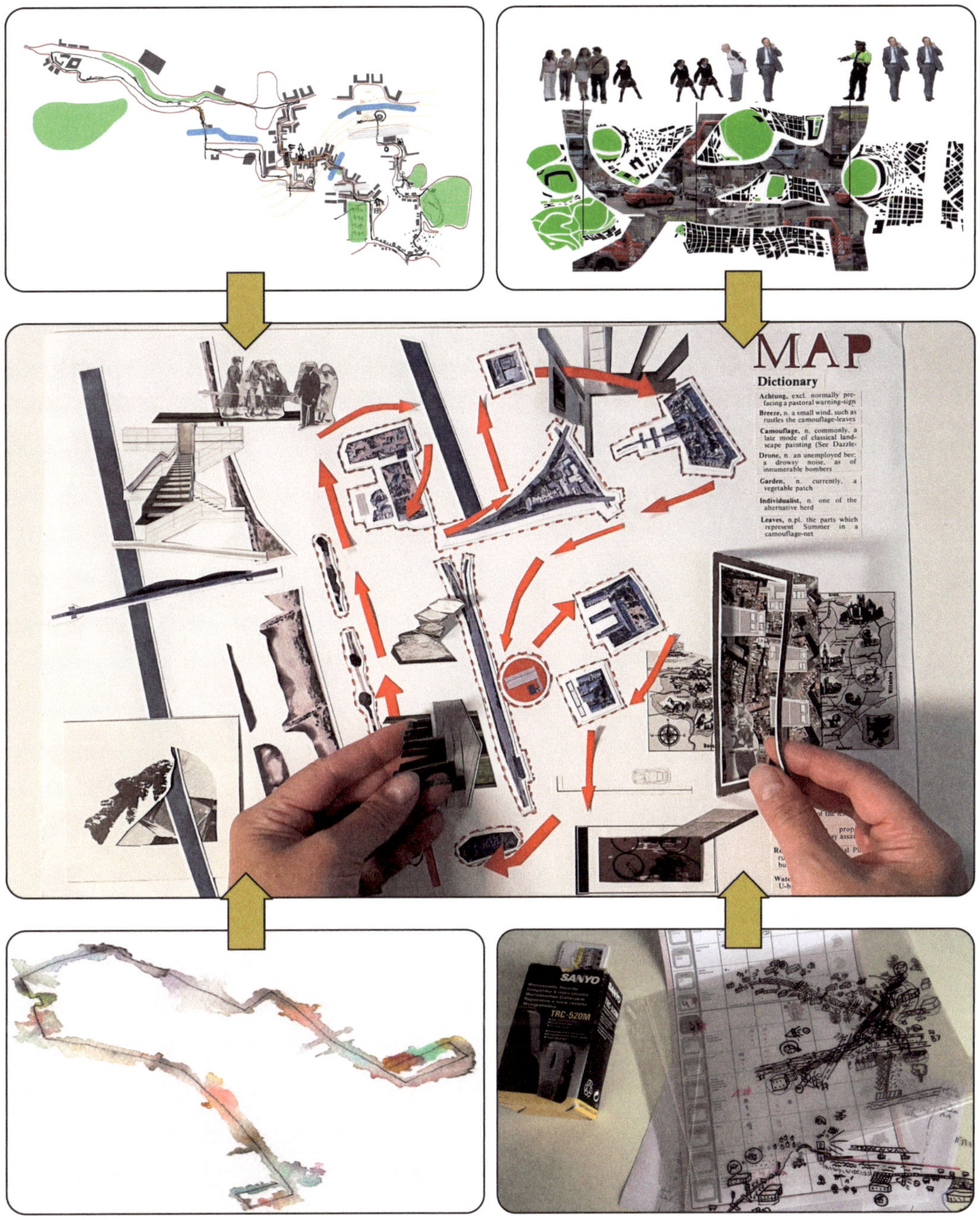

Toolbox of materials for illustrating a dérive

render such evaluations clearly visible. Thus, they are not bound by the rules of realistic plan representation and can display existing conditions in an exaggerated or transformative manner. The mapping type that offers the greatest degree of freedom is the psychogeographic map of a dérive. Such maps capture the spontaneous experience of a situation in order to integrate it as a factor in plan illustration.

Situational urbanism – dérive as an analytical evaluation tool

The dérive plays a special role, due to its character as a free, intuitive tool. Beyond the previously described methodical approach within the analysis and evaluation phases, a dérive can serve to evaluate further defining elements of urban space. In contrast to existing or newly established maps, plans, or data, a dérive creates new information for the further design process, due to a situational analysis of existing conditions in the context of a planned drift aimed at exploring invisible places. The method of dérive was created in the late 1950s and early 1960s by the Situationists, a group of creative individuals from the disciplines of art, literature, film, and architecture who employed it in the urban context in the form of a social space. Students at the Sorbonne University in Paris joined forces in order to create awareness of the outdated "top-down" university structures. The students' political protest was not expressed through an aggressive form of demonstration, but instead, through artistic activity: creative action, such as the dissolution of the fixed and standardised language of figures of literature by using collages on posters, or poetic slogans inscribed on walls as mural poetry. Or, when film students disassembled audio and video sequences and reassembled these materials, viewers were able to witness the resulting new interpretations. These creative methods are based on cultural and artistic approaches to aesthetics. They were employed as instruments of political protest to peacefully promote social change. It was important to the activists that art could be manifested within the public space of society and unleash its impact upon it by repeatedly generating new situations.

Such interactive urban actions resulted in the development of situations in theory and practice in order to advance societal change and, by creative means, transcend a social reality perceived as technocratic and hierarchical. In this context, individuals such as Guy Debord or Daniel Cohn-Bendit are of great importance. In different ways, they supported these processes for many years. Guy Debord in particular is an important figure for urban exploration and the development of a creative urban design process. In 1957 he created a city map collage of Paris, the first psychogeographic guide. His folded map features arrows as orientation for separate areas. However, it is designed in such a way that users of the map loosen their positioning or orientation inside the city fabric and therefore drift through the city. This created detour allows them to newly experience and interpret the urban and spatial construct.

Applying the dérive to the design process

Topical dérives can be employed productively in order to perceive the environment in a different manner and rediscover situations by using different senses. In this way, patterns of movement can also be investigated and evaluated differently. The conscious perception of the place under development can, by using our senses as sight, hearing, touch, smell, and taste, lead us to discover new urban situations and capture them within maps or tangible collages. Further information can also be gathered virtually, in online forums or exchange platforms, by actors, including associations or other local groups on site. In the manner of a perceptive dérive, equipment such as wheeled walkers, wheelchairs, goggles that limit the field of vision, weights distributed along arms and legs, or stuffed suits can be used, to assume the role of an older person or an individual with disabilities. This allows the environment to be perceived and examined in a more differentiated manner.

The Master's created a city map as a psychogeographic guide for the urban design assignment aimed at the Wuppertal districts of Elberfeld and Vorwinkel. In the vein of Debord, urban structures reimagined in exploded-view drawings, "escape" the previously constructed urban context and reassemble and newly interpret the remaining fragments. By using this method, the students, in the role of flâneurs, identified interesting and different links within the urban fabric. This further step within the analytical process of filtration can result in the creation of maps as an outcome of emotional, subjective experiences. In Wuppertal, for instance, the compiled psychogeographic map defined new patterns of movement, which were tested during the dérive by using the different available modes of transport as walking, riding a bicycle, the elevated monorail, the bus or a car. The resulting maps and plans created by the students comprise descriptive illustrations, such as observation-based sketches and mental maps. Beyond that, these studies of movement comprise qualitative designs of situations in urban space from the viewpoint of the observer, wich serve to identify the potential and deficits of the existing urban system. These results were depicted within diagrammatical plans or speed maps.

Investigations on site or in the digital realm

Beyond that, online investigations can be conducted in the digital realm, without being present on site, yet interrelated with the immediate urban context. Interactive 3D maps or web pages featuring detailed information on a neighbourhood, quarter, or district, as well as forums maintained by urban actors can support the evaluation process. They can assist further investigations of the area under observation and lead to a renewed interpretation of the spatial environment. Further methods, for example a fantasy journey, can also contribute to gathering experiences within a virtual tour, to include the insight gained within the investigation at a later date.

To efficiently conduct a sustainable urban investigation using a dérive, the following procedure is proposed: as preparation, the areas of the neighbourhood, quarter, or district that are intended for further investigation and are relevant to the detail phase of the urban strategy are selected from the urban design analysis. The dérive is an analytical method used to explore cities, to approximate the "unconscious" parts of the area beyond the urban design investigation. The area in which the dérive is supposed to take place needs to be clearly delineated beforehand. It is also necessary to define the aspects according to which the scientific exploration is supposed to take place. Once the parameters, characteristics, and the space intended for investigation have been determined, the relevant areas in terms of urban structure are detached in the form of separate "urban islands" and reconnected according to the previously determined criteria. The criteria can include questions on the distribution of functions, residents, or users as actors, plant and animal life, or deal with environmental factors, such as sun, wind, or water. The areas determined for the scientific exploration are connected through new pathways that are symbolised as arrows within mapping. When designers follow this newly created city guide of the area intended for development, they

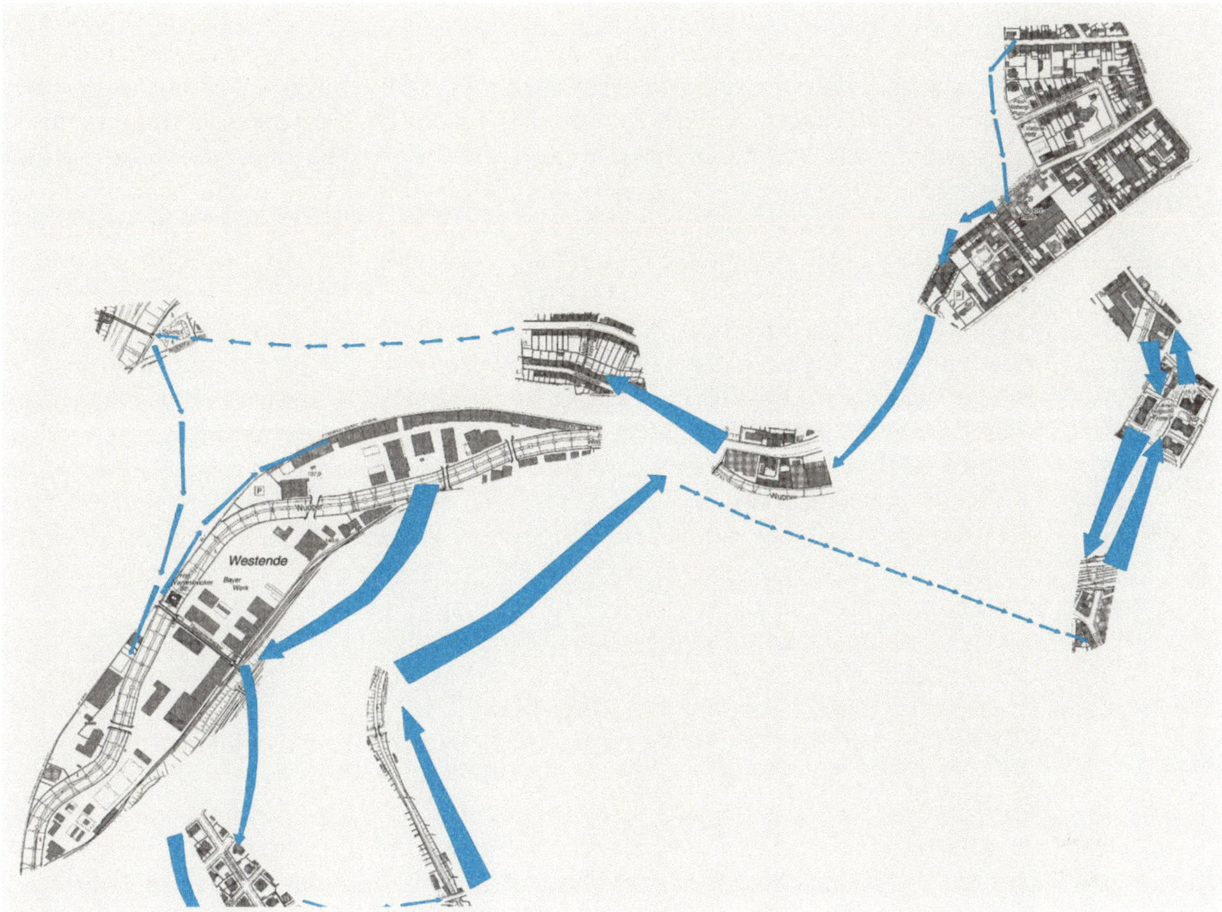

Psychogeographic map of Wuppertal-Elberfeld

will discover completely new characteristics of the area previously subject to elaborate investigation and captured in maps. Also see the illustration of the visual and tangible map of Cologne.

All these impressions can be compiled using diverse methods of illustration and depicted according to alternatives in order to gain results for the urban strategy. Depending on the design assignment and goal, a dérive can be conducted in different ways. Typically, the intended area is delineated beforehand by determining start and finish lines. Whether the dérive will be conducted by one person or a group based on a chosen theme, whether it will last three hours or the entire day, and whether participants will walk through the area in a targeted manner or randomly, are all defined by the urban "operation" and its actors. Within this process of sensual experience, the compilation of the psychogeographic map is of paramount importance. It shows the existing built structures and the manifest urban layers and represents these, as well as the newly discovered situations, in a manner comprehensible to experts and laypeople alike, by using selected graphic means of illustration. They can be tested on site within photo safaris, field studies, or city rallies.

Superimposition of urban layers of the urban system

Within the evaluation phase, an intensive deliberation on the individual urban layers takes place by interrelating and evaluating the mapping compiled previously by using multi-layered graphic illustrations. Further, the analytical statements are tested with regard to their capacity for implementation. Axonometric illustrations or exploded-view drawings as graphic illustration types can be helpful in displaying a comprehensible superimposition of urban layers. In an initial step, an axonometric illustration can serve to superimpose the mapping of the analysis phase. Between these layers, references, discrepancies, and evaluations can be compiled and once more generate information relevant in urban design terms.

The different types of superimposition can either be considered as a merging transformation of urban elements, or as a visualised superimposed layering of interdependent, yet additive layers. In this way, urban design-related strengths and weaknesses can be identified and the potential of urban layers can be displayed.

Exploded-view drawings as a further instrument of evaluation go beyond a layering of separate strata and establish connections and links within the entirety of an image. In this

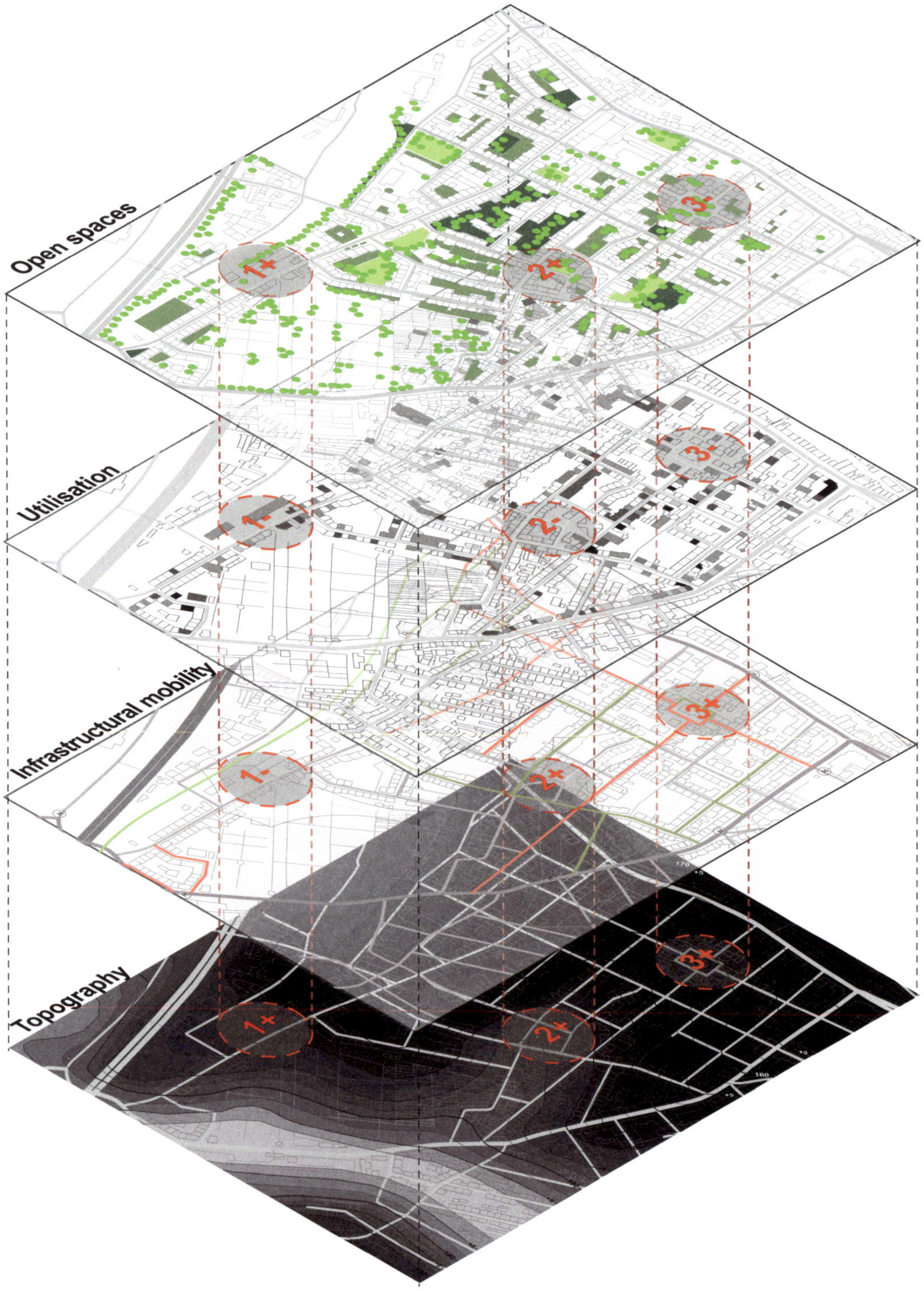

Axonometric illustration as an evaluation tool of urban layers

way, the linking of all urban elements and their influence on the totality are made visible in an evaluative manner. In the complex urban fabric, the interplay of individual elements can reveal deviations and weak spots, as well as obstacles, dominant elements, and transformative strengths.

The targeted superimposition of mapping already created in the analysis phase can, by using this method, serve to draw new conclusions on the urban design-related and infrastructural situation. During this design step, the evaluation of the different types of superimposition and layering generate a new characterisation of the area under deliberation. Depending on which mapping is layered, new information can be elicited which, in return, is potentially helpful to the development of the urban strategy.

A superimposition of mapping of vacancies and those of separate building classes can, for instance, by indicating renovation needs, lead to the creation of a new map that can become relevant to the design and the development of related concepts at a later point. Such mapping can display buildings that are subject to renovation measures due to their age

Process model as discussion platform for experts and lay persons

and vacancy and which are intended to receive a new functional programme. The renovation map identifies all buildings that are supposed to undergo necessary renovation measures. A renewed site visit and study of the building structure allows repeated testing and revision of this map. A further superimposition, for instance, of the newly compiled renovation map and a zoning plan can, as a result, generate a land-use conversion map. Correspondingly, the potential options for different-use conversion can be displayed and employed to develop a future-oriented, urban adaptive reuse strategy.

Superimpositions can generate planning needs

Other types of superimposition within mapping can produce statements on infrastructural planning needs. Linking maps on topography and traffic networks can, for instance, lead to conclusions on barrier-free access. In the first step of the superimposition, barriers within the street network map are identified and flagged, for instance kerbs without drops or cuts. This allows maps to display that the opportunity for a barrier-free transition from pavement to street, such as one for a crossing, does not exist. If mapping of the topography is included for purposes of evaluation, it becomes clear that a barrier-free transition between other areas within the neighbourhood, quarter, or district are not guaranteed: places are displayed clearly that do not adhere to the maximum 6 per cent slope for wheelchairs or wheeled walkers. The urban design strategy and the architectural concept can allow designers to demonstrate how design can address these deficiencies. The method of superimposition of maps thus creates a basis for new solutions to existing problems through design. The design itself can specifically show how overcoming the barriers can take place in terms of planning and construction and how a concept for district-wide, barrier-free access can be realised as part of the strategy.

In sum, it is necessary to display the existing structures of the separate urban layers of the urban system in a restrained manner. Too much information inhibits the ability to make clear statements on urban design within the strategy and the concept. Diagrammatic means of illustration within the evaluation phase support the management of the enormous amount of data through consolidating and scaling down information on data and facts from the analysis phase.

In conclusion of the evaluation phase, the conducted evaluations of the existing urban conditions and situations, as well as illustrating these within the evaluating maps, support the formulation of initial concept ideas. The illustration of, and deliberation on separate urban layers permit the complex urban system as an urban design- and infrastructure-related fabric to be communicated and conveyed in a comprehensible manner. The comparison and layering of these structures can lead to an understanding of new comprehensive urban systems that can be sustainably advanced within a neighbourhood, quarter, or district.

Working model for developing the concept

Capturing the decision-making process

The described applicable tools for evaluation can support decision making within the design process and also precisely depict it: urban design tools, such as a logbook or a process model, ensure that the decision-making process is represented in a comprehensible way. A process model comprises a dynamic and creative tool within this creative process. It employs elements of analysis and, at the same time, by using these elements, initiates a testing phase aimed at new ideas for developing the concept.

The process model enables, for instance, the placement of existing and supplemental urban basic elements and produces new interrelations between them. These elements can possess different origins. Due to their arrangement, they are permanently subject to discussion, and thus allow renewed reading and interpretation. A process model can, as in the teaching example of Berlin Teltow (Fig. 54), serve as detailed explanations and scale representations, and thus systematically juxtapose different structural elements on site for purposes of evaluation. Further process models can display particular material studies of investigated elements in spatial terms. To be useful as an evaluative tool, clear framework conditions and evaluation criteria should be part of the process model. Aside from grids, templates, patterns, and scales, digital and virtual tools may also be useful.

For decisions made during this phase to become visible and comprehensible beyond the model, it is helpful to create and regularly update a logbook as an account of the evaluation process from the very beginning of the design assignment. Keeping a logbook within the evaluation phase means more than simply documenting variables, workflow, and responsibilities. Documenting decision-making steps using text and images allows all involved actors to retrace the individual steps according to fixed goals. In order to enable verifications, the logbook must be kept in a comprehensible and systematic manner. Used in this way, a logbook can become an important basis for the design and can support all further strategic planning steps. The urban tools and instruments of the evaluation phase presented in this chapter are intended to help planners and students develop different scenarios for the urban design and architectural concept in the steps to follow.

CONCEPT PHASE:
GENERATING URBAN STRATEGIES

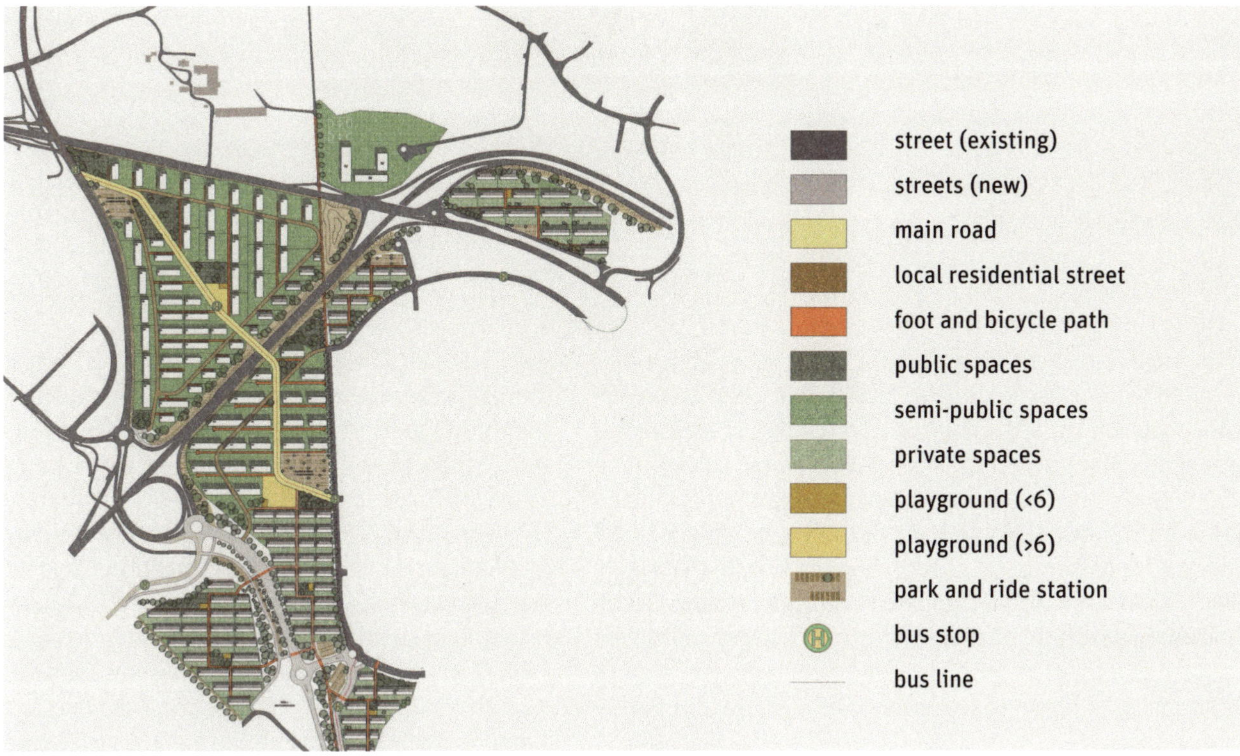

Master plan for the development of the Øvre Rotvoll neighbourhood in Trondheim

The urban strategy plan proposes applicable approaches to solutions for urban design problems that have been analysed and evaluated during the preceding steps within the design process. It serves as a basis for the ongoing discourse, and allows deviations and detours, while aiming for the creation of a master plan. This master plan comprises recommendations for action that are intended for implementation within a particular framework and according to a particular schedule.

In the concept phase of the design process, different alternatives are established early on and evaluated according to the required scientific criteria, in order to develop a comprehensive urban strategy. The foundations for the development of the design are laid during the first two phases. Within the successive concept phase, the resulting extensive collection of materials is evaluated again for the analysis of problems and deficiencies. As a result, approaches to solving them are generated for the architectural and urban design concepts. In the first two design phases, the as-is conditions are displayed extensively in plans, evaluated by mapping, and documented by graphic illustration. In the following concept phase, various visionary proposals are developed that become later on part of the urban strategy. After formulating the urban strategy, the functional programme of the urban design is specified, to propose a precise master plan for the development of the neighbourhood, quarter, or district.

Within the master plan, the process of planning and construction is displayed by graphic means in a comprehensible manner, indicating which concepts are intended for further development, and according to which schedule and within which construction phases they should be realised. In this phase, the position and composition of the different urban design-related settlement types, the determination of how functions are distributed within the urban typologies, the development of a comprehensive traffic- and landscape-oriented design concept, as well as the creation of a sustainable, technical building services infrastructure are all under deliberation. The degree of detailing is defined by scales of 1:2,000 to 1:500 and displayed in plans and physical models, as well as digital 3D-models, or sketched and substantiated by means of collages, montages, and diagrams (not to scale).

Different graphic plan illustration techniques displayed during a project presentation

Project discussion using an urban design model

Beyond that, decision-making processes are documented in the concept phase in order to retrace every decision made throughout the design process at a later point. In methodical terms, a logbook offers the opportunity to record this decision-making process. It serves to capture every design step based on the evaluation criteria by using graphic illustrations and text. Within the first three phases, a feedback loop is employed that permits precise testing of the accuracy of the design decisions made. Only these indispensable feedback loops will allow the management of a design; only in this way can a phase of reflection take place within the design and follow every creatively directed production step.

In this phase of the design process, decision-making criteria defined during the preceding analysis and evaluation phases can be recorded within a process model, documented in a logbook, and further developed within every phase.

Testing ideas with process models and logbooks

Urban design tools, such as process models or logbooks, can support decision making by serving as instruments of evaluation. They can further precisely document and illustrate decisions and, as a result, ensure that related processes are retraceable.

For this purpose, the process model comprises a dynamic and creative tool. It incorporates the elements from the analysis and, at the same time, uses them to test new ideas for the development of the concept. The process model is formed in a way that allows the different alternatives of the built structure, open-space planning, or street layout to be tested continually.

Models as elements of the test phase are useful to visually manifest designs beyond the concept and test their applicability. Due to their versatility, models are a central instrument for the development and communication of urban design schemes. Comprising actual "objects", they incorporate the initial spatial realisation of ideas which thus become something to experience and modify during the design process, while allowing design intent to be communicated. Scales of either 1:2,000 or 1:1,000 are suitable to capture the urban space "from above", in its entirety. By assuming this "creator" role, it becomes possible to navigate a confined realm, acquire a certain position, or focus on specific elements. Partial areas, objects, or situations that are illustrated within a process-oriented model can thus be repeatedly arranged and modified. Models are, therefore, an important element of discussion within a creative work process.

Different from a model that is part of a final submission and can no longer be physically altered, process models employ materials that are sufficiently flexible to alter the model at any point within the design process. Materials such as lightweight cardboard, Styrofoam, mount boards, graphic stickers, and adhesive foil are suitable for this purpose. Process models thus permit the placement of existing or supplementary basic urban elements and the creation of new interrelations. These elements can be of diverse origins, can be rearranged, and as a result enable renewed reading and interpretation. A process model can, as described in detail in the teaching example of Berlin, comprise a scale representation, and can therefore enable a systematic comparison of structural elements on site, in order to evaluate them. Further process models can incorporate information from analysis plans and precise material studies of identified elements in a spatial manner. In order to be useful as an evaluating tool, clear framework conditions and evaluation criteria should be included in the process model. Aside from grids, patterns, templates, and scales, digital and virtual tools can be used.

In order to ensure that decisions made by the students during this phase are not exclusively documented within the model, it is helpful to create a logbook at the beginning of the design assignment in order to record and illustrate the evaluation process. The logbook serves to document and illustrate the design process across the entire phase of concept development by using graphics and drawings. In parallel with all phases of the design process, all relevant steps are recorded in the logbook, for instance the formulation of the urban design-related infrastructural and architectural concept; the employed references and case studies; as well as the data collection and evaluation, the select means of graphic illustration, or the model examples. This enables the design ideas and concepts, and the decision-making principles they were based on when completing the design, to be retraced.

Within the process-based development of design ideas within a team, the logbook constitutes an important and decisive tool that ensures the transparency of decisions made for the further development of the urban strategy, the master plan, and the architectural concept. In contrast to a simple working protocol, a logbook serves to enable developments to be retraced in their entire diversity, and depict interrelations between them. It makes use of various media: aside from correspondence or protocols, a logbook always contains drawings, sketches, or diagrams, as well as other explanatory visualisations of procedures. The documentation indicates more than a linear process; it also visualises alternatives subject to discussion, and deviations within the development that can be revisited, if necessary. Logbooks also make it clear which actors participated in these developments and which responsibilities they bear. In this manner, logbooks constitute an important tool in order to manage the multi-layered approaches within an urban design process and correct them, as required.

From urban strategy to master plan

The urban strategy indicates initial solutions that can be illustrated by means of collages, montages, diagrams, or sketches. It serves to formulate precise recommendations for action regarding sustainable urban development that are localised within the master plan on the basis of a site plan. Based on the mapping of the first two phases, the master plan can be used to make statements on expanding or limiting the development of certain areas – whether an expansion of an area produces separations or connections, or whether a limitation employs demolition, or whether redensification requires expanding building structures through rooftop additions or by developing vacant plots. Within the existing building structure, targeted adaptive reuse strategies can produce temporary or permanent differentiation aimed at a diverse set of user profiles. The adaptation of ground-floor uses is particularly important in this regard.

Within the concept phase, the urban strategy and the master plan are developed, including their structural, infrastructural, and landscape planning-oriented programmes. For the urban strategy, the preceding collection, disassembly, and reassembly of information and related evaluation allow new parameters relevant to the design to be generated. It is important to give consideration to which particular needs exist, which actors require recognition, and which natural conditions of plants and wildlife exist. These factors are visualised by using different graphic illustration techniques, tested on the basis of previously determined principles and, as a result, integrated into the strategy. By doing so, additional simulations or augmented reality tools can be employed as digital instruments for the formulation of the strategy. Analogue techniques are also suitable for supporting this process, such as urban strategy round tables or interactive models.

Plans as a conventional method display the existing and planned structures and spaces in the form of an overview "from above". Most building volumes, open spaces, and infrastructure are depicted in their context according to scales from 1:2,000 to 1:500. Information derived from preceding phases and mapping can be integrated into the urban strategy and the master plan. At related scales, the principles formulated in the evaluated plans from the evaluation phase according to existing structural and infrastructural conditions are predominantly employed for the development of the master plan. They allow the display of deficiencies in a neighbourhood, quarter, or district depending on urban structure or traffic, as well as related proposals and solutions. The consideration of external factors that influence an area, its topography, size and structure, identity, location, and connection are of significant importance, as is the determination of settlement functions in the context of the entire urban fabric. A use conversion due to functional, spatial, or social circumstances can lead to creating a unique identity for an area, which can then assert its role within citywide processes of resource allocation.

A suitable example for the implementation of an urban strategy within a master plan is the concept of the "Urban Cluster" developed by the students Tim Hecker, Jan Philipp Heidenreich, Manuel Kramm, and Timon Nüsken for the Kreuzberg district of Berlin. The aim of the strategy was to create a new identity for the urban district, its historic character, and its established social structure by proposing a central and state library as a new urban centre. The students generated a comprehensive concept for the masterplan that manifests the library within the existing, unique urban design context as a place for the communication of information and knowledge, for cultural activities and communal engagement.

During the development of the design concept for the Kreuzberg district of Berlin, we provided a framework comprising analytical approaches that were applied in order to specify a comprehensive strategy which, in return, was supposed to lead to an innovative architectural concept. For this assignment, the urban design analysis and the dérive served to filter decisive criteria for the creation of precise, applicable parameters for the architectural design of the library, based on the observation of urban space and its social char-

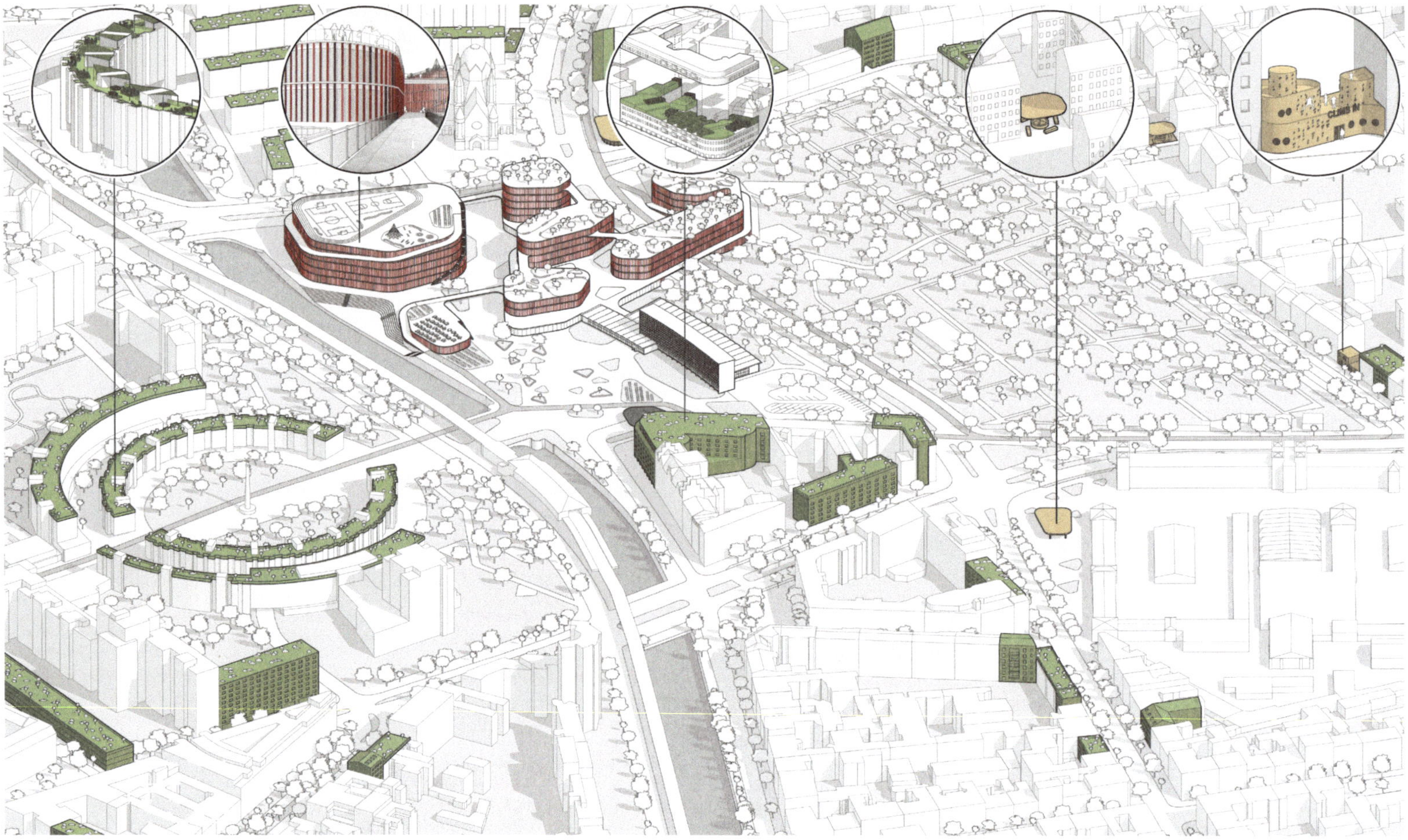

"Strategy plan" example: a concept for Berlin Kreuzberg

acteristics. The urban design strategy proposes a balanced mix of functions while efficiently using space within a projected thirty-year timeframe.

The steps designed for a yearly process are detailed in phases and colour-coded within the final master plan. For this purpose, urban interventions were developed and illustrated in yellow within a three-dimensional structure plan. The green-coloured areas comprise permanent infill development, remodelling of areas on top of flat roofs, as well as use conversions of vacant ground-floor areas. Items coloured in red indicate separately developed building complexes for the library and proposed links to the urban context. In parallel, the students spatially integrated the phased developmental steps that are depicted in the master plan within the physical model.

Storyboards as a tool for communicating interrelations

To communicate urban design interrelations within a master plan, further visualisation tools are of particular importance. A storyboard serves to create and present images of situations and processes. As a tool, it is mostly known for its use in the film industry, where its purpose is to visually represent and prepare filming of the scenes outlined in the script. As an instrument of urban design, a storyboard displays a view of the city from the perspective of an observer. In contrast to simple visualisation techniques, its view is not limited to isolated situations, but instead, emphasises procedures, dynamics, and interrelations in urban space. By doing so, it can establish visual interrelations of a narrative, social, or historic character within a greater context, and as a result create an overview – "at a glance" – of multi-layered and dynamic information.

Urban space always comprises multi-layered narratives

Moving pictures can serve to reproduce and visualise a spatial concept. As a result, it becomes an easily comprehensible tool for communicating and conveying information that supports a narrative of interrelations within a given time. Film as media allows different phases to be conveyed comprehensibly and in a simple manner, since many of the previously described tools can be integrated and linked. For instance, the data and facts contained in documentation can be portrayed in combination with interviews. Simulations or animations of new elements and designs related to plans and

Project film, exhibition of master plans for Offenbach

analytical data can be presented by layering them. This type of visual representation has the advantage that it can be presented and distributed in less than no time and in various ways, in a virtual online format or in the context of a presentation or an event. Used in this way, film can serve as a comprehensive medium for communicating and conveying information.

Manually drafted and computer-generated visualisations

In the disciplines of urban design and planning, experts often employ an aerial view. This choice of perspective allows them to reduce a tangible, three-dimensional space to a two-dimensional, predominantly flat space, to view it from a distance. A comprehensive display of the entire urban fabric with its complex elements, however, requires a four-dimensional form of representation that includes the factor of time, and thus is capable of illustrating processes.

Two- and three-dimensional visualisations are intended to demonstrate planned structures and designs to an observer. For this purpose, numerous objectives can be pursued, ranging from "artistic representation" to "artistic impression" and "verified illustration". An "artistic impression" ideally aims at the creation of a vivid experience based on the visualisation of the impression and atmosphere of a design. Such portrayals often include social situations, proposed materials, and atmospheric moods. Here, exaggeration as an artistic technique is actually permitted and anticipated. The "verified illustration" belongs to the other side of the spectrum: its intention is to offer a highly accurate, realistic representation of a planned design in a precisely determined context, with its exact viewing angle, geometry, and position verifiable by software. Social situations or atmospheres play no role here. The purpose of all of these types of visualisations is to offer a "promise of the future". They need to be highly dependable for purposes of the design and realisation process.

Beyond computer-aided visualisation, collages and montages can convey specific atmospheres within the design. The techniques of montage and collage are tightly interrelated, since they are both created using different media. They are employed in the most diverse creative disciplines: in fine arts, literature, film, audio recording, or photography, yet also in architectural visualisations, as well as urban design. A collage is a composition of materials and objects. It can comprise magazine and newspaper cutouts, pieces of paper, colours, textiles, or other found objects. It can also include text from books, or photographs. Source materials are glued to different kinds of substrate, such as paper, cardboard,

Atmospheric visualisation of an interior space for the Gyeonggi Museum

wood, or canvas. In the context of architectural and urban design pedagogy, a collage allows the use of abstract urban fragments for a recombination of these elements and, as a result, enables the renewed interpretation of a situation.

A montage, on the other hand, is a composition that is created by arranging a series of pieces of paper, photos, or other media, in order to produce an artistic image. This technique is mostly applied for the purpose of creating a new composite whole from image, text, or music fragments. The montage technique is used in film production in order to express different perspectives within a sequence by creating striking edits between different scenes. This technique of assembling fragments can also find use in urban design and architecture. It offers observers and analysts different perspectives of a situation or of spaces: architectural and urban design montages can present a new and recognisable context by assembling previously defined elements and parameters.

The described tools and products are helpful in demonstrating and developing a concept within a group of people. Plans and models at different scales are as important as multi-dimensional renderings and visualisations, as well as atmospheric collages and montages. Further, storyboards and film can be used in this phase as means of illustration in parallel with the argumentation on how a concept was developed. For the generation of a design concept, students receive counselling from supervisors during this phase, as well as interdisciplinary input in the form of lectures from cooperation partners. In addition, interim presentations are held while experts and interested laypeople are present in the audience. Only in this way is it possible for students to receive feedback in the form of continuous commentary aimed at a comprehensive design process.

In the following detail phase, it is important that the steps required during this phase are not simply conducted in a linear manner with the available tools and instruments, but instead, by employing those during the next conceptual steps. Before making recommendations for the completion of the design assignment, once the urban strategy and the master plan have been elaborated, it is necessary to re-analyse and re-evaluate the results with the tools from the first two steps, to produce a precisely detailed concept in the final step of the design process.

DETAIL PHASE:
DEVELOPMENT OF ARCHITECTURAL CONCEPTS WITH ILLUSTRATION METHODS AND TOOLS

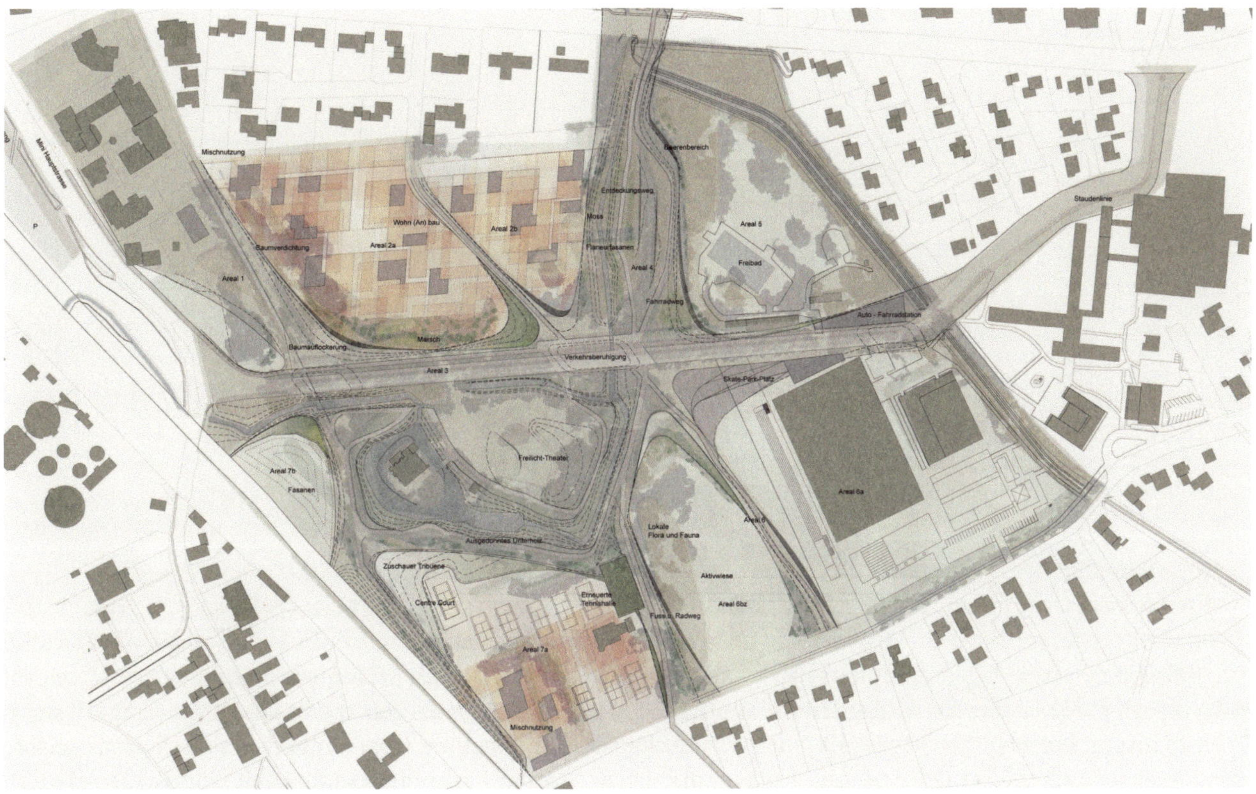

Development of a housing quarter in Voerde

The fourth and final design phase comprises detailing the entire concept of the design. In this phase, the architectural design is substantiated as a result of the further development of the urban strategy and the master plan. Within the architectural elaboration of urban design schemes, the focus is less on architectural design per se, and more on architectural elements that constitute the concept and the functions under development.

Floor plans, elevations, and sections are standard tools of technical visualisation for the illustration of architectural conceptual ideas. This systematised mode of representation allows architecture to be comprehended beyond disciplinary barriers, enables comparison, and eventually, implementation. Therefore, it is not necessary to explicate this in further detail. In urban design, additional challenges influence these architectural modes of representation. Floor plans, elevations, and sections need to be read and understood in a greater context. This is possible by depicting exterior spaces, yet most of all by referring directly to other scales, information, or forms of representation. The exclusive use of plan illustrations only offers limited opportunities for expression.

Suggested scales for zooming in to detailed illustrations of floor plans, elevations, or sections range from 1:200 to 1:100. To further substantiate design details, scales from 1:50 to 1:20 are suitable for drawings in order to optimally display technical details. Within the detail phase, the use of a matrix is helpful to depict close-ups of architectural and urban design elements, such as street or landscape profiles. This decisively increases the level of detail.

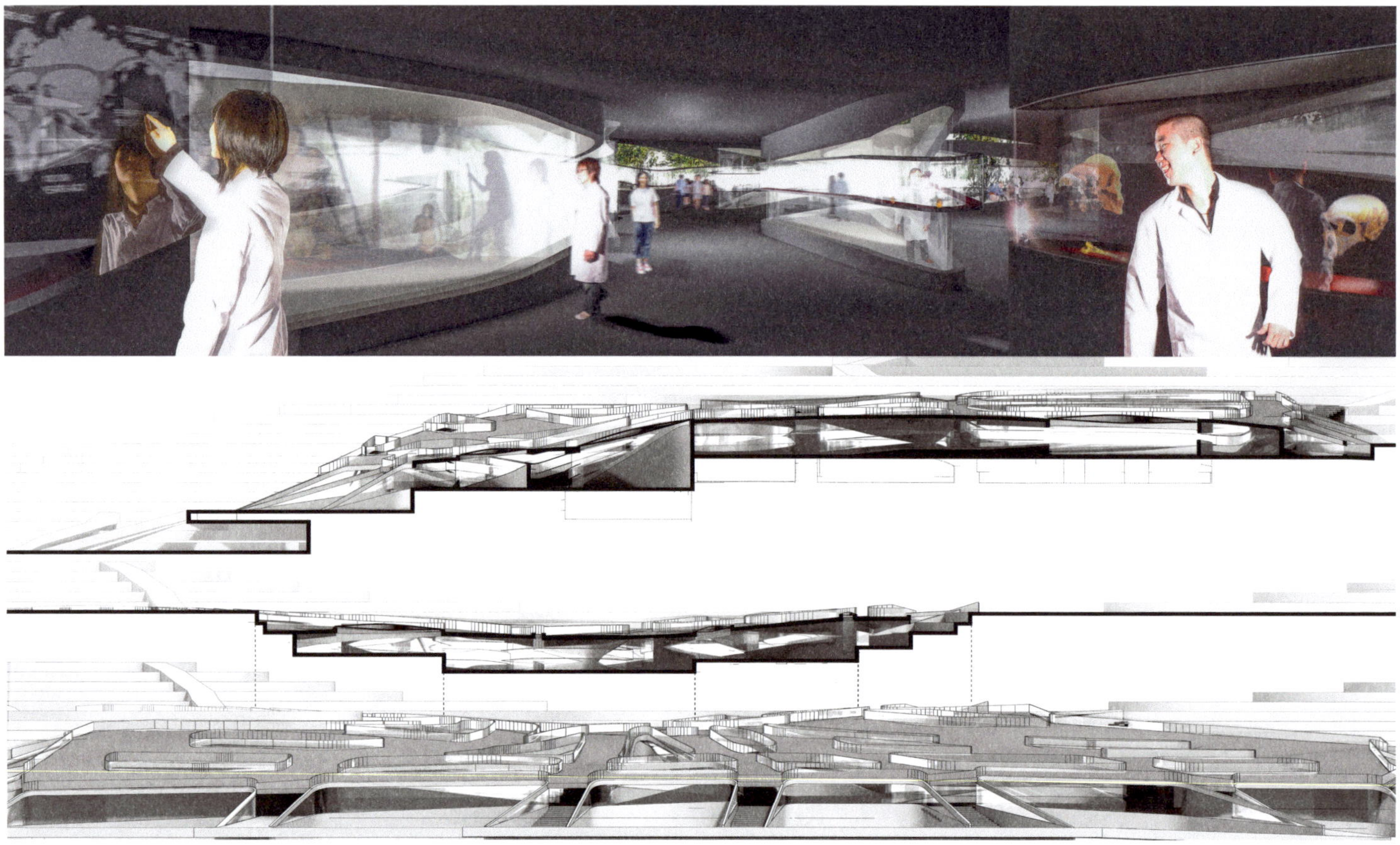

Elevation and visualisation for the Gyeonggi Museum

Urban design sections for displaying the context

Different types of sections depicting the urban context play important roles for urban design-related planning. They serve to display interrelations and conditions of different urban elements in a discernible and detailed manner. Landscape profiles visualise the relation between the landscape, either in its entirety or within a detailed view, and the building volumes and elements under planning. A street profile can, most of all, indicate the arrangement and orientation of the urban structure and the traffic infrastructure, as well as their relation to architecture and landscape architecture. Here, proportions and interrelations become clearly identifiable.

Aside from the architectural elaboration using sections, floor plans serve to visualise functions and connections to the urban design context. Most of all, this applies to the ground-floor plan. It always shows adjacent exterior spaces at the same level of detail and thus the connection to the urban design concept. The specific orientation of the respective design can be emphasised at this scale and in this way becomes legible.

A matrix for visualising typologies and floor plan alternatives

An urban design concept often comprises various functions and thus different floor plan alternatives. For this reason, merely representing them as floor plans within a plan format becomes insufficient. To visualise the different functions, it is helpful to create a systematic overview of the different typologies. Such an overview permits a comparison of floor plans, allowing their relevance in the context of the overall planning and evaluating to be assessed. Thus, in addition to functions, a floor plan matrix comprises quantifiable information, including size and number of residential units or workspaces, which would, under other circumstances, be hardly legible and comprehensible within a conventional floor plan. Using a floor plan matrix, it becomes possible to precisely integrate important principles of public and semi-public space into the actual floor plans. Linking a floor plan matrix to a process model can provide sustained support for the development of an architectural concept within the design process, as the featured matrix for an urban design concept for a district in Helsinki demonstrates. The combination of a floor plan matrix and a process model can contribute to envisioning and testing different modules and elements based on alternatives within different spatial, temporal, economic, and social processes.

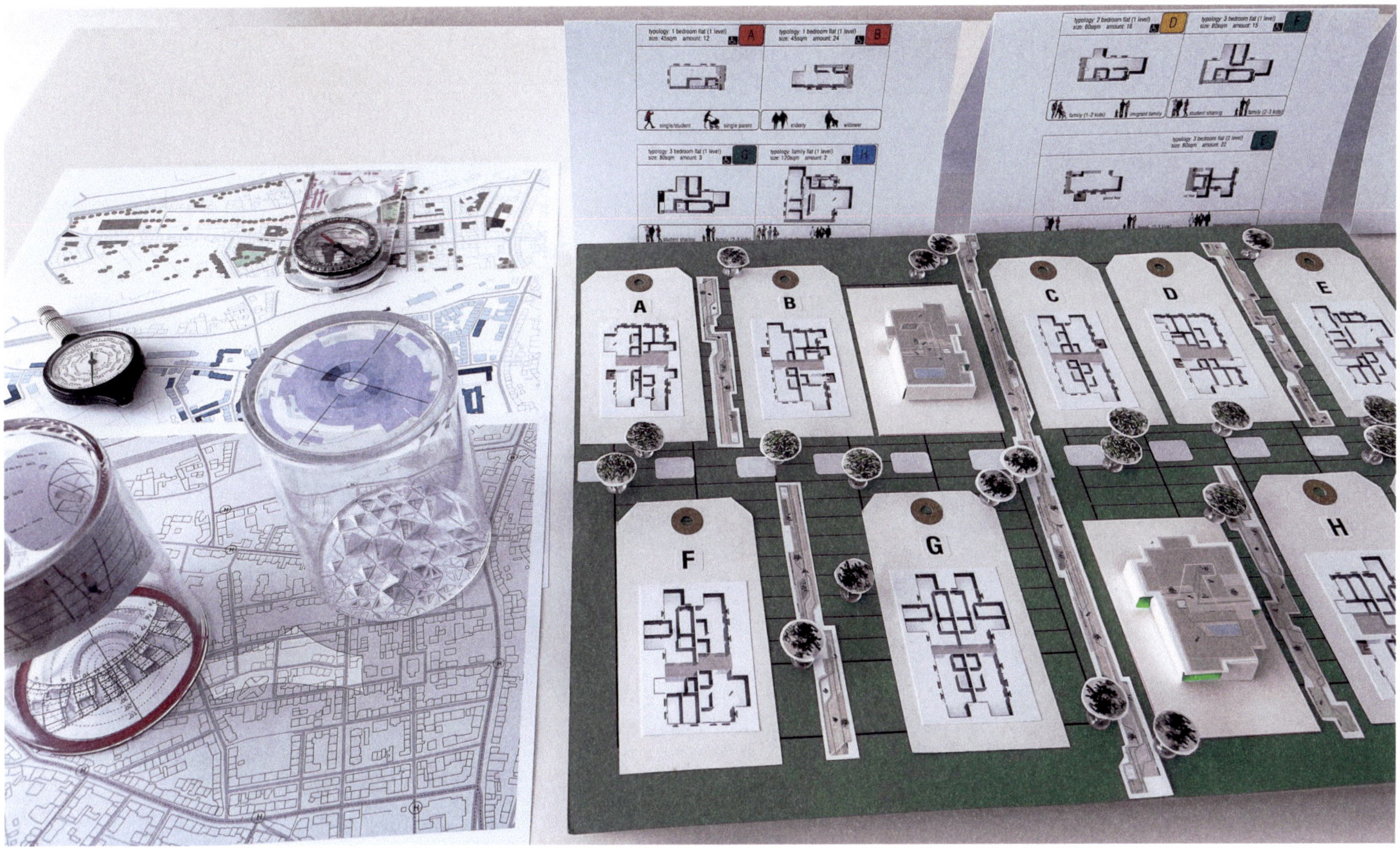

Floor plan matrix and process model for a district in Helsinki

Within this fourth phase of the design process, three-dimensional representations and visualisations are also characterised by different key aspects and focal points. Visualisations not only show the superordinate urban design situation or the atmosphere, but also detail the interplay between architecture and urban design by depicting specific situations of interior and exterior space within the urban fabric. Here, it is often useful to focus on the transitions between the different situations. Three-dimensional illustrations can also be used to display urban design elements in detail and integrate them into a matrix in the form of a catalogue.

Communicating design concepts through physical models

During this phase, different physical models can serve to effectively convey design concepts, ranging from small-scale to full-scale mock-ups. Architectural models at scales of either 1:500 or 1:200 allow for the display of elements of the urban strategy and the master plan that are relevant to the design at a higher level of detail. Such physical models offer additional information on the architectural intent, such as a detailed language of forms or a material selection. In contrast to models of purely architectural objects, urban design models maintain their interrelation to the context. It is thus important that these models are always considered complementary to and enter a dialogue with urban design models at respective scales. Detailed scales ranging from 1:50 to 1:5 can be selected for models showing urban furniture or other urban situations of limited extent and displayed in a physical, three-dimensional manner.

Developing and testing prototypes

Elements relevant to the design can be employed here by using full-scale instruments consisting of selected materials. Material studies and sample montages can, for instance, serve to demonstrate the tangible and sensory qualities of a detailed urban design concept, beyond a purely visual impression. Full-scale prototypes are useful for testing individual elements, such as urban furniture, and enable people to experience them easily, also on site. Numerous actors and users can jointly evaluate them – a scenario comparable to the previously described realisation project for Brussels.

In addition to architectural design tasks, the detail phase of urban design includes far-reaching specification tasks. Within this concluding design phase, sustainable concepts for the mobility transition, the energy transition, or water-sensitive urban design are integrated into the design in detail. To test the feasibility of the proposed architectural con-

Foldable booklet as continuous urban design facade elevation

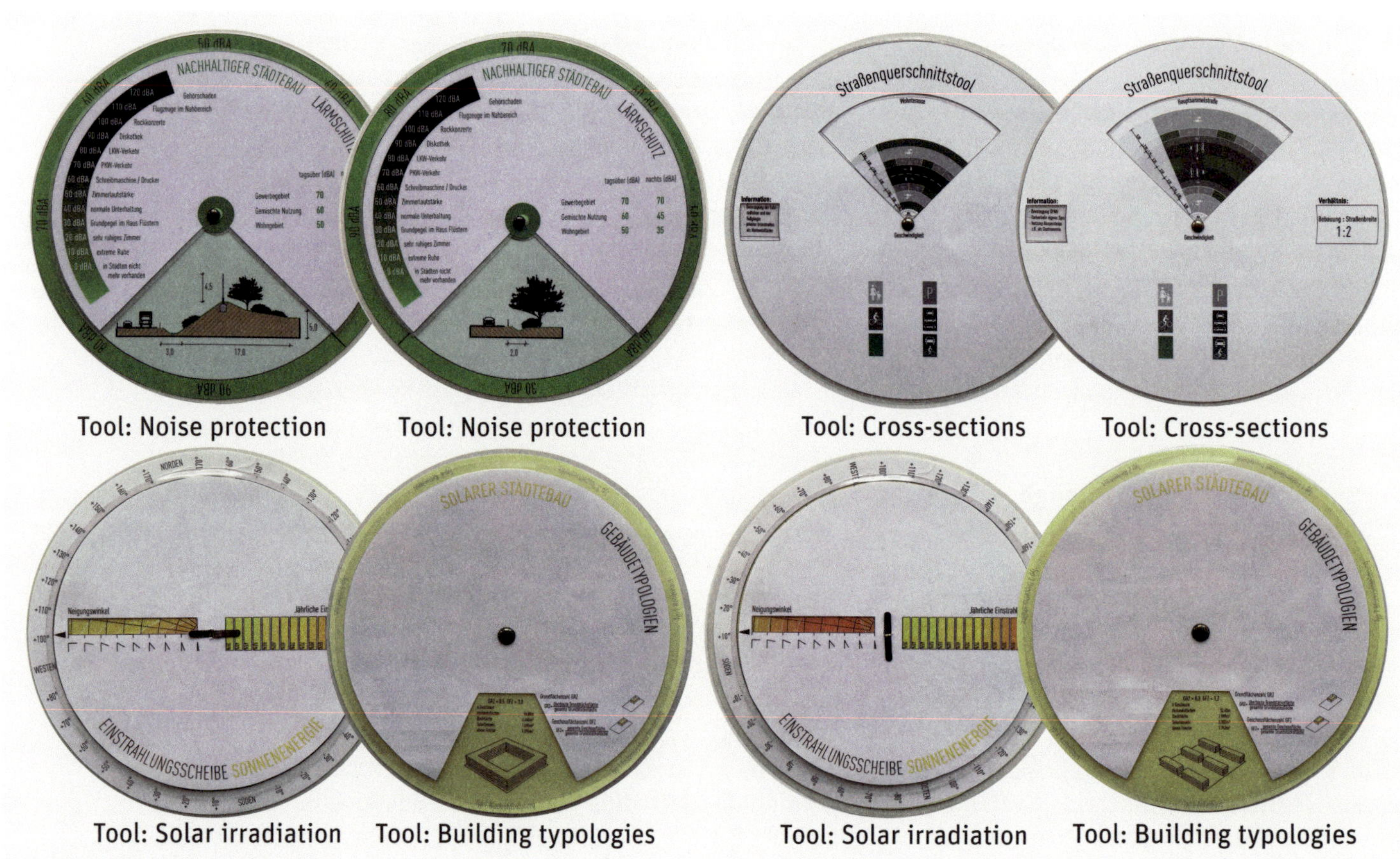

Evaluation dials for urban design parameters

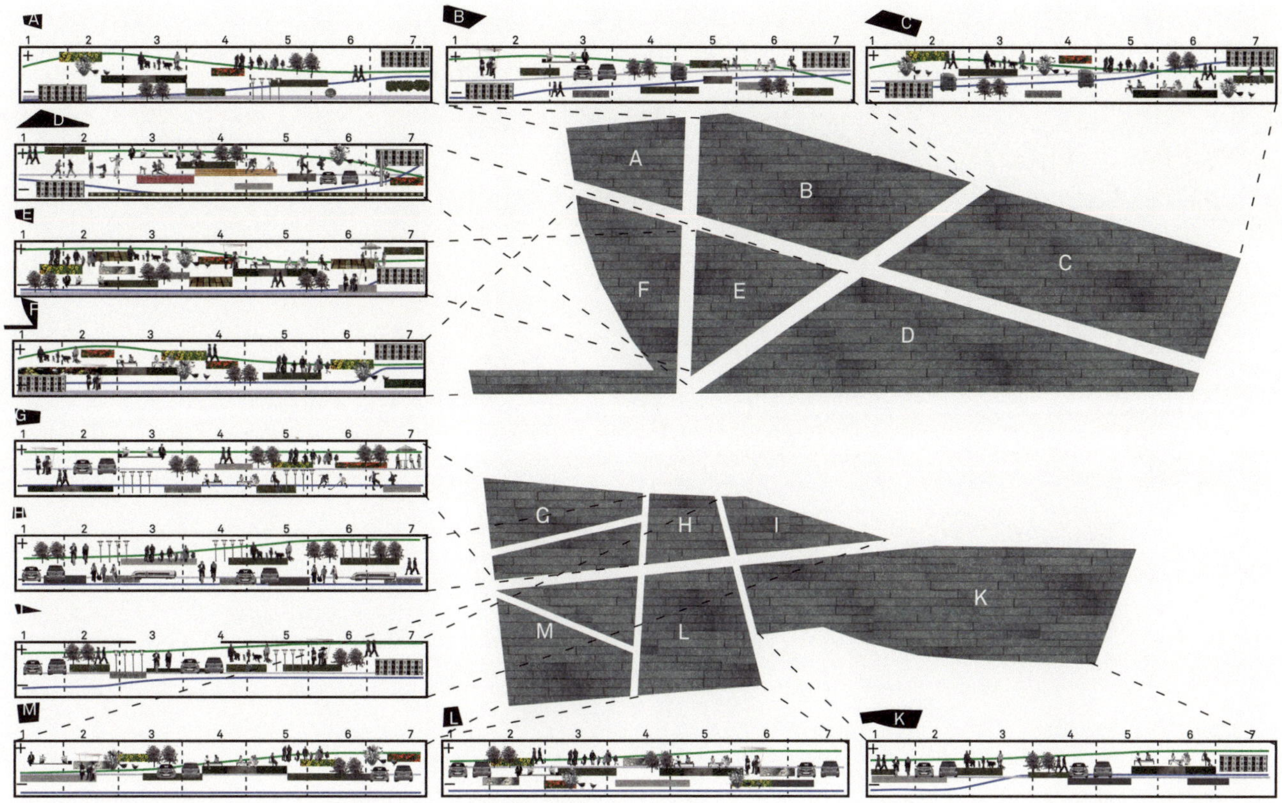

Diagrammatic illustration of functional street profiles for Cologne

cepts, such as the implementation of area-based conservation efforts, water-sensitive urban design, or sustainable energy conservation within the urban fabric, computer-aided simulations, as well as manual tools, are relevant for an evaluation. These analogue evaluation tools can include anything from graphic media, such as foldable booklets or exploded-view drawings, to decision-making templates. For instance, a solar gain diagram can be used to calculate sunlight intake in relation to a selected architectural typology, and thus offer precise design information.

Urban processes are complex; although they can be dynamic and fluid, they often betray static forms of visualisation. Thus, as successive elements akin to movement, they literally and practically require unfolding. An uninterrupted, continuous form of graphic illustration permits urban situations to be visualised at a single glance in temporal, as well as spatial terms, beyond a static and linear approach of creating separate sections. This type of illustration can be helpful in displaying the principle of water-sensitive urban design in open spaces for the purpose of open-space planning, based on urban flood zones impacted by flash flood events. It can also serve to depict greywater use within a designed water supply system for use in building interiors at architectural levels of detail.

PARTICIPATORY RESEARCH PROJECTS

3

Bergisch project profile

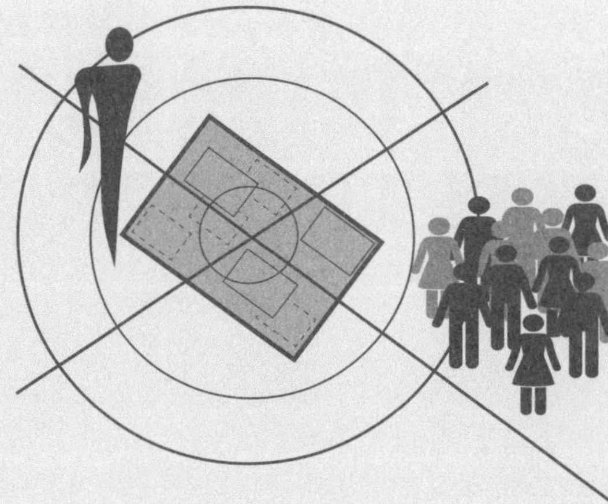

Project initiators and clients

BUW Chair of Urban Design – Urban Scape:
Ragnhild Klußmann, Bärbel Offergeld,
Tanja Siems

Participating partners and institutions

Christian Hampe, Utopiastadt Bahnhof Mirke (Utopiastadt / GmbH Wuppertal)
Carsten Zimmermann, Bergische Entwicklungsagentur (BEA GmbH Solingen)
Local and regional actors as well as initiatives from the cities of Remscheid, Solingen, and Wuppertal, institutions such as the Wuppertal Institut, Düsseldorf regional government, Region Köln / Bonn e.V. and the Ruhr special administrative district
Sponsors: funding was granted by foundations including the Dr. Werner Jackstädt-Stiftung and the Ulrike u. Klaus Krebs Stiftung, as well as regional corporations including the Wuppertal-based tool manufacturer KNIPEX, the modular shelf producer STOCUBO, and the Witten-based art supply provider BOESNER.

Research project timeline

Concept phase: definition of research topics, comparative studies, and networking within the region (0.5 years)
Developmental phases and publications: bergisch.paper, urban design implementation strategies jointly developed within workshops with experts and students in summer schools in the cities of Wuppertal, Solingen, and Remscheid (1.5 years)
Realisation phases: urban labs in Wuppertal-Mirke, Solingen-Birkenweiher, Remscheid-Bahnhofstrasse (1.5 years)

Important data and facts

The region of Bergisches Land comprises the district of Mettmann, the cities of Wuppertal, Solingen, and Remscheid, the Rheinisch-Bergisches district, as well as the Oberbergische district. The three cities of the Bergisches City Triangle are characterised by polycentric settlement structures. The settlement spaces have long since merged together. Their historically rooted settlement cores, however, still maintain a presence as discernible regional centres. The municipalities of Remscheid, Solingen, and Wuppertal combined cover 332.5 square kilometres with a population density of 1,878.91 per square kilometre. In 2019 the Bergisches City Triangle comprised a population of 624,736, of which 53 per cent were female and 47 per cent were male. In comparison and at the same time, the Ruhr metropolitan region alone was home to a total of 5,112,050 people. Demographic change in the region indicates a strong increase in the number of older people. Far less than 20 per cent of young residents aged 0–20 live in the Bergisches City Triangle. The percentage of residents aged 65 and older is 26.5 per cent and is greater in all three cities than in the entire state of North Rhine-Westphalia.

Project objectives and goals

The Bergisch Project consists of a diverse set of activities, including interdisciplinary workshops, symposia, and seminars with local actors and associations, in combination with international events and academic programmes, such as summer schools with universities and other scientific institutions. The project concept is understood as an open developmental process intended to flexibly respond to required changes within the methodical approach and topical orientation and permits adaptation to the current body of knowledge. Experimental teaching formats and innovative didactic approaches are supposed to be tested and evaluated within this context, in order to propose alternative perspectives on how to think about the future-oriented development of the entire region.

The region as an experimental research lab
"Bergisch Project"

The Bergisches Land is one of Germany's oldest industrial regions. It also features a unique cultural landscape, due to a combination of its existing natural environment and historical industrial development. For a number of decades the region has been experiencing far-reaching structural change. To the three metropolises of the Bergisches Land – Wuppertal, Solingen, and Remscheid – it has been important, ever since, to cooperate within a cultural landscape, and for economic and societal reasons. Based on the structural development programme of the Regionale 2006, the cities officially founded the Bergisches City Triangle. The initiative cooperates with neighbouring urban networks that were created in the 1990s, such as ANKE (Arnhem, Nijmegen, Kleve, and Emmerich), the EXPO-Region, the city triangle Enschede-Münster-Osnabrück, as well as the regional cooperative comprising the city of Bonn and the Rhein-Sieg district.

The experimental research project served to follow this transformation process in collaboration with a diverse set of actors and institutions within the Bergisches City Triangle in the form of different assignments and approaches. Our experimental and interdisciplinary approach employed new tools for analysis and planning to mediate between different professions and topics and generate joint strategies for sustainable urban development. By using temporary interventions and workshops, easy to implement directly on site, new impulses were set for a shrinking region. Based on different methodical approaches, the insights gained from the different events were deepened in the course of time and, eventually, led to precise project proposals and recommendations for action. The "Bergisch Project" is understood as a continuous, multi-year project that is supposed to be expanded and complemented by numerous partial projects, allowing it to become firmly rooted in the region.

Interdisciplinary approach to foster knowledge transfer

The concept described a teaching and research project that offered, on the one hand, a basis for a large-scale scientific and interdisciplinary approach. On the other hand, it offered the opportunity to test innovative methodical approaches and ideas in the context of teaching projects that bring students and experts from the region together. This approach allowed the project to contribute to knowledge transfer and its increasing importance for complex urban planning processes, not only within planning pedagogy, but also in practice. The idea of a cooperative project allowed us to intensively deliberate on spatial transformation processes within the region by using experimental methods and cooperative formats, while exploring possible developmental perspectives for the selected urban spaces. As supervisors and planners, at the beginning of the project we asked ourselves the following questions: what is the significance of this small and unknown area, located between the Rhine and Ruhr regions? What does the model of the Bergisches City Triangle mean for the people living in the region? Can the citizens, actors, and their cities identify themselves with the model of a city triangle in their region? How can we help the three cities of Wuppertal, Remscheid, and Solingen and their citizens look to the future in an optimistic way, despite a shrinking population and vacant buildings?

The Bergisches City Triangle is characterised by a very high degree of engagement on the part of citizens and the business sector. This is further indicated by its high number of existing associations. This allowed us, even before the project began, to approach interested citizens, local actors, associations, and businesses, to secure their involvement in the project. Due to its experimental approaches, the "Bergisch Project" generated research questions and results that were tested within different formats, for instance symposia including the participation of experts and the interested public. These events spanned multiple days. The results were explained within panel discussions, in workshops, and at summer academies, together with students and local actors, across multiple weeks and with daily counselling by supervisors and experts. This also included formats such as "students in residence" or "studies in urban labs" that enabled students to conduct work and research directly on site for numerous months.

Innovative solutions for a sustainable transformation process

Before we, as representatives of a scientific institution, began our creative interventions in the three cities, to develop innovative approaches to solutions for the transformation process, the project started with a comprehensive investigation and evaluation of the region. By using experimental methods and instruments, we specified and evaluated the urban design situation and its qualities, deficiencies, and

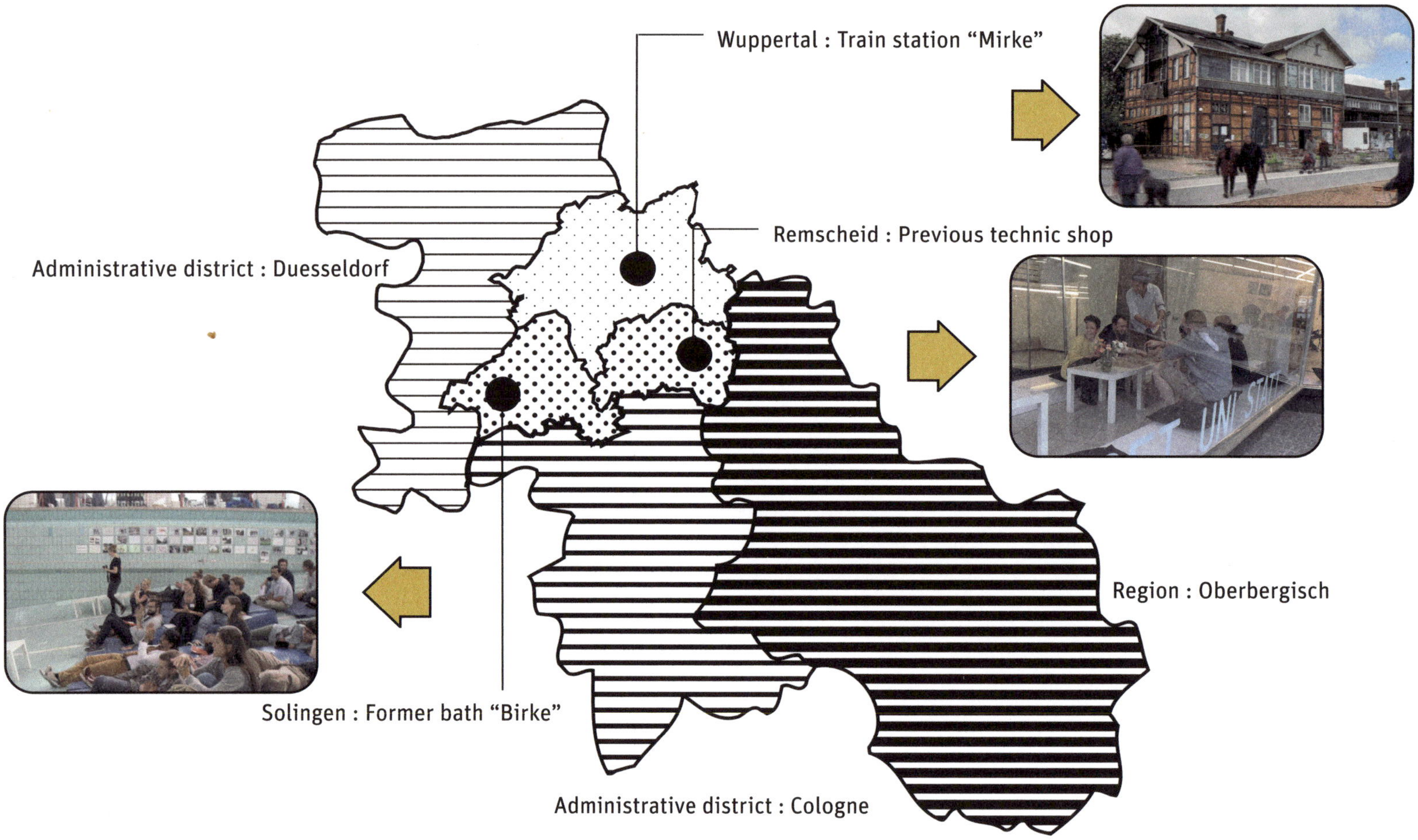

Overview, "Bergisch Project": labs in the cities of Wuppertal, Remscheid, and Solingen

potential. Supervisors and students were required to explore, read, and wander through the area, to identify what defines the essence of the Bergisches City Triangle. Instead of renting a bus and a tour guide, as is often the case when conducting field research, we created the "bergisch.taxi", not only as a means of transport, but most of all as a research tool. The "bergisch.taxi" was driven by the most diverse types of regional specialists in order to receive the most intensive and authentic insight possible into the Bergisches Land. The more informative and the more intense it was to familiarise ourselves with the region and the people living there, the more we were able to precisely evaluate regional topics later on. The "urban chauffeurs" showed us their personal cultural and culinary highlights of the Bergisches Land. Project participants discovered and identified unique characteristics and exceptional peculiarities.

We began our journey on board the "bergisch.taxi" and spoke to people on site in order to find projects that impressed them or that were essential to the "Bergisch" character of the region. This allowed us to deliberate on the region in analytical terms and, most of all, to conduct networking. We listened to the diverse range of stories and retold them, in combination with our own experiences. The "bergisch.blog" was an important element of this communication. As an online platform, it continually displayed the state of our operations. Most of all, it was used to include news in real time from all parties involved. The "bergisch.blog" supported our public outreach campaign for the research project. It also featured background information on the entire project, the most current project status, and planned actions, in a visible and informative way.

Further, the question was raised regarding what other urban methods or new tools or products we could develop and test during the "Bergisch Project". We knew that the "typical" instruments of urban design would be of little help in understanding the multi-faceted region in its entirety. Thus, we as supervisors needed to improvise, organise, and most of all moderate, to discuss the content under development with the students, the local actors, and the regional organisations – in a professional way.

Instruments and products to advance the process

The following tools and products can support the research process in a sustainable manner. To display the multifaceted mosaic of the region and its actors and systematise it, the creation of an atlas comprises a suitable approach. The "bergisch.atlas" was intended to show as much information as possible on the region and its people. To depict phe-

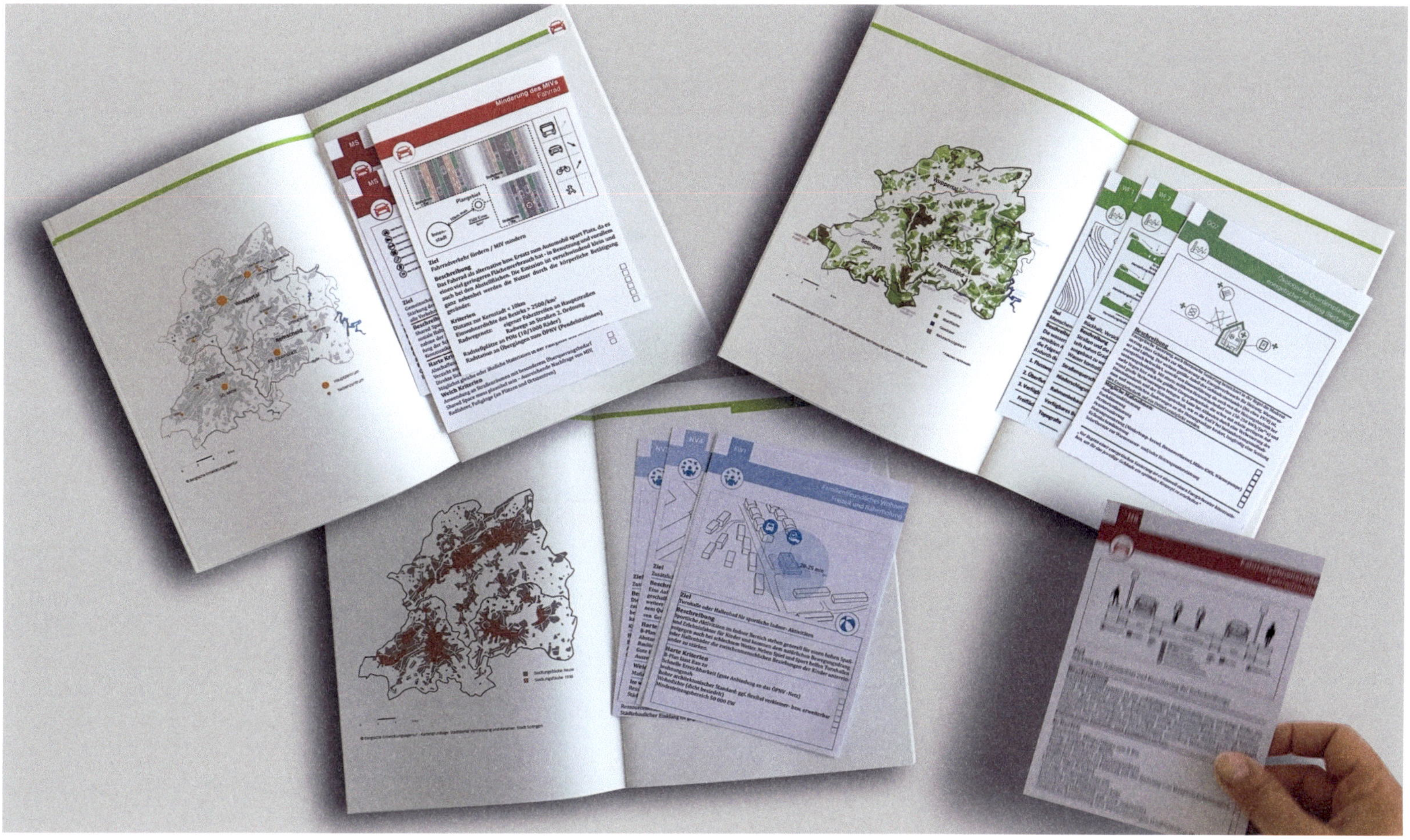

"bergisch.atlas" as systematic analytical tool for the evaluation process

nomena of everyday life was just as important as professional projects. Personal experiences and insights became components of the "bergisch.atlas", just as did the analytical and systematic illustrations that served to document the Bergisches City Triangle. Beyond commonly available statistical information and datasets, we attempted to gain an intentionally personal and methodically heterogeneous view of the region. The "bergisch.atlas" as a catalogue and inventory of regional conditions became a template for the formulation of research questions within the different working groups. The creation of the "bergisch.atlas", depicting stories, images, experiences, thoughts, and interviews conducted on site, allowed us to further advance the project process in a decisive manner.

For the next step, it was particularly important to create a place of gathering – a place to transform the academic project into an applied creative project, while also creating a place for participation, to launch and maintain the conversation between the teaching institution, the actors, and the organisations. The "bergisch.box" served to establish this place of gathering and discussion: an exhibition space that became the meeting point and information carrier of the project. Vacated spaces in the region, for instance the decommissioned train station in Wuppertal-Mirke, the closed public swimming pool in Solingen, and a vacant shop in Remscheid were used for this purpose. The "bergisch.box" was accessible to all residents and local actors as a place for communication. Anyone who had ideas for action, events, talks, or projects received the opportunity to appropriate the space. Once the atlas had been compiled as a basis for discussion, we were able to begin with the different events directly in the three cities. First, in Wuppertal in the Mirke train station, the previously defined research questions and topical fields were discussed and revised in a multi-day workshop with numerous experts from the region, from the municipalities, and from the scientific community.

TEACHING AND RESEARCH – "URBAN LAB"
WUPPERTAL'S OLD TRAIN STATION MIRKE

Mirke train station, prior to the founding of Utopiastadt

The Mirke district in Wuppertal has been, for many years, a centre of civil society engagement. The decommissioned train station had long since been a place of identification for the area. It is situated directly next to the repurposed railway track of the Nordbahntrasse, now a combined bicycle, pedestrian, and skate lane. Thus, it became a juncture between the district and the city of Wuppertal and its two centres of Elberfeld and Barmen. The Mirke train station is in the entire region a centre of activity for cultural and creative businesses and therefore an open place of gathering and exchange. The vacant spaces of the historically listed building were eventually reused by regional initiatives and the non-profit association, Utopiastadt.

This association has been acquiring funds from different public and private bodies to make this place step by step available to the population. The gastronomical services on the ground floor are part of this place of exchange, available to building tenants, residents, and users of the Nordbahntrasse, which is a former rail track. Anyone can, in less than no time, become acquainted with the creative centre of Utopiastadt. To date, the building has become home to workshops for regional crafts, a cooperative that sells the design and label products of different local and supra-regional businesses, as well as rehearsal spaces and studios for music and dance in the former train station offices. The impressive former waiting room became an innovative event space. Further areas for studios and workspaces will be created on the ground floor in the coming years.

In the context of the "Bergisch Project", it seemed obvious to make these active spaces in the train station the centre point of the events that would allow us, as an academic institution, to network with local actors and interested parties. In this regard, the task was less to create new spaces for dialogue than to make visible the existing place in its current structure, emphasise its qualities, and enable others to experience them.

Site visit by the charity "Wuppertalbewegung e.V." of the Nordbahntrasse

Tour with experts to Mirke train station

Former train station spaces as a place of conversation

During the two-day expert workshop, the train station as a place of conversation offered us different opportunities to distribute the working groups, each focusing on different topics, throughout the entire building. For this purpose, the building comprised spaces for individual working groups that would enable intensive, interruption-free discussions, for instance, due to their specific arrangement. Further spaces presented inviting opportunities for a public exchange with passers-by, based on their prominent position. The size and height of spaces, ranging from conference rooms to small, angular chambers, comprised the methodical framework for the workshops by defining their capacity and atmosphere. The selection of spaces allowed us to determine the number of participants and the interdisciplinary mix of the individual working groups. The podium of the former train station waiting room as a place of gathering had the feeling of a cosy living room, and thus led to various degrees of intense discussion between experts and laypeople on the proposed topics.

The working groups comprised a diverse range of scientific disciplines, including supervisors and students from the University of Wuppertal and experts from the Wuppertal Institute.

Both local and regional actors from associations, organisations and institutions joined the discussion, as well as young regional creators: artists, designers, architects, urban planners, landscape planners, and engineers. The interdisciplinary expert workshop at the Mirke train station was intended to confront common scientific modes of operation with perspectives from practice, to identify topics relevant to the future of the region, beyond the atlas. Location, accessibility, and capacity for orientation within the Rhine-Ruhr metropolitan region formed one set of topics. The topographical isolation and the small scale of settlement cores also played significant roles in the discussion, with the aim of focusing on the future developmental potential of a shrinking region. The interdisciplinary make-up of the working groups served to evaluate these topics and tasks, as well as the particularities and potential of the City Triangle, in order to formulate initial recommendations for action. A returning focus of the discussions within the individual working groups was the specific way of dealing with recent processes of transformation, especially within a region defined by industrial production.

Formulation of research questions and subject areas

The interdisciplinary working groups were separated into discussion groups according to the subject areas of "identity, quality, and networking". At the end of the intensive rounds of discussion, one working group that predominantly dealt with the topic of identity reached the conclusion that the Bergische City Triangle, as a comparatively small and compact region, was overshadowed by the surrounding regions. Regarding urbanity, appealing residential space or cultural attractions, it was currently not in a situation to adequately compete with the neighbouring regions. This mirrors the results of the working group that selected the topic of quality as basis for their discussion. Following a comprehensive evaluation of facts originating in the atlas and the successive discussion between local actors and experts, the group was able to determine that the "Bergisches Land" as a cultural landscape, due to its situation within the natural environment and its cultural and industrial developmental history, has a unique profile. The Bergisches City Triangle, however, finds itself in a situation where it needs to compete with the established Ruhr area's industrial culture and the cultural hubs of the neighbouring metropolises of Cologne and Düsseldorf. In sum, the observation was made that the amalgamation into the Bergisches City Triangle certainly offers many opportunities, but that no single city can benefit from them, because spatial cohesion is absent. As a result it becomes necessary to question the Bergisches City Triangle and whether it is an appropriate model for a sustainable regional development in terms of its identity, quality, and network. Within pedagogy and in the context of the successive public events, such as workshops or summer schools with experts and students, this resulted in the task of continuing research on the historical cultural-spatial developments and affiliations within the region, its historical development, as well as the actual everyday life of residents. The aim is to identify which degree of spatial expansion actually makes sense for the region and which supra-regional affiliations should be extended.

In a further working group, intensive discussions took place regarding networking between people and the existing built systems in the region. Within all networks, a significant contribution to the success of initiatives was to maintain an adequate balance between individual identity and superordinate identity. This becomes apparent in the integration, submission, or mutual benefit of existing strengths on all levels, within active networking systems, ranging from creative and scientific networks to economic interrelations. Often, successful networks display manifold interrelations that strengthen individuals, while also creating a common basis for the advancement of sustainable transformation processes in urban and rural regions. For the Bergisches City Triangle, this mostly asks: How can the characteristics of the individual cities and of the Bergisches Land be emphasised and used, while generating a synergetic network based on shared interests of involved actors that can advance the entire region and provide it with a strong shared framework? Within the network of cities, we ask ourselves what should be connected and for which purpose. In the areas of infrastructure and natural environment, the Bergisches Land features manifold qualities of industry and cultural landscape, as well as energy potential: the aim is to interlink them in spatial or media terms within strategies and concepts. In the following steps of the research project and the public workshops, the intention was not to work in overly pragmatic terms, but instead, in a visionary way. For this purpose, regionally active, competent, experienced, and unbiased actors who demonstrated long-term engagement were integrated into the process.

The research questions formulated in the expert workshops and the identified subject areas were deepened within a diverse set of urban design models created in the following semester by students of the Bachelor and Master's programmes. The subject area of "reprogramming" the region was of relevance. Differently composed groups were supposed to deliberate on this topic within seminars and design assignments. One significant aspect for the investigation and the development of sustainable strategies and concepts was the question of how to deal with the existing vacancies and the extreme processes of shrinkage experienced in recent years in the cities and within the region. Different teaching modules, for instance the year-long research studio on "experimental urban research" in the Master's programme, served to develop conceptual and applied solutions for specific places to set productive impulses for the entire region. In this regard, it was of particular importance to us to directly visit the region, teach there, work there, learn from it, and research it. Only in this way were the students able to think outside the box of everyday pedagogy in scientific institutions and leave the lecture halls and seminar rooms to work on designs, concepts, and case studies, on site and together with experts and interested individuals from the region.

INTERDISCIPLINARY TEACHING LAB – "CREATIVE LAB"
BIRKER BAD, SOLINGEN

Swimming pool as lecture hall and exhibition space

We organised the interdisciplinary Urban Summer School in an empty public swimming pool in Solingen during the semester break. Here, we deliberated on the topics surrounding the characteristics of the region, together with more than thirty students from fourteen different universities. The interdisciplinary structure of the workshop allowed us to produce new modes of interpretation of the region at the intersection of art and science.

The topical basis for the Urban Summer School comprises Bachelor and Master's programme student contributions featuring urban design elaborations from seminars, urban design assignments, and the Research Studio of previous semesters. Some students from the University of Wuppertal also participated in the summer academy and thus were able to convey to the other participants the results of their intensive deliberations on subject fields of spaces of potential, atmospheres, regional networks, idiosyncrasies, and stories. These student strategies and concepts were subject to review and critique from the supervisors and students from different disciplines who participated in the ten-day summer school. Discussions and workshops produced new information and approaches to solutions for different subject fields: sustainable urban districts, landscape as resource, energy development potential, and cultural identity.

Summer school in the Bergisches City Triangle

Prior to the summer school, we had already developed and tested instruments and products. Within the summer school, they were reused, to once more test their suitability as methodical formats in the context of the multi-week academy. As an introduction to the region, all participants boarded the "bergisch.taxi" for an informative field trip. The work-

"Bergisch Project" expert discussion on the future developments

Students presenting their urban design projects

shop began with an open call in local newspapers aimed at the local population in order to introduce the Bergisches City Triangle to the students, in a multi-faceted and manifold way, using the "bergisch.taxi" – considering the region was, for the most part, unknown to them. The intention was to find people who were willing to introduce "their" region to one or two students during a three-hour taxi ride.

The rides – each of which was unique – and the related walks and round trips were documented by the students and compiled in the "bergisch.wall", an exhibition wall comprising photos, sketches, and text. The results were presented and discussed two days later and with the participation of regional experts during the occasion of a public event. The diverse ways of deliberating on the region, the participation of all involved parties, and the presented results were impressive and, in many cases, advanced the individual research interests of the students during the entire summer academy week and inspired further experimentation.

The "bergisch.talk", a symposium with impulse lectures from regional supervisors, experts from different institutions, and local actors, created a topical basis, in order to begin with the successive interdisciplinary workshops, which included students, supervisors, and regional experts. The students from different disciplines and different universities formed working groups that changed on a daily basis. At a final culinary closing event, the "bergisch.dinner", the results they had discussed and recorded in the "bergisch.log.book" throughout the process were presented. The produced content of the individual groups was compared during the weekend within a representative exhibition format and displayed to the public in an open-house format.

Ideal spaces for intensive exchange

The mix of different disciplines was of specific importance, as was the selected location. The Birker Bath was an ideal place for the workshops and symposia. It fostered an intensive discussion between individuals and groups consisting of supervisors, students, and experts. We used the swimming pool as a lecture hall; the dressing room lockers became exhibition cabinets; and the entrance area served as the kitchen for a culinary space of exchange. The students slept on foldable beds in the former shower area and dressing rooms. They worked in the swimming pool and the bordering gallery. They presented interim results for public discussion within this variety of spaces.

LEARNING AND COMMUNICATION – "NANO LAB"
STOREFRONT IN REMSCHEID

Storefront in Remscheid used as an on-site Lab

Remscheid's inner city has always been characterised by local small businesses. The spaces used for shops and built during the era of the German postwar economic miracle are particularly reminiscent of the tradition and the past vitality of this location. The former radio store, with the address "Markt 13", is such a case. Its glazed facades and its mezzanine floor express the pride and modernity of its time, and thus permitted us to present innovative processes and ideas, instead of technical appliances and radio sets. The institute with its staff and students, therefore, moved into the shop in Remscheid, together with its entire semester curriculum.

In the form of a small urban living lab, we assumed the role of an academic interim user and, perhaps even more important, as a mediator between the city, the local administration, and the residents. Not only did we teach different urban design modules here, but also organised public round table discussions and events. The "bergisch.nano.lab" was projected to last for multiple months and dealt with the topic of the identity of the city of Remscheid amid a shrinking region. The lead topic was how to deal with the increasing rate of vacancies of shops in the historically rooted pedestrian area of Remscheid and how this related to the construction of a new shopping mall.

Storefront as an urban showcase

The earliest urban design strategies and concepts that were developed by the students, presented in the shop window, and thus publicly presented, indicated a strong interest in changing the current situation through innovative projects. Residents, local actors, association members, and indi-

Round-table discussion with local actors and regional experts

viduals from district institutions, the city, and the region visited us daily in order to exchange ideas in our lab. The public interest and the support of dedicated individuals allowed us as supervisors to immediately generate different strategies and concepts for projects together with the students and, as a result, directly discuss these with actors and experts and test them, based on interventions in urban space. In doing so, we provided an opportunity to examine possible participative design patterns for a diverse set of urban spaces, together with the students and directly on site in the vivid inner city. The "bergisch.nano.lab" initiated conversations between students and actors even beyond the lab and therefore inspired further innovative ideas and projects for the city.

The Evaluation is the important aspect, it serves to identify which particular topics and projects can be broadened in the future and eventually lead to realisation. The Chair of Urban Design – Urban Scape is dedicated to continued service to the city of Remscheid as a moderator or initiator of ideas, based on its expertise – even without a lab.

LEARNING BY TEACHING AND RESEARCHING ON SITE – A SUMMARY

The urban process is unique. Thus, related procedures and instruments require repeated definition and adjustment. This is particularly the case in the context of the participation of local actors and residents. The spaces intended for participatory exchange are not neutral. Their purpose as such is to inform the conversation. Thus, it is often alienating and detrimental if participation processes take place in the spaces and conference rooms of institutions detached from the actual area under discussion. As a result, it is difficult to identify and understand far-reaching ideas and concepts – or even discuss them. It is also difficult to enable this experience in others. The selection and design of "spaces of negotiation" are significant factors in the conceptualisation of participation processes. Participation requires time, as well as adequate space. The selection of a space and its quality and character, from the very beginning, sets the tone for the cooperation between actors. The three examples in the cities of Wuppertal, Solingen, and Remscheid clearly show the different character of the spaces used in the context of the "Bergisch Project" and indicate the potential and versatility of space as an instrument of design within urban conversations.

The space of participation should also represent certain values. It is no coincidence that momentous political negotiations and agreements often take place in impressive spaces, to emphasise the relevance of what is happening. The space used for the participation of the public should, therefore, be taken seriously as a space of identification. Which place within a neighbourhood, quarter, or district stands out in particular? Which place represents the public and its notions of community? In Solingen, we identified the vacant Birker Bad as such a unique place. The historic building of the public baths had always been a space of gathering and wellbeing. The empty pool was suitable for use as a "pool of thought" and an exceptional space for joint work and creativity. Participation not only means to take part, but also requires a transparent portrayal of its underlying process and further development. The storefront in Remscheid also offered a suitable space for this purpose. The transparency of the space permitted members of the interested public to easily witness the actions taking place inside, as well as their results – an invitation to become active and join the process. Here, crossing the threshold did not mean to enter a public institution or city hall, but to simply enter a space, just like entering a shop. The former shop consequently became a place for an interactive exchange of ideas.

In contrast to the appropriated vacant spaces of the "Bergisch Project" in the Bergisches City Triangle, the following chapter will present approaches to mediating spaces in the context of our research on the realisation of a "participatory spatial constructs".

The participatory spatial construct

Project initiators

T2 Spatialwork Ltd., London, directors: Theo Lorenz, Tanja Siems
Lob-Design / Studio Fezazi Architekten, Wuppertal, director: Mohamed Fezazi

Participating partners and institutions

BUW Chair of Urban Design – Urban Scape and Institute for Environmental Design (IUG):
Elli Börgener, Mohamed Fezazi, Alexia Radounikli, Tanja Siems
AAIS Theo Lorenz, Interprofessional Studio, Architectural Association School of Architecture, London
TallerDE2 Madrid, directors: Arantza Ozaeta Cortázar, Álvaro Martin Fidalgo

Important data and facts

The participatory spatial construct is an inflatable temporary building. It can be set up as a stand-alone unit or in the context of existing buildings. Unit sizes range from 10 square metres to 150 square metres with a corresponding weight of 4.2 to 63 kilograms. The composition of the inflatable construction supports very small packing sizes and convenient transport. The construction is self-inflating and can be set up by unskilled individuals in a short amount of time without the use of tools.

Project objectives and goals

The participatory spatial construct was developed within an interdisciplinary process involving students of different disciplines in cooperation with two further European universities in Madrid and London. Actors of different professions cooperated, including architects, urban planners, artists, engineers, designers, supervisors, and students. The prototype of an inflatable structure was built and tested in different urban space-related and architectural situations.

Design project timeline

Analysis phase: cooperative strategies including workshops, lectures, interviews, and surveys to determine spaces of potential in the urban context and in the interior of large-scale institutional buildings. Identification and integration of the most important actors (1 year).
Consolidation phase: conceptualisation, design, and construction of the inflatable participatory spatial construct. Deployment within different spaces of potential, including use for cooperative teaching and research events. Evaluation of deployment and transformation of the spatial construct (1 year).
Application phase: deployment of the transformed spatial construct in different scenarios with different actors from research, teaching, and practice. Evaluation of deployment and publication of results.
As a result, the spatial construct is available for use by a municipality, a university, or an association for related functions (test phase 1.5 years).

A PLACE FOR COMMUNICATIVE ACTION: THE DEVELOPMENT OF A PARTICIPATORY SPATIAL CONSTRUCT

CONTRIBUTION IN COOPERATION WITH MOHAMED FEZAZI

The participatory spatial construct operates as a spatialised form of cooperative practice at the intersection of science, pedagogy, and society. As an experimental space, it permits the testing and optimising of its effectiveness during deployment. It creates a shared space that can be deployed in a diverse set of spatial contexts. Its defining characteristics, such as size, location, or function can be changed by its users.

During cooperative processes, actors of different professional and cultural backgrounds can, by using participatory methods and spaces, work together successfully. The space in which this work takes place receives specific importance. Beyond particular recommendations for action regarding implementing cooperative measures, we intended to develop the concept of a participatory spatial construct. We defined architectural criteria for it, to describe the typology of a participatory structure. This resulted from its strategic and practical requirements. Throughout our investigation, it became apparent that a participatory spatial construct is always defined by its relation to common building typologies and only permits description within this relation. The spatial construct, therefore, refers to other buildings and existing situations in urban space. In this regard, form and exterior appearance, functional programme, and construction type are defined by strategies of cooperative action.

The methods of cooperation described in the previous chapters are the point of origin for the development of the form and superordinate aesthetics of this new typology. We base our hypotheses on a series of experimental buildings that were developed during the last twenty years at the AAIS of the Architectural Association School of Architecture in London and at the Chair of Urban Design – Urban Scape in Wuppertal in cooperation with students, citizens, artists, architects, actants, and urban designers. Gaining results within this process was only possible by realising these projects.

The diagrammatical illustration of the projects within a project matrix reveals this fact. While this matrix certainly can't replace an actual trial run, it allows us to describe the manifold interrelations between the depicted experimental buildings, their users, and the surrounding spaces according to defined criteria. Particular attention is paid to the capacity of the building to support participation, to develop a related typology.

MATRIX OF TEMPORARY PARTICIPATORY SPACES

Based on the matrix, we assign the following criteria to different experimental spaces: functional programme, type of use, construction type, as well as production method. These spaces are derived from completely different scenarios. In our matrix, the Bauhaus Lab, for instance, constitutes a temporary expansion of a theatre stage including an interactive building envelope. The SAMUWA-LAB for our research project "The city as changing hydrological system – steps towards adaptive management of the urban water balance" addressed the topic of water-sensitive development in the urban context and, during the entire research period, served as a mobile exhibition space to communicate this complex topic to the public and discuss it among involved partners. Other structures and constructions produced performative spaces that interacted with dancers and their choreography by means of movement. The project for the "Junior Uni" in Wuppertal was created as a mobile companion of outdoor teaching spaces for schoolyards. In the context of the regional structure initiative "Regionale 2006", the built pavilion served to present related developments to citizens. Afterwards, the building remained in use as a temporary space, open to appropriation by local associations and schools.

The matrix indicates the functional programme as well as the type of use, the topics of the events, and the interactive character of specific elements. The interactivity refers to the capacity of a structure to register and process sensory stimuli. This can include input or movement created by users, values of air quality, indoor temperature, or the number of users in the space.

Based on the site of installation, the relation between the specific structure and its environment became a topic of investigation. Some spaces expand the scope of functions of existing buildings or reformulate interiors, resulting in the reprogramming of existing spatial configurations. Other structures function in an autonomous manner and engage in a dialogue with the surrounding urban space. Depending on the site of installation and the position of entrances and openings, these spaces can accommodate, accompany, or interrupt flows of traffic, such as in the case of the "kids-driving-school" created by the Wuppertal-based office Lob-Design.

All spaces have in common that the selected construction type produces a space that enables easy access to communication. Due to their configuration and design, they also create a point of contact or a communicative platform, based on their flexible structure and appearance, that continually invites users to participate.

All these buildings, located on various sites of different kinds, are only in use for a limited amount of time. In this regard, as the matrix shows, they allow comparison in terms of parameters of transport expenditure, required time for set-up, and construction type. Spaces featuring a low transport volume and permitting set-up with little effort have an advantage. Thus, inflatable construction types find use more often than structures that are, for instance, built from materials such as timber or steel. In relation to the space they enclose, their package volume in dismantled condition is very low. Some of them can even be transported using small carrying cases or can be easily installed and altered by laypeople. Their production is simple. Prior to installation, prototypes can be produced quickly and tested. Completed spaces can be expanded or replaced with very little effort, as required.

Institutional spaces and power

Within a cooperative process, it is specifically important to enable all actors to understand the big picture without any inhibition. Against this background, the participatory spatial construct serves as a platform for cooperative action. It provides a space for discourse that welcomes the diverse set of actors, and thus mutually sensitises them with regard to each other's interests. Such spaces permit easy overview and are intuitive. The range of uses follows an architectural rhetoric that everyone can understand and remains free from connotations of power. In contrast, institutional spaces such as city halls or banks articulate, based on their sheer mass and complexity, a superordinate type of aesthetic, and thus a related claim to power: "In purely physical terms, architecture is enclosure and border. Once built, houses and walls have a causative power. [...] What is built creates or contours a social topography based on rules of access and, thus, on the transition from prohibition to imperative, from preventing to enabling. In architecture, the monumental and the colossal are the preferred rhetorical figures for the expression of power" (Zimmermann 1992).

If information events take place, for instance, in the conference room of a public city hall, it will seem perfectly suitable for this purpose at first, due to the available infrastructure. It features a large projection screen, proper lighting, and sound amplification, as well as tables and chairs to accommodate many interested visitors. The mayor can simply walk down the hall from their office in order to enter this space. All other involved parties are required to travel by public transport from the urban fringe to the city centre and, in a certain way, enter the mayor's domain. Municipality and mayor are guided by their own interests during such processes and can strongly influence the way a discussion unfolds. If public participation is to take place in city hall, the municipal representatives likely determine how the process unfolds. Perhaps they are the only people who know how to control the lighting and sound equipment, and thus decide who may use a microphone and who may not. Visitors enter city hall as the abstract territory of an institutional body with a mayor who has been voted into office based on free elections, while the institutional structure as such, in its complexity, remains impenetrable. Our guests enter the conference room by passing a stone portico, traversing labyrinthine corridors, and after having to explain to the doorperson what they desire. They are intruders, strangers – those who are not accustomed to the enforced spatial "code" of the building. Such are the sentiments among visitors who, similar to all other interested parties, follow the statements made during the session, where issues are negotiated that impact their personal environment.

Visitors of other institutional buildings can experience similar situations, for instance in corporate buildings, sacred architecture, or financial institutions. In such cases, these effects also reinforce power and influence of a corporate, financial, or religious kind. For employees, staff, and members of these institutions, the related buildings represent their own domain. They know their way around; they control building services technology and have permission to access all areas. They can suddenly vanish and appear somewhere else, similar to old castles of lore and their secret passages and hidden chambers. Citizen associations or initiatives that represent needs of a neighbourhood, quarter, or district, however, hardly command similarly representative spaces. Perhaps their meetings take place in a musty gym, in an improvised community centre, or a smoke-filled bar. Here, time and again, improvisation meets an institution and the result is inequality.

However, there are useful influences exerted by institutional spaces that can benefit the unfolding of a cooperative process. Such spaces communicate to visitors the everyday life of their occupants. A visit to a city planning department can indeed give the owner of a small neighbourhood restaurant an impression of the basic principles that guide daily business within such an institution. Visitors gain insight into such working environments. The reverse case is also true, when actors visit that small neighbourhood restaurant. This is only one reason why taking a stroll through an area is a popular method to be able to better understand an area under planning. Despite precise guides and plans, digital models, and aerial photography, many phenomena can only be experienced on site. Visitors gain access to an area and experience the atmosphere and the aura with all senses, intuitively. Architects and urban planners use the term "genius loci" to describe this phenomenon, meaning "the spirit of a place".

	Project	Institution	Location	Material	Production	Budget	Transport
P1		AAIS	Jena	Polyamid tex	Sewing	€€	VAN
P2		AAIS	London	Holz-rinde	CNC	No budget	LORRY 7,5 t
P3		BUW SU	Stuttgart	Polyamid tex	Sewing	No budget	VAN
P4		AAIS	Cologne	Polyamid tex	Sewing	No budget	COURIER
P5		Junior Uni	Wuppertal	Polyamid tex	Sewing	€	CAR
P6	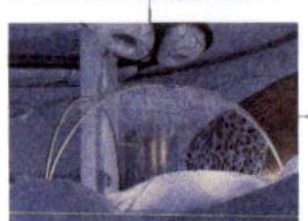	AAIS	London	Tiber+ Fabric	Lasercut	€	VAN
P7		AAIS	London	Timber+ Plywood	CNC	€ - €€	VAN
P8		AAIS	Girona	PVC Honey-comb	Tool	€	COURIER
P9		Oper: Der Liebestrank	Wuppertal	Polyamid tex	Sewing	€	COURIER
P10		AAIS	London	Polyamid tex	Sewing	€	BACKPACK
P11	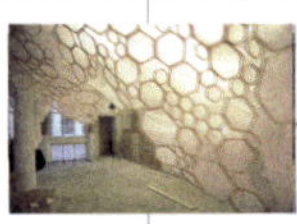	AAIS	London	Timber+ Gauze	CNC	€	BACKPACK
P12		AAIS	Madrid	Timber+ Metall	CNC	No budget	COURIER
P13		Kids driving school	Berlin	Polyamid tex	Sewing	€€	LORRY 7,5 t
P14		Info Pneu Regionale	Remscheid	Polyamid tex	Sewing	€€	CAR

AAIS = Interprofessional Studio BUW SU = Urban Design Institute

€ =< 10.000 € €€ =< 100.000 € €€€ =< 500.000 €

Matrix, performative and mediating pavilions

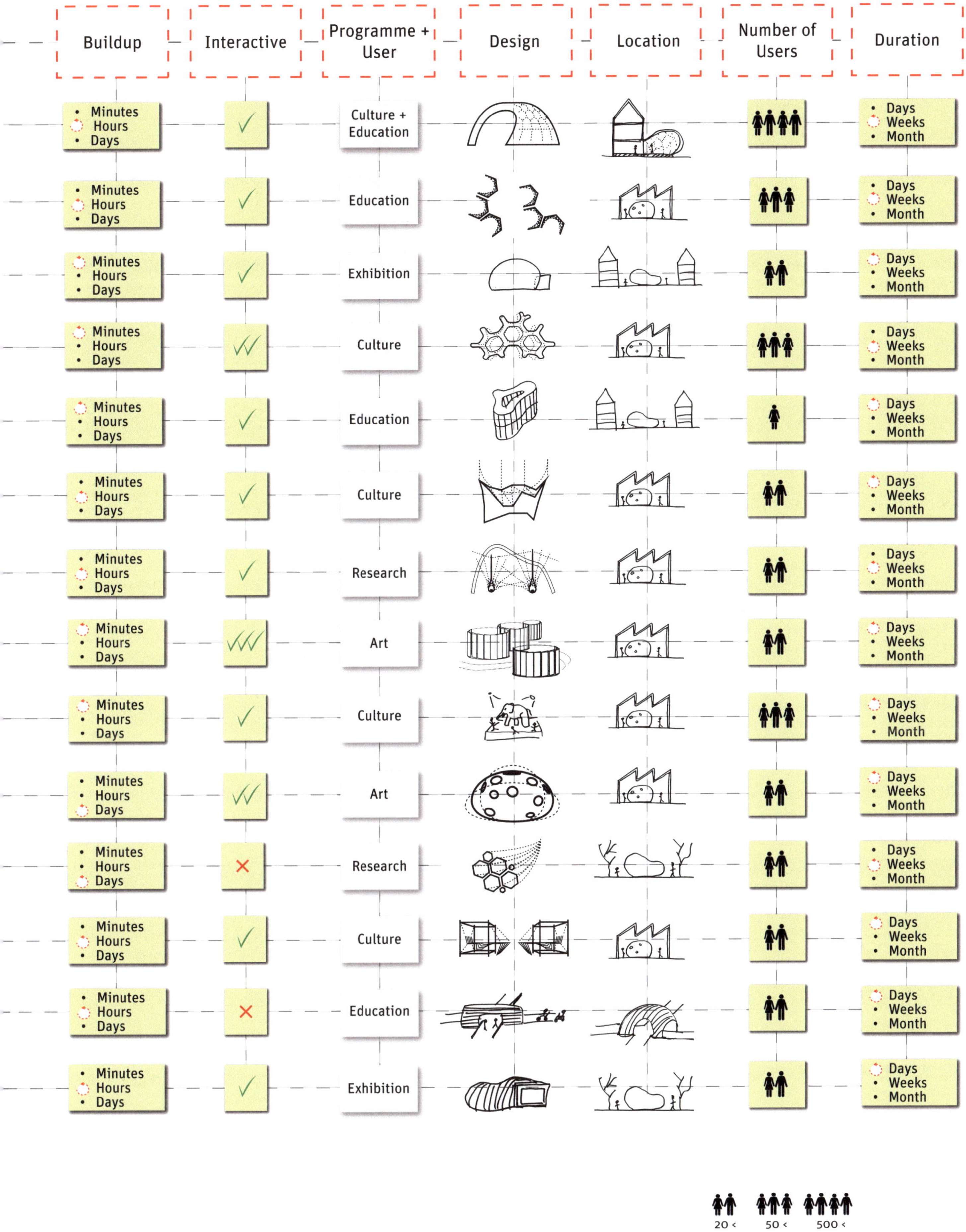

Buildup
Interactive
Programme + User
Design
Location
Number of Users
Duration
Minutes Hours Days
Culture + Education
Days Weeks Month
Minutes Hours Days
Education
Days Weeks Month
Minutes Hours Days
Exhibition
Days Weeks Month
Minutes Hours Days
Culture
Days Weeks Month
Minutes Hours Days
Education
Days Weeks Month
Minutes Hours Days
Culture
Days Weeks Month
Minutes Hours Days
Research
Days Weeks Month
Minutes Hours Days
Art
Days Weeks Month
Minutes Hours Days
Culture
Days Weeks Month
Minutes Hours Days
Art
Days Weeks Month
Minutes Hours Days
Research
Days Weeks Month
Minutes Hours Days
Culture
Days Weeks Month
Minutes Hours Days
Education
Days Weeks Month
Minutes Hours Days
Exhibition
Days Weeks Month
20 <
50 <
500 <

MEDIATING SPACES AS PLATFORMS FOR BRINGING PEOPLE TOGETHER

How does a participatory spatial construct influence the process of bringing people together? Certainly, such spaces cannot resolve all contradictions and inequalities embedded within related processes. Instead, they mediate between the individual spheres of life and create a level playing field for users who can interact on equal terms. On an urban scale, they occupy forgotten sites or temporarily rededicate well-known places and green spaces. The form as such, or the construction type, actually play subordinate roles. More important to us is how these spaces produce interrelations with the given situation of the urban context. A participatory spatial construct can help access antithetical places for intermediary uses, expand them through media, or re-programme them.

These principles can be explained easily according to the example of the circus wagon. Most people know that circus wagons are both space and enclosure. The timber cladding appears ephemeral and slightly improvised, allowing alteration by simple means. The naive aesthetic of these wagons is self-explanatory. They comprise timber construction with glazed bar windows, and the interior is subdivided into different rooms. They are reasonably dimensioned and set on wheels. In the manner of an *architecture parlante*, this type of architecture clearly communicates its function. Such enclosures will soon disappear from the site and appear elsewhere. For some observers, they radiate the refreshing creative energy of a continuous new beginning; for others, the magical restlessness of the circus world. The observation and interpretation of these spaces intersect in the imagination of all users in decisive aspects. This is true for many similarly trivial spaces, such as covered wagons, tents, or bouncy castles. Everybody understands these decisive aspects at a first glance. Without requiring lengthy discussion, they can agree on the employed architectural rhetoric.

Spaces as media

The previously mentioned *architecture parlante* is, perhaps, the most immediate form of a self-explanatory enclosure. The designs of French Revolutionary architecture, such as the planetarium sketches by Étienne-Louis Boullée, describe the building as a walkable sphere that depicts the star-studded sky. This cenotaph places humans in the star-lit centre, becoming part of a virtual experience based on directing light in a highly sophisticated manner across the interior of the spherical building envelope. The historical rotundas of the eighteenth century signalled their function due to their geometry and, as a result, acted as a medium. On the interior of the cylindrical form, observers gazed in wonder at painted panoramas. Thus, the hypothetical reality of an immersive landscape was revealed to them in the form of a vision of a new reality.

The many information pavilions that accompany large-scale construction sites also function as media. One of the better-known examples is the Red Info Box by schneider+schumacher that was located at Berlin's Potsdamer Platz during the 1990s. This building was clearly a temporary one, set on top of stilts and clad in facade elements reminiscent of construction site containers. It comprised a lookout and referred to the visual connections that were under development on the construction site. However, participation is no more than a simulation here. Planning is revealed to visitors who may glance at the unfinished work in an intimate way. They become passive confidants who never actively co-design. Such spaces assign a fixed position to their users. They are limited to the communication of prepackaged impressions where the user serves as consumer.

Participatory methods as strategy of communicative action

Cooperative approaches to urban design-related planning processes can be described as a form of communication, which permits them to be discussed in the context of the theory of communicative action as Jürgen Habermas formulated it. The underlying principle refers to non-hegemonic communication. This method of exchange aims at a cultural process that principally facilitates community. All participants receive the same opportunity to engage in the conversation – on equal footing – which requires a shared vocabulary, opportunities for the initiation of the conversation, actual participation in the conversation, and appropriate quality of interpretation and argumentation (Habermas: 1981).

Simple terms such as "quarter", "place", or "neighbourhood" can trigger completely different perceptions of everyday urban life. Here, it is important to find agreement on the shared meaning of terms that allow individuals to act on equal footing, notwithstanding the professional jargon that every discipline brings to the table and remains unintelligible to the uninitiated.

The space in which such discussions take place can be understood in a similar manner. Its architectural expression should follow the principles of a shared rhetoric. In doing so, it fosters non-hegemonic communication and itself remains free from the exercise of power. We can ask ourselves two simple questions that help categorise such spaces: do they provide all users with equal opportunity with regard to participation and interpretation? Does their aesthetic expression project power?

Aside from the way the building is perceived in functional and programmatic terms, further soft factors are required to declare it a participatory spatial construct. In principle, spaces are free of doubt when they demonstrate clear ephemerality and express aesthetics of improvisation. This relates to spaces that invite users to contribute without fear or anxiety and to be creative. This also relates to sustainable spaces based on simple means of construction that can be used by many people, also for their own ends.

The ideal participatory space is understood by all users directly and in the same manner. Even children can assign to it simple characteristics. It remains free from architectural connotations of power. Naive forms are highly suitable for this purpose, similar to the previously described circus wagon. However, abstract structures can also follow the same rhetoric, as long as the scale remains palpable and the functionality and technology of the space permit intuitive handling. A participatory space recontextualises its surroundings: it confronts accustomed patterns with a new context, and thus provides an opportunity for unbiased observation to all. Such spaces inspire intuitive associations, like the circus wagon or the bouncy castle.

Our comparative matrix reveals that lightweight, transparent structures in particular meet many of these criteria. Inflatable structures allow an objective reading of the construction which, at the same time, triggers an intuitive response. Every child knows how a balloon works and immediately understands the principle of an inflatable building. In the 1960s, avant-garde architects and urban planners designed new, inflatable means of building as a response to new notions of society. The Expo '70 world's fair in Osaka featured numerous inflatable buildings. The most ostentatious of these buildings was the Fuji Group Pavilion by Yutaka Murata, with its yellow inflated double-layer textile building envelope. These buildings certainly are indebted to the historical and societal context of the 1960s and 1970s. They represented a new beginning and a desire for the future. Spaces of this kind and which follow this tradition have, once more, become highly visible and embody similar values.

Design of a participatory spatial construct in teaching and research

For this specific project, the participatory spatial construct is both the research topic and objective. We intended to develop the structure of an inflatable, participatory space within a cooperative process. As a result, the participatory spatial construct as a flexible spatial structure for cooperative learning, research, and action became the goal of an interdisciplinary process. The design and the development of this construct was the product of students of different disciplines from two further European universities. The actors included urban designers, artists, schoolchildren, and interested citizens of different professional and cultural backgrounds. In cooperation with the Architectural Association School of Architecture in London, the Polytechnic University of Madrid, and further actors from civil society, we engaged in this cooperative experiment. Its complexity was highly comparable to the expected diversity of actors one would encounter in practice. Within university pedagogy, the participatory spatial construct serves as a didactic instrument that allows supervisors to convey and research significant mechanisms of effectuation of cooperative processes in a shared manner. Thus, in the field of participatory urban research, insight can be generalised and applied to other disciplines.

Within the phase of concept development, students are tasked with generating detailed user profiles and scenarios of use. For this purpose, prototype spaces of potential in the urban context are researched in order to identify characteristics that permit generalisation. The goal is to propose a highly diverse set of different scenarios of use to initiate and research the potential of effectuation. At the beginning of concept development, the partner universities of our network also follow this procedure in their respective urban context. This allows different types of influence to be observed directly on site and assumptions that permit generalisation to be formulated.

We derive principal requirements from the insight gained within the projects described in this book. The participatory spatial construct is intended to transcend the simple appropriation of existing spaces: instead, these spaces are supposed to be occupied by a stand-alone structure that recontextualises the hierarchies between actors, as well as related spatial connotations. An autonomous space of experience is created that serves as a constant experimental set-up for a diverse range of scenarios.

This concept demonstrates measurable influence on the course of cooperative processes on multiple levels. The space itself fosters communication on equal footing, and thus the success of related approaches. At the same time, the selection of the space, the positioning of the participatory spatial construct in urban space, and the resulting interrelations already constitute an analytical operation. The spatial construct and its deployment on site continually represent the identification with, and the transformation of possible spaces of potential. Critical urban situations are quickly revealed and directly integrated in a cooperative strategy through temporary appropriation. The participatory spatial construct produces comparable datasets for the scientific evaluation of what the places actually are.

URBAN PROGRAMMING AND ARCHITECTURAL SPATIAL CONCEPT

The inflatable construction allows us to reconfigure and temporarily rededicate these spaces in the urban fabric by simple means. New interrelations of meaning and context are the result. The intention is to enable a new look at existing interior and open spaces and, following that, to support the scientific analysis of new contexts. The further development of this spatial function prompts us to ask certain questions: is the space of potential an interior or open space? Is there an interrelation between it and the surrounding context? Is it located at an infrastructure hub or is it relevant in infrastructural terms in any other way? What is the composition of the social structure in the area?

The functional assumptions for this spatial lab are, during the first step, limited to simple criteria. In the steps that follow, these assumptions are verified by a cooperative procedure. The space is intended for a maximum of twenty to thirty occupants. It is supposed to serve cooperative approaches and permit deployment in interior as well as exterior spaces. Further, it needs to allow the inclusion of media in order to communicate programmes and topics and to support the use of projections or monitors. Sensor technology is optional, to capture data on indoor temperature or air quality. The profiles of possible functions, required media, and technological equipment can be tested while in operation and revised as required.

The designing actors operate within a tight network of interrelations that refers to the following questions: how do we develop the space in a cooperative and interdisciplinary manner? How do we gain new insight from the operation of the spatial construct? How do we integrate this insight into defined profiles and criteria? And finally, how do we actively alter the spatial construct in order to meet, change, or amend defined criteria? All involved actors receive equal opportunity to participate in the conversation for purposes of comparable quality of interpretation and argumentation. The newly conceived spaces remain free from institutional connotations of power as usually projected by a building made of stone. Thus, they are supposed to challenge users to develop new approaches and methods of participatory research.

The participatory spatial construct is in constant exchange with the actors, as well as the possible spaces of potential. Insight that is gained in the context of the spatial construct permits generalisation and application to comparable situations in the urban context. The flexibility of the structure supports the continuous adaptation and alteration of spatial configurations. For this purpose, changes to the structure of the space, its accessibility, or technical equipment are supposed to take place immediately and be tested in operation. From this point of view, the space remains incomplete and resembles an open system.

Simple application for urban actors

Its equipment is limited to simple components that permit easy handling in order to be accessible to all actors at any time. The intention is to make available a basic range of equipment for new cooperative approaches. This includes, as previously described, a simple audio and video media system, a projector, to cast images onto the surface of the structure, as well as non-technical tools for writing and sketching. App-based solutions are also possible, to use the cameras of individual smartphones to transmit live recordings and video to the projector and onto the walls of the space, thereby sharing these media. Further technical requirements result from the cooperative process.

The inflatable construction permits interior and exterior spaces alike to be occupied. For this purpose, existing interiors are superimposed with an additional new surface. The surface itself is translucent and allows existing lighting and daylight to pass through the material, into the interior. The surface can be directly used for projections from the exterior or the interior. The structure itself can be moved using controllable ventilators or can be adapted to the geometry on site. Based on sensory data, air quality, temperature, or the number of occupants can be registered and transmitted. The aim is to expand the space of potential using the technological options provided by the participatory spatial construct. For operation, the construct can be set up on the most diverse sites by the actors themselves. Due to the low packing volume, a parcel service can deliver it to other cities or municipalities.

Participatory capacity of the spatial construct

The approach demonstrates how participatory and scientific methods can be combined in order to lead to new insight in both areas. In the field of participatory research, this refers to the development and application of cooperative methods, but also to research based on applying participatory strategies. The spatial construct can accommodate both options. It can foster participatory research and it represents the outcome of participatory methods. Participatory research can also be understood as the development of interrelations and networks. Interrelations are created between researchers and supervisors, between universities and communities, between experts and laypeople, between adults and children, and between working space and living culture. The construct creates an independent system of reference that relates to its users and its surroundings, while permitting alteration of its system as soon as references change. The participatory spatial construct offers room for discussion between different interest groups. In this manner, the development of interrelations can be observed and measured very well to evaluate its effectiveness.

The evaluation of the participatory capacity of the spatial construct demonstrates how all criteria of the matrix interact. They can be present to differing degrees, but it is important that specific characteristics are present in all. Our comparative matrix displays how a series of quantifiable characteristics enables the creation of new typologies. The functional programme is directly derived from the local calendar of events, the actions and measures undertaken, as well as the cooperation between actors. For this purpose, the functional requirements are not considered uses in the conventional manner of a functional programme, but instead, they primarily describe the underlying processes. The spaces can be used for workshops, conferences, or seminars. Exhibitions or lectures can take place there, as well as cultural presentations, cookery courses, or dance lessons. A diverse set of uses can typically occur on the same day or even at the same time. Everybody has something to show; anybody can pick a chair and sit in with the group.

Parameters for a participatory spatial construct typology

››› The structure needs to support an open functional programme to ensure uses can take place according to formats such as workshops, round-table discussions, impulse lectures, cooking and dining events, or other cultural presentations.

››› A flexible site is beneficial since structures can occupy different areas within the urban context. Setting up the space requires only a small amount of time and expenditure. The construct should be independent of the ground or soil conditions on site, ceiling heights, or traffic infrastructure. The space should respond to user input or external data on temperature, air quality, or number of occupants.

››› The exterior form of the building follows a discernible logic in terms of temporality, function, and construction. Easy assembly and disassembly are required to allow laypeople to set up the space. Low packaging volume guarantees easy transport.

››› The construct is comprised of components that permit separate assembly. Modularity allows the structure to be connected to an existing building. An open range of media equipment creates an interface for all participants to simply project and communicate information by using video or audio files.

››› The participatory spatial construct does not require any dramatisation of an architectural syntax in terms of orientation, perspective, or lighting. It is free of excessive complexity and representational elements. Instead, spatial sequences are clearly legible and can be experienced intuitively in terms of scale. Exterior impressions from the surrounding environment related to noise, smell, or lighting can reach the interior. Access is not regulated and is always barrier-free. Passers-by receive a spontaneous impression of how and why the space functions due to their "intuitive experience" of the space related to its techniques, functionalities, and dimensions.

››› The participatory spatial construct supports a dialogue with its surroundings and responds to urban programming. It creates a lookout post and a point of contact for interested individuals who happen to pass by, coincidentally. As a result, the spatial construct becomes an ally that supports its users in their redefinition of urban space. The spatial construct establishes new connections between open spaces and infrastructures, between interior and exterior, between public and private, as well as between individual actors. It occupies antithetical domains, connects them, or rededicates them for a limited amount of time. The actual form and composition of the participatory spatial construct remains indeterminate. Each structure constitutes a new alternative within a broad range of possibilities of producing similar characteristics. In principle, spaces are suitable that display unambiguous ephemerality. Beyond that, they express an aesthetic of improvisation. They comprise sustainable spaces based on simple construction types that permit use by many parties. Most of all, they welcome freedom of expression without fear or anxiety, and inspire creative contribution.

››› A mediating, communicating process always deals with providing all actors with barrier-free access to decisive information. The participatory spatial construct is a platform for cooperative action. It provides room for discussion. It can reach a diverse set of actors in their own living environment. It can sensitise actors with regard to the interests of the other. Such spaces are clearly comprehensible and intuitive. The range of functions they offer corresponds to an architectural rhetoric that everyone can understand, free from connotations of power.

Lisbon project profile

Project initiators

Teatro Aberto Lisbon: João Lourenço and Vera San Payo de Lemos
T2 Spatialwork Ltd., London, directors: Theo Lorenz, Tanja Siems

Partners and participating actors

Theo Lorenz, Interprofessional Studio (AAIS), Architectural Association School of Architecture, London
Institute for Urban Design: Tanja Siems, Elli Börgener, Mohamed Fezazi, Alexia Radounikli, Bergische University Wuppertal
Paula Cadima, Sustainable Environmental Design (SED), Architectural Association School of Architecture, London

Project goal

Development of a comprehensive cultural urban open space for the Teatro Aberto in Lisbon's Bairro Azul neighbourhood. Conducted within an international partnership between different disciplines from socio-cultural and planning institutions. The theatre is located directly adjacent to the Praça de Espanha infrastructural hub and near the internationally renowned Fundação Gulbenkian. The park of the Fundação Gulbenkian, which offers room for contemporary Portuguese art, temporary exhibitions, and colloquiums, as well as a concert hall with orchestra and choir, is supposed to be connected to the theatre by means of landscape planning. It is therefore essential, in spatial terms, to open the public area that borders the theatre, and thus the theatre building itself, to the city.

Important data and facts on the origin of the theatre

The Teatro Aberto opened on 24 February 2002 with a performance of Ibsen's *Peer Gynt* (director: João Lourenço, composer: Eurico Carrapatoso). It is a new building, owned by the municipality of Lisbon. It replaces an older building, previously located on a different site adjacent to Praça de Espanha, that belonged to Grupo 4, an independent group of actors and directors. The municipality of Lisbon had offered a site for the construction of the building and its use within a limited timeframe. Based on their own funding and design, Grupo 4 erected a simple building, yet with adequate technical equipment. It was opened on 25 May 1976 in the pioneering spirit of the Carnation Revolution, which ended forty years of dictatorship in Portugal. The Novo Grupo collective was formed in 1982 by two former members of Grupo 4, João Lourenço and Irene Cruz, together with former members of other independent theatre groups. It was home to their partnership until 2001.

In 1984 the city of Lisbon intended to redesign the entire Praça de Espanha and build a new structure for the Banco de Portugal on the property occupied by the Teatro Aberto. The theatre needed to be demolished for this purpose. The negotiations between the directorship of the Novo Grupo and the city's mayor at the time led to the following solution: the city of Lisbon would build a new Teatro Aberto at Praça de Espanha. Within the project, the Novo Grupo as experts, worked with the architects commissioned by the city. The Novo Grupo then received the right to use the new building as their place of work for twenty-five years. The fact is noted that cultural life in Portugal and the city of Lisbon owes the existence of the new theatre most of all to the vision, stamina, expertise, and negotiation skills of director João Lourenço, who founded the theatre and served as its creative director. The theatre is excited about the future collaboration with the students to creatively collaborate and conceptually transfer the spirit of this place into the urban context.

Project timeline

Analysis phase: cooperative strategies including workshops, lectures, interviews, and surveys with experts and important local actors (1 year);
Concept development phase: concept development, design, and realisation strategies for the theatre and the surrounding urban context (1 year);
Application phase: redesign of the building through temporary structures, testing structures in cooperation with different actors from practice, research, and teaching, in the context of international festivals, local events, summer schools, and workshops (1 year).

PARTICIPATORY OUTLOOK: AN INTERDISCIPLINARY CONVERSATION ON COLLECTIVE INITIATIVES

FEATURING **VERA SAN PAYO DE LEMOS** (VSPDL), **THEO LORENZ** (TL) AND **TANJA SIEMS** (TS)

It is the aim of this publication to develop practicable guidelines within the framework of a participatory and applied urban mediation, in the way of a creative and open-ended experiment without adhering to rigid and established rules. To achieve this in a convincing manner, it is necessary to substantially expand the framework of the discussed topic. For this purpose the following methods will be applied: it is necessary to consider not only realised and past projects and design-task as case studies, but to also speculate on how these individual approaches could develop into future projects.

This should not occur according to hypothetical and generic descriptions, but through using a specific model of actual project development examples. This applied approach has already been described in the previous chapter about the "participatory spatial construct" as a temporary and non-site-specific instrument. It is an additional basic principle to this extended approach to look beyond the field of the planning disciplines and to set up new initiatives with other professions, exchange knowledge, and to learn from each other through site-specific projects.

An example of such an applied initiative can be seen in the envisioned collaboration between the Institute for Urban Design at the Bergische University, the Interprofessional Studio and the Master's of Sustainable and Environmental Designs at the Architectural Association in London and the pioneer theatre the Teatro Aberto in Lisbon. This conversation shows the common ground between the different participants and demonstrates that an approach based on initiatives and shared principles can be implemented across the genres, and has the potential to achieve sustainable and innovative results.

TL "To achieve changes, one has to act." This is the basic principle of any collective creative work. Within such a framework mere ad hoc activism however is not enough if one wants to achieve lasting change. To allow multiple voices to be heard and to enable sustainable action, it is necessary to develop a systematic, yet open framework that gives such ideas a "home" without erecting obstacles and bureaucracy. "What do you have to do to change things?"

TS This could be an interesting theoretical concept if applied to projects and collaboration within an urban context. What forms of collaboration can be developed between different municipalities? Could, through communal networking, as for example took place within our "Bergisch Project" in Wuppertal, Remscheid, Solingen and its Region, project concepts that were developed by one city equally be applied to a different municipality? One could re-evaluate such developed frameworks within a different context and create through different approaches additional improvements and feedback within communal structures for a similar project.

The aspect of the localisation of a project within a "house", as the theatre provides, affording a reliable and available institution and its infrastructure, that guarantees a lasting and comparable quality as a framework, remains an important approach to the project. The location of upcoming events, the "venue", as demonstrated by the projects of the Interprofessional Studio as well as the "Bergisch Project", is a significant factor within the quest to find a common ground.

VSPdL A systematic and open framework would for example entail the openness to develop partnerships and thus the possibility to collaborate with other theatres and institutions. This would enable us to show plays that were developed at our venue at other playhouses. However, one would have to assume that these other theatres co-finance the production. This should encompass not only the creative process, but also the overall logistics if the production is shown at different playhouses, in a different city. It would be implicit that, for example, the set design is designed from the outset as easy to transport, not only because of the related cost, but also because every theatre has a different technical set-up.

TS If you want to avoid using a city hall or other institutional places of assembly for participatory events, as we tend to do, spaces that are available for this purpose and feature the required infrastructure and logistics, in contrast to an established theatre, are different every time. The participatory spatial construct as a mobile module is an important element of such a framework. The question that remains is an interesting one: which tools within the framework can guarantee consistent quality, as it is in the case of a theatre set-up with a clear infrastructure comprised of stage, with a set-up of spatial sound and lighting systems etc., yet without limiting the desired level of a spatial openness?

VSPdL Obstacles often arise due to the gap between the different generations of artists and their different points of view. Also, financing mostly implies bureaucracy. Where do we get the money from to realise projects? Which application forms need to be submitted? When will we receive the funds?

TS In urban development projects, many of the obstacles lie primarily in mediation and communication between the many actors. Generational changes are less apparent in terms of individuals, but more apparent within existing legislations, authoritarian frameworks, and bureaucracies that are slow and persistent.

A necessary challenge lies in replacing these with new and more flexible frameworks and instruments that prevent you from reverting to the old way of doing things. It is a constant challenge to find a balance to determine a dependable framework that permits verification and within which multifaceted ideas can be developed in a non-bureaucratic manner. Once this balance has been established, it becomes simpler to create a wide-ranging support network, and thus produce synergies and new approaches in relation to new funding opportunities.

TL Is this approach applicable independently of genre or discipline? In particular, when it comes to creative disciplines, it has been consistently demonstrated that applied and systematic approaches best support cultural and creative tasks when they are not designed in a predictable and rigid manner, as that would limit the diversity of the results. How can we compare participatory approaches in the realms of the theatre, of spatial design, and of urban design? What can we learn from each other in a process of exchanging knowledge? And, most of all, how can different approaches complement each other?

VSPdL In order to produce a play or build a building, the project must be described, the application must be submitted, and the costs must be calculated. Whether we receive funding that allows us to realise a project, remains open. Mostly, the realisation of a project is highly dependent on the partners, the circumstances, and the approaches that emerge within the process. You can present a summary of a play, but it is difficult to foresee how the performance will be. It is exclusively a result of collaborative design on the part of the artists, established through rehearsals. The same is true for the materials that are required to build the stage set: which materials will actually be used? How expensive will they be at any given time? Creative work is always a process, a form of togetherness. That is why it is difficult to precisely describe the result in advance.

TS Creative work is a promise made that requires building trust among all those who are involved. This could be archived by projecting and visualising ideas but also by creating ideas through substantiated basic preparations. It is also the case when to accentuate these ideas, by showing best practice projects which could be self-build project examples showing the previous demonstrable successes or other similar case studies.

VSPdL Realising a performance requires participatory approaches from different disciplines: dramaturgy, set design, costumes, lighting, sound, music, video, choreography, acting, design (posters, flyers, programme booklets, programme leaflets, commercials, press sheet, online communication) and directors coordinating all disciplines. Spatial design is comparable to set design and how directors organise the actors' movements on stage. Directors and dramaturgy define how actors inhabit this space. During rehearsals, everyone comes together and develops new ideas and solutions. Cultural and creative tasks are enabled by applied and systematic approaches. The diversity of results is related to the dramaturgy of a play and the way that a team of artists interprets the play within the rehearsal process.

TS In terms of interdisciplinarity, architecture and urban design on the one hand and the theatre on the other display certain differences. All of this happens within a limited timeframe and, as an immediate form of experience, permits application to a successive project. These are the decisive advantages of playhouses and the performances. Architectural and urban design processes often last for years and rehearsals are non-existent. We attempt to structure these moments of rehearsal within participatory events and constructs. The applied and systematic approaches that our publication presents are an indispensable precondition to achieve such processes similar to rehearsals in the theatre world that can produce open and creative results.

TL What inspires us to act? What responsibility do we have in our field of work? What are the related historical and cultural dimensions?

VSPdL Communication as an actual form of sharing questions with others – questions that are inspired by a play and, in return, inspire people to reflect, to think with an open mind, to empathise, to adopt new perspectives – is an important participatory element. This also informs the selection of plays, the compilation of the play schedule, as well as the forms of communication (media, internet, post-performance conversations with the audience) and communication materials (advertisements, posters, flyers, programme leaflets, programme booklets, performance photos available at the ticket office, foyer commercials).

TS All too often, architectural or urban design tasks are viewed as solutions to challenges or problems formulated beforehand. It is desirable to expand this notion and, similar to the theatre, formulate a research or design question first, in order to inspire reflection and thereby open up new perspectives. This is indispensable for a sincere participative process. Here as well, involved actors need to be confronted with open questions and suggestions. Communicating these processes is a fundamental issue. However, in the field of planning, the use of media for this purpose is neither common practice nor visually comprehensible in the manner of how theatres and accompanying media achieve it. Unfortunately, communication is often viewed as a necessary add-on and not as an integrated and valuable expansion of a project.

VSPdL In terms of historical and cultural trends, nowadays the range of cultural activities in Lisbon is very broad. Theatres no longer have ensembles and most theatres develop their programmes based on productions by different artist teams. These productions are performed three to ten times and then concluded. Mostly, the audience is composed of members of the theatre scene. The Teatro Aberto is one of the few playhouses that presents a production for at least two months, to give a broader audience the opportunity to see a play. Most of all, this happens to fully utilise the team's work, as well as the public funding. When you rehearse a play for two months, it should remain on the play schedule for two months as well and attract a greater audience. The theatre defines itself as an "author's theatre"; the performances are of plays by contemporary playwrights. Currently, the general trend is to produce popular plays, projects, rewrites, and other types of performances.

TS The kind of specialisation found in the "author's theatre" can be considered as something very valuable. A specific identity is capable of reaching a certain depth within a particular topical area. It is important to ensure that specialisation does not lead to isolation, but instead, to intersections with other trends and ideas. The Teatro Aberto in Lisbon is very interesting to us as a collaborative partner for the Urban Design Institute in Wuppertal and the Interprofessional Studio in London precisely due to this openness. Such intersecting networks demonstrate their success according to different scales. Identities of cities or their districts, quarters, and neighbourhoods become particularly important when they serve to initiate further development, and thus increase in range and innovation capacity.

TL In terms of cultural frameworks, what do we need in order to act? How can culture unfold, unshackled by bureaucracy and slow procedures? Which alternative frameworks can foster open-ended results?

VSPdL Alternative frameworks mostly comprise partnerships. A network of like-minded people can co-finance a production and include it in their programme, while cooperatively working on the production concept. The bureaucratic limitations and slow procedures result from the need to submit applications for funding to the Ministry of Culture. For this purpose, many details that are impossible to foresee require precise description, while jury decisions are, most of the time, oriented on fashion trends. A further shortcoming is that, often, funding is not provided in a timely manner.

TS The solutions to these challenges are related to the hierarchy embedded in connections and partnerships. Partnership on equal terms, based on a diverse set of shared and multi-faceted goals, permits all involved actors to engage in the design process and become creative actors. If structures of dependency are present, such as in the case of financial limitations, liberties become constrained, and thus creative results as well. Therefore, one of the main tasks of each creative process is to achieve this form of equality and consider it the foremost task of all. Even if we can't avoid all hierarchical structures, it is nevertheless possible to minimise their effect or even use them to our advantage within broadly and openly structured partnerships.

TL In terms of basic preparations: what is the relevance of analysis and research in the development of sustainable creative projects and their implementation?

TS In particular, regarding the previous question on frameworks, sustainable basic preparatory work, research, and analysis are the preconditions for developing a diverse set of projects according to a broad knowledge base and in an informed manner. Knowledge is the best tool to overcome gridlocked structures. The described case studies and best practice work in research, teaching, and practice presented in this book make this particularly clear.

VSPdL In regard to research to create and compile the programme of a play, it is important to read and analyse various plays, or to receive suggestions from a network of translators of contemporary plays. Those could be for example provided by the German International Theatre Institute (ITI). This institute organises different kinds of workshops and, recently, it launched an online platform for the exchange of translators. To conduct research effectively, reading theatre magazines, visiting different festivals, and travelling to events are all very important.

TL In terms of knowledge conveyed through text, image, and design: how is knowledge conveyed in the context of each project? Vera, could you dwell on the strengths and weaknesses of media such as text, images, and design, in relation to how to use these media in order to sustainably advance knowledge. How can we use them as basic components for results that exceed expectations and produce serious and durable results?

Everybody who has worked for, or in a performance learns something new. We are confronted with new challenges, need to solve unexpected problems, and develop new ideas. To convey knowledge to a broad audience, materials are developed for each play (flyers with play summaries, programme leaflets, programme booklets, commercials for the theatre website). They are intended to make the potential audience interested in the play and contribute to post-performance tasks.

Programme booklets are available for free download at our website, featuring a new design and online links. While a play is included in the programme, one or two conversations take place between the team and the audience regarding the performance following the Sunday afternoon presentation. The theatre works with a professional designer: she creates the different materials and, additionally, cooperates with a professional director who films the commercials and also documents the performance for the theatre archive. Sometimes both, coming from different disciplines, create elements that are integrated into the dramatisation at a later date (e.g., text or video footage).

TL Can you also emphasise how important the artistic and professional precision and quality of these media are. What is the "package" of information that is required for the development, implementation, and post-performance tasks of projects and how are they comparable? In that process how can we reach a broad audience or even get the audience involved in this process?

VSPdL Our theatre offers walking tours and conversations with the technical and artistic teams to interested individuals, schoolchildren, or students who want to know more about the professions involved in the theatre or want to know what it is like behind the scenes. Every year, two students from the department of dramatics and communication studies at the Faculty of Humanities of the University of Lisbon work as interns at the Teatro Aberto. Some of them stay with us and, after concluding their studies, work as stage assistants or assistant directors, or in the archive, where we organise and digitise all materials as historical documents for purposes of research or studies.

In order to reach a broader audience, we invite for the final rehearsals prior to the premiere, representatives from associations, groups, and non-profit organisations, and discuss the performance with them. This special audience is integrated into the communication process and acts as a multiplier. The theatre also offers audience tickets that allow visitors and one family member to each purchase a theatre ticket at a discount. Prior to each premiere, these audience members receive information on the current play. There are also discounts for schoolchildren, students, seniors, and groups. During post-performance activities, the materials are stored in the archive and performance reviews are discussed. This alternatively happens on the occasion of presenting the play at another playhouses, or at a festival, and thus in a different context.

TS It is interesting to see which parallels exist in the theatre and urban design disciplines in terms of instruments used for the preparation, implementation, and revision of concepts and projects. Preparation is mostly about basic research and the contextualisation of a project. Here, instruments are oriented, most of all, towards producing material that allows related tasks to be scientifically substantiated. The cooperative instruments for implementation tasks are mainly oriented towards conveying, mediating, or triggering action and participation among actors and the audience. The review process deals with integrating experiences and lessons learned into a knowledge pool for future projects and developments, in order to make instruments readily available in the “urban design toolbox”.

TL How can we establish facts through manufacturing objects? Durable artefacts such as buildings exemplify the outcomes of initiatives and movements. Should the creation of spaces, as in the case of the Teatro Aberto, built by artists, become part of the applied tools, in order to visually create precedents and realise far-reaching results? How important is the topic of “designing the design process”, which was also the underlying principle of the participation pavilion for Brussels?

VSPdL The original theatre was planned and built in the 1970s by João Lourenço and a group of actors, based on their own initiative, after the events of the revolution in Portugal. Following the success of this free theatre, from the 1990s onwards and despite all the political and bureaucratic processes related to public construction projects, they continued promoting the construction of a permanent building. The current Teatro Aberto was opened in 2002. It comprises two stages. The Sala Azul, or blue hall, features 400 seats in an amphitheatre arrangement and an orchestra pit for sixty musicians. It is suitable for dramaturgy, music, dance, film, and opera performances and presentations. The Sala Vermelha, or red hall, comprises 100 seats and is used for limited or experimental productions. Both can be programmed in different ways. We use the foyer for colloquiums, exhibitions, and book presentations. Our theatre further houses a workshop where parts of the stage sets are built and another workshop for creating, cleaning, and maintaining costumes. Twenty years after opening the theatre, João Lourenço made suggestions for the renovation and “green remodelling” of the theatre and its spaces.

TS This long-term process, in a certain way, resulted in the fact that we are now starting a joint initiative in collaboration with diverse institutions and their multi-layered objectives and positionings. We are actually building upon what João’s group of actors had created in the 1970s. Based on their self-initiated project for a performative building, they established facts which, much later, led to the current building and the related new ideas for remodelling it. In return, these ideas are the basis for the current discussion and our future teamwork networking during the project.

TL Speaking of networking and collaboration: our previous questions dealt with commonalities and differences regarding approaches in different disciplines. Besides the various given backgrounds, we can develop a project that transcends disciplinary boundaries in the format of an initiative. How, in this case, can disciplines learn from each another? How can we expand the related instruments of the disciplines? How can we achieve a result that is more than an assembly of parts and makes innovation visible?

TS The cornerstone of this partnership and the initiative needs to comprise a broad selection of mutual interests and overlapping objectives. However, a necessary degree of differences and individual, professional specialisation is required to learn from each other. And also approach the task which lies ahead together in a greater and more audacious way than anyone could attempt on their own. Most of all, it is a shared endeavour for creating new things and generating lasting effects that inspire all of us.

VSPdL This partnership will newly develop many intersecting opportunities. We can jointly design architectural concepts for the renovation of the existing building in its urban context. We can also jointly develop a festival and explore new approaches. These activities can lead to dramatisations and performances created in collaboration with international students and institutions.

TL Our conclusion: finally, what else is there to say?

TS This conversation shows that the conversation itself

is one of the most important instruments. In its brevity, it isn't required to offer comprehensive answers. Instead, it is supposed to trigger questions and offer inspiration for further discourse and action. The significant precondition for this is that institutions, groups, or individuals are always capable of responding to initiatives with project-specific connections and approaches. Establishing a broad range of interests, networks, knowledge, and instruments is also the goal of our experimental approach to teaching and research. While this abundance of information and data can often seem unmanageable, conversations and specific applied projects give them focus. Each expansion of the area of discussion is not only welcome, but also significant. In my opinion, this is the most important objective of a participatory process. Actors should not only contribute to a project once, but instead, feel invited to contribute to an ongoing conversation that sustainably expands the existing scope of ideas and networks.

VSPdL Your teaching methods – the ones I witnessed – include research conducted by the students on site. In doing this, the students gain sensual experiences, speak with people, and learn how these spaces are used and inhabited. This activity on site, the act of witnessing the space and the people within it, and the sensual experience of space itself, are all foundational methods for the development and elaboration of an interdisciplinary project. Much of it reminds me of the images and dialogue of the introduction to the reading primer by the theologian and teacher Comenius, titled *Orbis sensualium pictus (The Visible World in Pictures).* Teachers and students are in an open field; all pathways are open to them. Behind the teacher, we see the city, society, order, buildings, and civilisation. Above them, we see the sun, clarity, illuminating thought, and knowledge. Teaching is like a road, along which steps are followed by pauses to reach one's destination. The walking stick is a symbol of experience, of a type of knowledge based on experience. The teacher possesses experience, because they have travelled widely, treading many roads. Teacher and student travel this road together and talk. The teacher leads, providing the student with orientation. They travel the world, survey all things (particular, empirical, sensual, by perception), and give them names (abstract, by using language, providing words that guide their thoughts).

I admire this dialogue for its progressive and pragmatic concept of wisdom and knowledge. Knowledge is a global goal, but it is divided into specific objectives. Knowledge means everything that is necessary to adequately understand something (to listen and to read), to adequately express something (to write and to speak), and to do justice to it and act. That reminds me of your introduction and what you mentioned earlier in our conversation: "What do you have to do to change things? You have to act."

A DICTIONARY: TERMINOLOGY OF METHODS RELATING TO THE URBAN DESIGN PROCESS

4

 # Brainstorming and Brainwriting: brainstorming refers to the spontaneous utterance of ideas in a group without dismissive criticism. This helps to collect numerous ideas relating to a certain problem. Participants in the group can help each other to form new idea combinations. Every idea is welcome; it is not necessarily the quality of proposals that matters, but rather the quantity. It is not permitted to voice criticism or self-criticism of proposals. Everybody in the group is allowed to pick up somebody else's idea and continue it. As opposed to brainstorming, in brainwriting the thoughts and ideas are not communicated verbally but are written in a collective logbook. In brainwriting, the participants note their ideas and proposals on their own paper; this gives everyone a chance to reflect on the subject. In brainwriting, the participants also share their ideas and use this process to mutually inspire each other. *(Source: Fürst/Scholles, 2008)*

 # Cause-and-Effect Analysis: this type of analysis is also called an Ishikawa diagram or a fishbone diagram. It is a simple method of investigating and determining the causes of problems. Potential causes that trigger certain effects are subdivided into primary and secondary causes. This leads to a graphic, fishbone-shaped structure of causes that provides a general overview. In this way, it is possible to identify all causes of the problem and show the dependencies between them; the resulting diagram is easy to understand and makes the problem easy to comprehend. The results can be presented directly and form the basis of work to be carried out. *(Source: Drews/Hillebrand, 2007)*

 # Checklist technique: this technique can be used to list tasks and processes, which are then carried out in the listed sequence. There are standardised lists that are used as such or in modified form. Checklists reveal thought processes and tasks and are used as reminders or documentary evidence. When tasks on this list are carried out, this is visually documented. When it is necessary to justify a decision process, it is useful to employ this method. This means that all aspects of a decision are checked and remain objectively comparable. The checklist technique is a valuable instrument for personal organisation and for quality control; it enables the creation of unequivocal and transparent evidence. *(Source: Simon Walter, 2004)*

 # Citizens' jury: the members of a citizens' jury are selected randomly and produce a "citizens' report" that is based on their own experience and knowledge. The participants make recommendations and assessments from the point of view of the common good. They do not have to represent special interests in the process because there are experts who can be relied upon for specialist issues. Usually, the proposals contained in the citizens' report are accepted without bias by those inhabitants of the project's catchment area who are not entitled to take part and are also often accepted by politicians and administrators and adopted in the ongoing planning process. *(Source: Peter C. Dienel, 2002)*

 # Coding: in quantitative social research coding is described as the encryption of information, which can be done using figures or letters. In this process it is important to establish allocation rules in order to be able to decrypt the information again. Theoretical coding is an analysis method that can develop reasoned theories in the form of codes on the basis of the collected data. The process of coding creates a conceptualisation of the collected data. Within the coding steps, the constant and systematic comparison of similar and different events in the data material is essential. *(Source: Uwe Flick, 2012)*

 # Cooperation methods: these are applied methods that create the basis and precondition for joint action and thereby lead to certain cooperation objectives being achieved. The cooperation methods include all forms of institutionalised communication, such as consultations, agreements, conference resolutions, and contracts. The cooperation has a defined end and is carried on until the prerequisites for the realisation of the jointly defined objectives are in place. *(Source: Jörn Altmann, online reference)*

 # Cost-Benefit Analysis: this is a popular method for evaluating different action alternatives and measures in the planning and implementation processes of projects. In order to be able to carry out a cost-benefit analysis, parameters such as likely costs, probable benefits, and possible income are set in relation to each other. After comparing the expenditure and result of the alternatives under consideration, those that most effectively fulfil the overall objective are selected. This is an important tool for decision-making and allows a better assessment of successes and risks. Cost-benefit analysis is primarily used in investment planning; however, it is also of significant help in the design and implementation of urban development. *(Source: Drews/Hillebrand, 2007)*

 # Cost-Utility Analysis: this method is used to evaluate alternatives in order to make the best possible decision in a rational manner. When the evaluation of alternatives does not primarily rely on concrete facts and figures, it is possible that subjective parameters come into play. An important part of the weighted sum analysis is that alternatives and variants are compiled in the form of a list. The following steps must be observed: firstly, the list must not be too long, otherwise the method takes too long. Secondly, evaluation criteria have to be defined; this should be a list of approximately ten criteria that sum up the requirements for the product. Next, a percentage is allocated to each criterion, which reflects the importance of that criterion. Then the criteria are evaluated by allocating points to them, from very good to inadequate. The sum of the individual weightings reflects the total number of points for the respective alternative. The best alternative is the one that has the highest number of points after evaluation. *(Source: Meise/Volwahsen, 1980)*

 # Diagrammatic illustration: a diagram is a graphic illustration of facts and information. Diagrammatic illustrations are used to communicate content such as statistics or facts in an easily interpretable way. Examples are histograms, bar charts, line and pie charts, and also more complex illustrations – for example those that involve facts relating to time and space. A certain degree of abstraction and reduction is necessary to be able to convey complex facts, circumstances, and problems. In the field of architecture and town planning, this method can be used to visualise complex processes and facts, dependencies, and interactions. It follows that different levels of information can be illustrated at the same time. By applying the reduction process to the information to be presented, the diagram creator may discover new findings. *(Source: Bauer/Ernst, online reference)*

 # Documentation: methods of documentation and publication can be used to record useful facts about research approaches, planning and building processes; as examples of best practice they can also be used in teaching, research, and practice. Such methods can be used to make written or otherwise recorded information on a subject retrievable. Examples are articles in reference books and journals, as well as information archived in a database. In architecture and urban development, this method has numerous advantages that are critical to the transfer of knowledge: one of them is that a detailed and structured archive of information makes it possible to retrieve that project information at a later point for another project. In this way, documented information is helpful in the context of future design processes. Furthermore, it is a legal requirement to retain plan documents for a certain period. In the case of defects occurring, it is useful to be able to refer back to information relating to the project; retention of such information may even be a mandatory requirement. Disadvantages result only from incomplete or inaccurate documentation. *(Source: Wilhelm Gaus, 2003)*

 # Documentation through photos: this method produces high-quality evidence and can also be used to supplement quantitative methods of recording information. The method is used to establish background material also for the purpose of presentations. Photos can record facts, such as the condition of a building, as well as changing processes; they capture impressions of places that we cannot get from maps or written descriptions. Photographic evidence can be digital or analogue and is a helpful resource during a later evaluation of contexts and situations. Photo documentation captures changes occurring over a longer period, documenting them for comparison. *(Source: Eichhorn/Nage, 2009)*

 # Flowchart: a flow diagram is a graphic device to illustrate and analyse the sequence of actions and processes. This device can be used to analyse, structure, and optimise existing systems, or develop new ones. In this diagram, process lines between connected symbols indicate the path and the sequence in which certain tasks and processes are carried out. This creates a simplified, schematic view of the system. These diagrams are well suited to the design of buildings; for example, by evaluating day-to-day or work processes it is possible to make statements about new uses of the building. The method is also used to support the documentation and presentation of processes or results. *(Source: Georg Schreyögg, 2012)*

 # Mapping: the mapping method is an important component of geographic research and town planning and helps to analyse space structures. Mapping can be used to illustrate the contents of structural, infrastructural, and free-shape objects and to highlight their deficiencies and qualities. In this way, mapping creates the basis for planning and controlling future urban developments. Mapping is one of the diagrammatic illustration methods that visually presents data, including the spatial relationship between various data, and selects, interprets, and highlights important aspects. This method is used to illustrate complex urban development content and relate it to different plan sections. It is a useful tool for evaluating analysis in the creation of urban development designs. *(Source: Georg Glasze, 2015)*

 # Mental maps: these are used to capture individual impressions, usually not to scale, which are subjective and potentially strongly deviate from reality. The term is used in the literature on urban and regional planning. A mental map is a type of map that translates into drawings the subjective idea held by one or several people of the perceived environment or a certain spatial situation at a certain time. Owing to the simplified representation of the complex reality, these maps can make understanding easier. They are a good method for describing, investigating, and evaluating a spatial situation. *(Source: Frithjof Benjamin Schenk, 2002)*

 # Mind mapping: this is a working method for ordering ideas, thoughts, or notes in a clear way. It is a very effective procedure that increases the flexibility of thinking. Mind maps can be used as part of a presentation in order to illustrate the source of inspiration and thought processes involved. As a rule, people develop their own presentation style over time. The advantage of this method is that no special materials are needed and that it is uncomplicated. To look at, mind maps consist of labelled tree diagrams that show connections and links between items. The result is an easy-to-read map with an image-based illustration of thoughts, which immediately makes the key subject recognisable. The point is that not only are the thoughts themselves expressed, but also the relationship between the various thoughts and their importance in the mind map. Mind mapping is an illustration method that can be applied in various fields and combined with many different working methods. *(Source: Higgins/Wiese, 1996)*

 # Moderation and Mediation: moderation can be used to support group work and should be neutral and stimulating. The method can be used to structure and guide discussion and work processes, with the aim of achieving satisfactory objectives for the whole team. The moderator involved in this process needs to apply a methodical approach, asking structured and inspiring questions that do not control but help to stimulate the discussion. It is important for the moderator to hold back with their own opinion so that the individual participants are free to contribute their knowledge to the discussion; the moderator should support and facilitate the communication of the group's ideas and proposals. This can be done by collecting input from the participants on small cards that are attached to suitable panels ready for discussion by the group. In this process, the suggestions from the participants are categorised, ordered, and finally evaluated in a creative dialogue with the aim of formulating shared proposals for a solution at the end of the process.

In contrast to moderation, mediation is a method that aims to find solutions where there is a conflict of interest. Mediation is a method for formulating results and finding alternatives and in this way differs from the traditional conflict resolution process. This process opens up new ways of communication and brings to light the true interests of the different parties. The focus of mediation is on those involved taking responsibility, because they themselves have the greatest competence to end their dispute and to find the best solution to their problem. Encouraging the parties to assume responsibility in working out a solution is an important objective of this method. In this way the team can jointly develop solutions that are satisfactory for all involved. The idea is not to come to a poor compromise, but to find an overall solution that benefits all parties and takes account of their interests. *(Source: Apel/Kettner, 1996)*

 # Monitoring: monitoring is an activity that covers all types of minuting, observing, and supervising of processes, using technical aids. An important aspect is that it is regularly carried out within an investigation in order to be able to draw concrete conclusions by comparing results. The important function of monitoring is to observe a process and to intervene should it not proceed as intended. For example, in construction site supervision, ongoing monitoring is recommended to control the progress of investment projects. The emphasis here is on recognising difficulties and defects at an early stage to prevent these from jeopardising the execution of a project. *(Source: Christoph Motzko, 2013)*

 # Morphological box: morphology refers to the study of shapes and their order. In a morphological box a grid is used to allocate variables that are then linked selectively to create a structure for potential solutions. The morphological box is an analytical and systematic creativity technique that is primarily used in product and process development. The objective is to create an ordering system for any task or problem in which all possible sensible solutions can be found in a systematic manner. The relevant criteria are defined beforehand and are presented as an overview table in an ordering system. The objective of this technique is to develop and analyse as many alternatives of potential solutions as possible. By combining possible solutions relating to specific elements it is then possible to solve the overall problem. Ideally, the whole spectrum of solutions should be covered in this process. *(Source: Billing/Schawel, 2011)*

 # Networkengineer-Plan: this planning technique is a critical path analysis, which can be used for planning, controlling, and monitoring processes during the building construction. These processes can run in parallel or be sequential. A network plan is a graphic device that is easily understood and updated and makes it possible to predict important deadlines with relative precision. For this reason, network plans are often used in planning and project management in a number of ways: for the purpose of control and for planning costs, time, and capacity. Even though it is relatively complicated to produce a network plan, it is a good method of presenting processes with their scheduled timing. The earliest and latest start and finishing times of processes are recorded, thus ensuring optimum efficiency of the overall process. *(Source: Erhard Motzel, 2010)*

 # Observation: participatory or non-participatory observation is an important working method for comprehending and depicting the surrounding environment. A number of different observation roles can be adopted. In participatory observation, the observer actively takes part in the process to be explored. In non-participatory observation, the observer is passively present and therefore has an unimportant role in the proceedings other than keeping the minutes. Observation can be carried out using the human senses and/or technical means. It is important for the observer to ensure that a certain distance from the subject matter is maintained in order to preserve appropriate objectivity. During a site visit, the fact that one sees and hears, or even smells and touches the physical surroundings results in quite a different qualitative impression of the situation. Photos and maps of a place cannot replace pure observation on site, but can be helpful during the analysis process. *(Source: Georg Glasze, 2015)*

 # Preference matrix: the preference matrix is a method for weighting objectives and as such is used to prioritise criteria, properties, or processes. The criteria that are to be decided upon are inserted into a table and compared with each other in pairs. The result of the decision is inserted into the arrow point that is created in the process; this ensures that the most frequently named criterion can be determined, and a ranking can be established in accordance with previously allocated weighting points. *(Source: Götz Schmidt, 2000)*

 # Prognosis: in a prognosis, scientific methods and statistical devices are used to demonstrate likely outcomes of events. This method can be used to make tangible statements about future events and developments. The method is helpful for discovering interrelationships and for agreeing on a focused strategy. It is possible to consider changes and interventions in order to produce hypotheses and predictions for the future, as well as forecasts and projections. Prognoses can provide important background information for the planning process. *(Source: Diederich, July 1971)*

 # Ratio-Delay-Study: this is a multi-moment process and can be used to collect data in a defined area of investigation. In this procedure, sample data collections are carried out to determine the frequency of previously defined events. The individual collection phases are short, without the observer necessarily being involved. Activities or events are observed and recorded; in order for the samples to be representative, it is important that the conditions in the investigated area remain the same. For the multi-moment analysis to be valid, the samples must fulfil certain statistical requirements so that the individual findings can be transferred to the whole. In addition, the necessary scope of the sample depends on the required precision of the result. Steps to be carried out in a multi-moment analysis: start by defining an objective; this involves the selection of systems and the definition of the situation to be observed. Secondly, define the processes and the viewpoints for observation in order to obtain a good overview of the processes to be observed. In the last step, evaluate how many samples must be taken in order to achieve a sufficiently precise result. *(Source: Federal Office of Administration, online reference)*

 # Round table: meeting for a round-table discussion is a course of action in which different institutions and stakeholders come together to discuss a certain issue and work out a shared solution. In this procedure, an intended objective should never be defined beforehand; the outcome must be open. The number of participants should be limited to between twenty and thirty; the group produces project ideas, establishes implementation concepts, and tackles the first steps towards realisation. Local resources are mobilised, professional competencies are bundled and networked, and innovative solutions are found through new cooperative initiatives. A round table can be organised for all kinds of subjects, whether it be the task of establishing a strategy for a sustainable urban development, a marketing concept for a region, or a new traffic concept. *(Source: Jürgen Wüst, 2018)*

 # Scenario: scenarios are used as part of the creativity methods and describe and develop relevant interrelationships. At the beginning, influencing factors are determined that characterise the problem. After that, the effects of possible actions or situations are analysed and evaluated, and development factors are identified. This makes it possible to project future developments as realistically as possible. Scenarios indicate alternative development possibilities, considering potential confounding factors. There are three basic types: the positive extreme scenario, the negative extreme scenario, and the trend scenario. Based on the scenarios created, it is possible to plan and decide on concrete measures and strategies to achieve a defined objective. In this way it is possible, with the help of scenarios, to show designs in a number of different versions in order to generate potential improvement proposals and recommendations for future action.

The normative-intuitive process is used in "future prediction research" and is one of the scenario techniques. In this process a basic idea is established at the beginning to define the intended direction of the scenario. To do this, factual information is gathered and, at the same time, personal experience is recorded in an imaginative and creative way; then both are used to knit together a storyline. Detailed accounts provide the reader with information that creates mental images and makes the future imaginable. This process can be supplemented with fictional newspaper articles that could have been written at some time in the future. The entire description is made from a present-day perspective, finishing with the end of the scenario to be created. *(Source: Popp/Schüll, 2009)*

 # Simulation: a simulation is a recreation of real events that matches reality as closely as possible. For reasons of safety and cost, it is almost always necessary to detach this from reality and recreate it in an abstract manner. This abstraction creates a model, which can then be used for experimentation in a focused way; the resulting outcomes are then transferred back to the real problem. In this way it is possible to explore systems and processes in different situations. The process requires a considerable amount of data in order to carry out the simulation realistically. This method can be developed analogously and checked digitally via a computer simulation. *(Source: Meise/Volwahsen, 1980)*

 # Simulation and role-playing games: analogue simulation and role-playing games can be used to simulate scenarios. Simulation and role-playing games are cooperative empirical working methods, in which the participants play the role of characters at the centre of the activity. In a given scenario, the participants always assume a role other than their own. The simulation of the situation is then carried out via an actual play on stage. The test-participants immerse themselves in the "simulated world" and, through the interaction, become part of this world. They identify with the adopted character in the role of the play and can act in this role in a playful manner. After the role play, a reflective discussion takes place in which the experience, observations, and assessments are explained and shared.

This cooperative method promotes dialogue and often enables teams to find solutions among themselves. Role play familiarises people with empathy and helps them to understand other people or situations. In particular, it enhances people's ability to resolve conflict and is often the means by which participants overcome inhibitions, existing prejudice, or the tendency to influence other individuals in the process. In a computer-aided simulation game the computer and the simulation game software play a key role. In that case, the simulation of the reality on the ground and the simulation of entrepreneurial decisions are made with the help of the computer: the participating simulation game groups use the computer as a planning instrument, for the purpose of documenting their decisions and as a database. In addition, the computer is used to communicate between the different simulation game groups and the moderator. *(Source: Klaus Selle, 2005)*

 # Stakeholder analysis: this analysis identifies people or groups of people, such as citizens, planners, investors, authorities, public bodies, and associations, who may be directly or indirectly affected by a project. In this analysis, the social environment in which the project is embedded is of particular importance, as are the persons and institutions that one has to deal with in the context of the project. These so-called "stakeholders" want to take part in the project because they have an interest in providing input and influencing decisions within the planning process. The stakeholder analysis can provide a platform from which it is possible to address parties interested in the urban planning process and involve them methodically in a communication plan. *(Source: Drews/Hillebrand, 2007)*

 # Statistical methods: quantitative information such as empirical data or urban development data can be systematised and assessed with the help of statistics. For example, urban design projects often require the collection and systematic processing of statistical data on development, on structure, or on social parameters. This makes it possible to carry out data collection, analysis, and evaluation, as well as planning, control, and processing in an organised fashion. The acquisition of information from existing databases, without collection on the ground, is currently mostly carried out in the form of internet research. Keeping statistics in the form of databases also provides a sound base for the strategic orientation of town development policies. *(Source: Horst Rinne, 2008)*

 # Strategy table: strategic planning makes it necessary to bring together as many actors as possible around a table in order to be able to jointly make decisions on the basis of existing facts and data. This form of arriving at a decision is well known and stretches from King Arthur's Round Table to board meetings in companies through to strategy tables in the military. This method makes it possible for a group of people to swiftly comprehend complex information, discuss it, evaluate it, and thereby to establish scenarios. In a complex urban development process, it is also possible to use a number of other planning tools in order to generate urban development alternatives. In addition to the currently predominantly analogue instruments, such as plans and drawings, it is nowadays increasingly possible to use interactive and digital elements, including parametric tools and software tools with AI algorithms, to obtain new findings from existing information. *(Source: Lorenz et al, 2011)*

 # Surveys and interviews (expert interviews): an interview is a specific method of obtaining data that allows the collection of additional information on planning and research issues that cannot be obtained in this form via literature research. Compared with a survey, an interview is more focused. A more specific form is the expert interview, which can help to provide additional knowledge. The special knowledge and practical experience of experts relating to a certain task or research subject can be obtained in a guided interview. Interviews proceed in an abstract manner without any limitation in terms of responses. Surveys are a scientific method of obtaining information on opinions, values, behaviour, or basic demographic data. It is possible to target the general population as well as specific groups of people, depending on the subject in question. A survey is one of the most important instruments in data collection. In addition, it is a helpful working method for finding answers to questions. *(Source: Uwe Flick, 2012)*

 # SWOT analysis: in this analytical process, the existing strengths, weaknesses, opportunities, and threats of the area investigated are listed. For example, in urban development this analysis may be based on the results of existing data, such as statutory plans, statistical data, or previously established concepts, as well as participation procedures. The format can also be used to establish the opinions, suggestions, and visions of the actors involved and evaluate them. Advantages of this method are that it is easy and simple to use, but also allows an intuitive approach. In addition the method does not involve weighting of the individual factors, which can be intrinsically subjective. *(Source: Drews/Hillebrand, 2007)*

 # Target-actual Comparison: this method is used as a planning and control instrument and compares the planned data with the actual data. The target-actual comparison can be used to find out the causes of deviations in order to be able to make improvements. Continuous improvement of scenarios or parameters is only possible on the basis of a continual comparison of the target with the actual data and the continuous review of control measures. The target-actual comparison is often used as an aid in controlling building projects (Source: Hans Jung, 2003). This process as an indicator formation takes place at several levels. It starts with an overall target, which typically expresses a guiding image for the improvement of the problematic situation, which is then used to define sub-targets. The overall target, which is also the project target, deals with the actual implementation level and the intended effects and expected benefits. Sub-targets describe the targets of all participating actors and contain descriptions applicable to the local conditions. The indicators define the point of measurement at which achievement of the target is confirmed. Indicators are used to check the degree of achievement. They should contain information on quality, quantity, and the anticipated timing required to achieve the target. *(Source: Robert Mager, 1975)*

 # Tree of Relevances: this analysis is a systematic method for identifying, analysing, and investigating complex tasks and issues. The relevance tree is used to structure problems and to depict systems and objectives. In a relevance tree, the basic characteristics of a project are classified in accordance with their relevance. In contrast to the preference matrix, this step is limited to the key characteristics and features. This method is well suited to finding and developing alternatives and is very useful for finding solutions to problems. The method requires specialist knowledge in order to depict complex problems in a clear manner. Individual target elements can be presented in a simple hierarchy and evaluated with the help of evaluation criteria. *(Source: Evelyn Boos, 2009)*

 # Working group: these working groups are parties of people who continually work on a certain subject in order to develop solutions to complex problems. The groups may consist of laypeople and experts who, over a longer period, lead a number of creative discussions in order to generate holistic results via these exchanges. Within such a group, the participants focus entirely on a certain question or a specific objective; the sharing of different viewpoints and experiences is an essential element of this process. Working parties are very important elements of communication that can be used in the participation process between town planning officials and citizens. For working parties to achieve concrete results at the end of a process and hence to allow quite different views and concepts to be taken into account in planning processes in good time, it is important for these groups to work in a target-oriented way. It can be helpful to appoint a moderator to support and drive the cooperation of the group and to lead and minute the discussions. *(Source: Klaus Selle, 1996)*

 # Workshops: these are events in which the participants evaluate certain subjects, with the help of practical exercises, and produce new proposals. They involve a methodical, didactic arrangement that takes participation seriously and values creative cooperation. In the urban development process, these workshops are primarily used for the purpose of creating ideas, strategies, and designs. The spectrum of participation workshops includes communication, problem-solving, and idea-finding workshops through to workshops on perspective, strategy, and the future.

In an ideas workshop, creative visualisation methods are used to find new solutions for a specific problem area. The collection, structuring, and combination of ideas and suggestions frequently leads to changed views and new approaches. Owing to their clear and straightforward structure, ideas workshops can be used for different areas of work and life. They are a suitable space for letting members of a heterogeneous team “take a mental walk” so that they can free up their minds and thereby enhance the creative process.

A perspective workshop is moderated by an external moderator and aims to achieve a consensus between the conflicting development objectives of various stakeholders. With the help of preliminary discussions and preparatory steps, a basis for communication is established with external moderators before the different stakeholders come together in the perspective workshop. The participants of perspective workshops include inhabitants, professional and lay actors, and people with a local interest, as well as external speakers on the specific issue in question. The speakers supply a professional assessment, which is further expanded by the views of the inhabitants and local actors. In the subsequent discussion rounds, deficits are highlighted and discussed, and proposals for further development options are produced. With the help of this method it is possible for moderators to deal with several hundred participants in working parties and round-table discussions.

Workshops on the future are primarily intended to support government planning and to empower those who are affected by this planning. The idea is that those affected cease to be the objects of the plans and become the subjects who, with the help of participatory workshops, obtain greater freedom and opportunity to be involved. The participant groups should reflect their various backgrounds and degrees of education as well as very different age groups – from nursery children to seniors. Interesting suggestions and proposals usually come from participants who have only scant experience of participatory processes and creative methods of coming to a decision. Workshops on the future always require careful preparation and support on the part of the moderators and planners, and should be applied in the context of specific target groups.

The objective of a planning workshop is to engage the interests and ideas of the affected parties in the planning process, allowing them to voice briefing and design ideas. Such workshops should be held locally within the planning area and should run for one or several days. The planners give advice to the workshop participants, who are given the opportunity to demonstrate their design proposals with the help of models and drawings. It follows that the planning workshop is an important participatory element in which the urban actors can contribute their interests and ideas to the planning process. *(Sources: Kuhn/Massing, 2000 and Dietz/Eißel/Naumann, 1999)*

 # World café: with this cooperative method it is possible, with low-key professional guidance, to create a safe space in which the actors are introduced to the subject and their varying views are crystallised through careful listening, questioning, and constructive discussion. It is important to ensure that all participants have a chance to speak in order to define shared objectives and strategies and thereby promote greater readiness to participate in urban development processes. A world café will last for at least forty-five minutes and can also last up to three hours in the case of more complex issues. The participants stand or sit in a room around small tables, ideally with four people each. To promote a creative dialogue, materials such as paper tablecloths and various pens and markers are placed on the tables; the participants are supplied with drinks and refreshments and a flipchart is used for summarising the proposals. In the discussions around the different tables, ideas, findings, and suggestions are collected and written on the paper tablecloths. During longer sessions it is possible for the table partners to change seats to promote their different recommendations. New participants in a round should always be welcomed and the elected host at that table should ensure that there is an open, clear, and friendly atmosphere.

Having created a range of suggestions, these are then brought together by hanging up the tablecloths, which then gives everyone an opportunity to discuss and evaluate the ideas proposed by the various tables in the group. In this step it is helpful when a table reporter summarises the most important results for that table and acts as the representative of their table group. The suspended tablecloths are then rearranged during the discussion so that at the end of this dialogue there is a type of "results gallery" that categorises and prioritises the most important statements. At the end, these should be evaluated and, on that basis, the various tables should formulate recommendations for action on the flipchart. In contrast to the moderation and mediation method, the table discussions in a world café are not moderated. Moderation tends not to be necessary when the description of the issue is clear and interesting enough for all participants and the size of the groups at the tables does not exceed six people. *(Source: Brown/Isaacs 2005)*

APPENDIX

BIBLIOGRAPHY

Apel/Kettner (1996) *Die eine Vernunft und die vielen Rationalitäten. Thesen zur diskursiven Vernunft*, Frankfurt am Main

Billing/Schawel (2011) *Top 100 Management Tools: Kreativitätstechniken*, Wiesbaden

Boos, Evelyn (2009) *Das große Buch der Kreativitätstechniken*, Munich

Brown/Isaacs (2005) *Das World Café. Kreative Zukunftsgestaltung in Organisationen und Gesellschaft*, Heidelberg

Comenius, Johann Amos (1658) *Orbis Sensualium Pictus (Die sichtbare Welt)*, Nuremberg

Dienel, Peter C. (2002) *Die Planungszelle. Der Bürger als Chance* (fifth edition), Wiesbaden

Dietz/Eißel/Naumann (1999) *Handbuch der kommunalen Sozialpolitik*, Opladen

Drews/Hillebrand (2007) *Lexikon der Projektmanagement: Methoden*, Munich

Eichhorn/Nage (2009) *Partizipatives Analyse- und Evaluationsinstrument*, Wiesbaden

Flick, Uwe (2012) *Qualitative Sozialforschung: Eine Einführung*, Reinbek

Fürst/Scholles (2008) *Handbuch Theorien und Methoden der Raum- und Umweltplanung* (third edition), Dortmund

Gaus, Wilhelm (2003) *Dokumentations- und Ordnungslehre. Theorie und Praxis des Information Retrieval*, Wiesbaden

Glasze, Georg (2015) *Methoden-Lexikon für die Sozialwissenschaften*, Wiesbaden

Higgins/Wiese (1996) *Innovationsmanagement*, Berlin

Jul, Diederich (1971) *Stadt- und Regionalplanung: Soziographie und Städtebau*, Berlin

Jung, Hans (2003) *Controlling*, Munich

Kuhn/Massing (2000) *Methoden und Arbeitstechniken*, Frankfurt am Main

Latour, Bruno (1999) *Pandora's Hope: Essays on the Reality of Science Studies*, Cambridge, Massachusetts

Latour, Bruno (2005) *Making Things Public: Atmospheres of Democracy*, Cambridge, Massachusetts; London, England

Lorenz, Theo et al. (2016) "Out of Thick Air", in: *Energy – Self/ie – Space*, Krakow

Lorenz/Staub et al. (2011) "Mediating Architecture", in: AA Agendas No. 11, London

Mager, Robert (1975) *Zielanalyse*, Weinheim

Meise/Volwahsen (1980) *Stadt- und Regionalplanung: Ein Methodenhandbuch*, Braunschweig/Wiesbaden

Motzel, Erhard (2010) *Projektmanagement Lexikon* (second edition), Weinheim

Motzko, Christoph (2013) *Praxis des Bauprozessmanagements: Termine, Kosten und Qualität zuverlässig steuern*, Berlin

Popp/Schüll (2009) *Zukunftsforschung und Zukunftsgestaltung: Beiträge aus Wissenschaft und Praxis*, Berlin

Rinne, Horst (2008) *Taschenbuch der Statistik* (fourth Edition), Frankfurt am Main

Schenk, Frithjof Benjamin (2002) *Mental Maps: Die kognitive Kartierung des Kontinents als Forschungsgegenstand der europäischen Geschichte*, Göttingen

Simon, Katharina (2017) *Implementierung der Solarenergie in den städtebaulichen Planungs- und Entwurfsprozess. Eine Evaluierung der Methoden, Instrumente, Werkzeuge und Akteurskonstellationen als studienbegleitende Entwurfshilfe*, Promotion, TIB Hanover

Schmidt, Götz (2000) *Organisation und Business Analysis – Methoden und Techniken*, Gießen

Schneider and Schumacher (1996) *Info Box: Der Katalog*, Berlin

Schreyögg, Georg (2012) *Grundlagen der Organisation: Basiswissen für Studium und Praxis*, Wiesbaden

Selle, Klaus (1996) *Planung und Kommunikation*, Wiesbaden

Selle, Klaus (2005) *Planen. Steuern. Entwickeln: Über den Beitrag öffentlicher Akteure zur Entwicklung von Stadt und Land* (first edition), Dortmund

Walter, Simon (2004) *Gabals großer Methodenkoffer: Grundlagen der Arbeitsorganisation*, Offenbach

Wüst, Jürgen (2018) *Bürgerbeteiligung in der Praxis: Ein Methodenhandbuch*, Bonn

Zimmermann, Gerd (1992) "Architekturen der Macht". Plenarvortrag, Bauhaus-Universität Weimar

ONLINE-LINK:

Altmann, Jörn "Kooperationsmethode", Springer Gabler Wirtschaftslexikon, https://wirtschaftslexikon.gabler.de/definition/kooperationsmethode-40547/version-263928, accessed 05.05.2021

Bauer/Ernst (2010) "Diagrammatik, Einführung in ein kultur- und medienwissenschaftliches Forschungsfeld" https://www.transcript-verlag.de/media/pdf/d2/20/3a/ts1297_19iipk2LV2bODI.pdf, accessed 05.05.2021

Bundesverwaltungsamt (2015) "Handbuch für Organisationsuntersuchungen und Personalbedarfsermittlung" unter https://www.orghandbuch.de accessed 05.05.2021

Online-Link für Abb. der Methodenkarte "Prognose" www.onvista.de/news/bitcoin-kurs-prognose, accessed 22.02.2022

FURTHER READING:

Baugesetzbuch: BauGB (2022) "Gesetzestext zur Bauordnung" (fifty-third edition), Munich

Constant Nieuwenhuys, Laura Stamps, Mark Wigley et al. (2015) *Catalogue: Constant New Babylon,* Museo Nacional Centro de Arte Reina Sofía, Madrid

Corner, James (1996) *Taking Measures Across the American Landscape*, New Haven and London

Corner, James (2014) *The Landscape Imagination*, New York

Habermas, Jürgen (1981) "Theorie des kommunikativen Handelns" Vol. 1: *Handlungsrationalität und gesellschaftliche Rationalisierung,* Vol. 2: *Zur Kritik der funktionalistischen Vernunft*, Frankfurt am Main

Koetter, Fred and Rowe, Colin (1979) *Collage City*, London

Lynch, Kevin (1959) *The Image of the City*, London

Minard, Charles Joseph, "Napoleons Russlandfeldzug 1812". Kartierung von 1869, in: Rendgen, Sandra (2018) *The Minard System. The Complete Statistical Graphics of Charles-Joseph Minard*, New York

Neurath, Otto (1931) *Atlas: Gesellschaft und Wirtschaft*, Leipzig

Nolli, Giovanni Battista, "Großer Plan von Rom. Kartierung von 1748", in: Arnold, Dana (2003) *Tracing Architecture: The Aesthetics of Antiquarianism*, Oxford

Perouse De Montclos, Jean-Marie (1974) *Etienne Louis Boullée: Theoretician of Revolutionary Architecture*, New York

Schneider/Schumacher (1996) *Info Box: Der Katalog*, Berlin

Snow, John (1855) *On the Mode of Communication of Cholera*, London

Vauthier, Louis-Léger,"Höhenlinienplan für Bevölkerungszahlen Paris", 1874, in: Stevens, James and Wilson, Susan (2006) *Dictionary of Architecture and Landscape Architecture* (second edition), Oxford

ACKNOWLEDGEMENTS

To the many individuals with whom I have had the opportunity to cooperate so creatively in recent years, I am sincerely grateful. For their decades-spanning, personal and scientific support, my heartfelt gratitude goes to my husband, Dipl-Ing. Theo Lorenz (AA MArch), and my parents, Elke and Dr. Horst Siems.

I would also like to express my cordial appreciation to Elli Börgener, coordinator of our institute, for her highly valued support over the years. Further sincere thanks go to my mentors, Dr. Schleife, Prof. Dr. Schwalbenhofer, Prof. Werner, Prof. Dr. Ackermann, Prof. Dr. Harder and Prof. Dr. Huber. I am grateful to my former colleague, Prof. Barbara Campbell-Lange, for her wonderful preface to this book, as well as Vera San Payo de Lemos for her highly valued interdisciplinary contribution, in particular to our conversation in this book.

My gratitude goes out to my institute team for our productive discussions and consistently interesting and creative exchanges in recent years. In particular, I would like to mention the scientific assistants who have contributed to the institute since 2009: Dipl.-Ing. Rocio Paz, Dr.-Ing. M.Sc. Katharina Simon, M.Sc. Dipl.-Ing. Ragnhild Klußmann, M.Sc. Dipl.-Ing. Johannes Geyer, M.Sc. Bärbel Offergeld, M.Sc. Dipl.-Ing. Julia Siedle, M.Sc. Dipl.-Ing. Hedda Vorwohlt, Dipl.-Ing. Dipl.-Des. Mohamed Fezazi, M.Sc. Alexandra Radounikli and Friedrich Gräfling AA Dipl. (Hons).

I am sincerely grateful to the Chancellor Dr. Roland Kischkel and the President Prof. Dr. Lambert Koch of the University of Wuppertal for their indispensable support in making this publication a reality. Further, I would like to express my appreciation to Alexander Felix and Katharina Kulke of Birkhäuser publishers for their highly valued cooperation in producing this book.

Professor Dr. Tanja Siems, University of Wuppertal

BIOGRAPHY

Tanja Siems is the Chair of Urban Design and Head of the IUG Institute for spatial design and planning at the University of Wuppertal. Together with Theo Lorenz she founded the interdisciplinary office T2 Spatialwork in London as well the AAIS Interprofessional Studio at the Architectural Association School of Architecture, a genre-bridging Master's in spatial performance and design.

Her work focuses on participatory urban transformation processes both in her research and applied work. The application of these approaches ranges from environmental and social topics to participatory methods and tools.

Tanja has led several national and international research programmes and applied projects within a transdisciplinary approach in the cultural, architectural, and urban fields. The research projects of the institute are tackle social, environmental, and political challenges to initiate and generate a dialogue between urban actors and stakeholders within the urban realm.

PICTURE CREDITS

Photos

Photo B612 Architectes, Büro Brüssel (p. 32 centre, p. 38, p. 39, p. 42, p. 44, p. 47 centre, p. 48 right)
Photo Valerie Bennett, Architectural Association London (p. 19 top, p. 20 top right, p. 20 centre left, p. 20 centre right, p. 24 top, p. 24 bottom, p. 26 top, p. 26 bottom, p. 28 top, p. 28 bottom)
Photo Uwe Blass (p. 116 left)
Photo Elli Börgener (p. 116 right)
Photo Mohamed Fezazi (p. 86)
Photo Gabriele Hillebrand-Knopff (p. 132, p. 133 left, p. 133 right)
Photo Theo Lorenz (p. 81, p. 41, p. 102, p. 108 centre, p. 113, p. 124 top, p. 136 left)
Photo Bärbel Offergeld (p. 57 centre right, p. 135, p. 136 right, p. 137, p. 138)
Photo Julia Siedle (p. 80)
Photo Tanja Siems (p. 18 top left, p. 18 top right, p. 22, p. 32 top, p. 45 top, p. 85, p.105, p.114, p. 119, p. 123)
Photo Li Mei Tsien (p. 32 bottom, p. 50 top, p. 50 bottom)
Photo Sue Jan Yeong (p. 20 top left)
Photo Yota, Büro Brüssel (p. 31)

Graphics

Graphic B612 Architectes, office Brüssel (p. 44 left, p. 46 right, p. 47 top, p. 48 left)
Graphic Ragnhild Klußmann, Bärbel Offergeld, Tanja Siems (p. 130, p. 131)
Graphic Theo Lorenz (p. 40, p. 41, p.45 bottom, p. 46 left, p. 56 centre right, p. 120, p. 121, p. 122)
Graphic Tanja Siems (p. 16, p. 30, p. 36, p. 37, p. 39, p. 53, p. 56 top left, p. 56 centre left, p. 56 centre right, p. 57 top left, p. 57 bottom right, p.60, p. 65, p. 70, p. 82, p. 97, p. 101, p. 104, p. 109, p. 112, p. 125, p. 128, p. 140, p. 150)
Graphik Tanja Siems, Theo Lorenz, Mohamed Fezazi (p. 144, p. 145)
Graphik Tanja Siems and Li Mei Tsien (p. 43)

Graphic Students Urban Design Institute BUW in Bachelor:

Antonia Sabisch, Eva Schreinemacher (p. 61, p. 63, p. 100 top)
Lukas Altreuther, Anika Pehl (p. 66)
Matthias Lehner, Georgi Vlahov (p. 67)
Niclas Engelen, Richard Haverland (p. 68)
Jacoba Istel, Kimberley Müller, Nadine Uiberall (p. 72, p. 74, p. 75)
Maximilian Berg, Carlos Camp, Sophia Leipert (p. 76)
Domenico Alberta, Finn Gandermann, Annika Porschen (p. 89, p. 94)
Burak Güller, Minh Khoa Nguyen, Clemens Oswald, Anastasia Pusch (p. 90)
Sayneb Abbas, Farah Alnihawi, Anna Ußler, Zhiyuan Wang (p. 91)
Filip Daust, Luna Emembolu, Tugba Kaya (p. 93)
Tim Hecker, Jan Philipp Heidenreich, Manuel Kramm, Timon Nüsken (p. 118)

Graphic Students Urban Design Institute BUW in Master:

Vassilissa Airaudo, Daniel Branchereau, Moritz Scharwächter (p. 55 top left, p. 55 top right, p. 55 centre left, p. 56 top right, p. 57 top right, p. 57 centre left, p. 78, p. 100 bottom, p. 103 top, p. 103 Mitte, p. 103 bottom, p. 107, p. 108 top)
Ias Daboul, Miftar Miftari, Nicole Regel (p. 55 centre right)
Alexandra Hollensteiner, Lukas Killisch, Lukas Salomon (p. 88)
Julian Rodenkirchen, Pia Weil, Christian Zeiger (p. 108 bottom)
Melanie Dahmen, Melanie Eichhorn, Katharina Holtkotten, Mona Kamalinovin (p. 111)
Entire group of master students in the winter semester 2014/2015 from the seminar experimental urban research, district development Øvre Rotvoll (p. 115 and p. 124 bottom)

Translation German into English: **Mark Kammerbauer, Hartwin Busch**

Copyediting: **Patricia Kot**

Project management: **Alexander Felix**, **Katharina Kulke**

Production: **Anja Haering**

Layout and typesetting: **hawemannundmosch**

Cover design: **Anja Haering**

Image Editing: **Repromayer GmbH, Reutlingen**

Printing: **Grafisches Centrum Cuno GmbH & Co. KG, Calbe**

Paper: **Magno Natural, 140 g/m²**

Library of Congress Control Number: 2022949310

Bibliographic information published by the German National Library
The German National Library lists this publication in the Deutsche Nationalbibliografie; detailed bibliographic data are available on the Internet at http://dnb.dnb.de.

ISBN 978-3-0356-2412-0 (Softcover)
ISBN 978-3-0356-2413-7 (Hardcover)

e-ISBN (PDF) 978-3-0356-2418-2

German Print-ISBN 978-3-0356-2410-6 (Softcover)
German Print-ISBN 978-3-0356-2411-3 (Hardcover)

P.O. Box 44, 4009 Basel, Schweiz
Part of Walter de Gruyter GmbH, Berlin/Boston

9 8 7 6 5 4 3 2 1 www.birkhauser.com